Children's Places

Children's Place ımines the ways in which children and adults, from their different ʒe points in society, negotiate the 'proper place' of children in both ıl and spatial terms. It looks at some of the recognised constructions (hildren, including cultural perspectives that do not distinguish chil en as a distinct category of people, as well as examining contexts *for* them, from schools and kindergartens to inner cities and war-zones. The result is a much-needed insight into the notions of inclusion and exclusion, the placement and displacement of children within generational ranks and orders, and the kinds of places that children create for them-selves.

Based on in-depth ethnographic research from Europe, Asia, Africa, North America and Australia, it challenges current Eurocentric theories of childhood.

Contributors include Eva Gulløv, Laura Gilliam, Francine Lorimer, Laura Hammond, Olga Nieuwenhuys, Hilde Lidén, Sally Anderson, Erick Otieno Nyambedha, Jens Aagaard-Hansen, Lotte Meinert, Anne Trine Kjørholt, Karen Fog Olwig and Vered Amit.

Karen Fog Olwig is a Senior Lecturer in Anthropology at the University of Copenhagen. She is author of *Global Culture, Island Identity* (Harwood, 1993) and co-editor of *Work and Migration* (Routledge, 2002). **Eva Gulløv** is a Senior Lecturer at the Danish University of Education in Copenhagen, and a co-founder of the Network for Cross-Cultural Child Studies.

Children's Places

Cross-cultural perspectives

Edited by Karen Fog Olwig
and Eva Gulløv

Routledge
Taylor & Francis Group

LONDON AND NEW YORK

First published 2003
by Routledge
2 Park Square, Milton Park, Abingdon, Oxon OX14 4RN

Simultaneously published in the USA and Canada
by Routledge
270 Madison Ave, New York, NY 10016

Transferred to Digital Printing 2008

Routledge is an imprint of the Taylor & Francis Group

© 2003 Karen Fog Olwig and Eva Gulløv for selection and editorial
material; individual contributors, their contributions

Typeset in Sabon by Exe Valley Dataset Ltd, Exeter
Printed and bound in Great Britain by CPI Antony Rowe, Chippenham, Wiltshire

British Library Cataloguing in Publication Data
A catalogue record for this book is available from the British Library

Library of Congress Cataloging in Publication Data
Children's places: cross-cultural perspectives/edited by Karen Fog Olwig and Eva Gulløv.
    p. cm.
  Includes bibliographical references and index.
  1. Socialization—Cross-cultural studies. 2. Child rearing—Cross-cultural studies.
  3. Place (Philosophy) I. Olwig, Karen Fog, 1948– II. Gulløv, Eva.

HQ783 C5427 2004
305.23—dc21   2003050009

ISBN 10 0-415-29640-4 (hbk)
ISBN 10 0-415-29641-2 (pbk)
ISBN 13 978-0-415-29640-3 (hbk)
ISBN 13 978-0-415-29641-0 (pbk)

Contents

List of illustrations   vii
List of contributors   viii

Towards an anthropology of children and place
KAREN FOG OLWIG AND EVA GULLØV   1

PART I
Place as a site of opportunity and control   21

1   Creating a natural place for children: an ethnographic
    study of Danish kindergartens   23
    EVA GULLØV

2   Restricted experiences in a conflict society: the local lives
    of Belfast children   39
    LAURA GILLIAM

3   The Smith children go out to school – and come home
    again: place-making among Kuku-Yalanji children in
    Southeast Cape York, Australia   58
    FRANCINE LORIMER

4   How will the children come home? Emplacement and the
    creation of the social body in an Ethiopian returnee settlement   77
    LAURA HAMMOND

PART II
Place as a site in the field of generational relations   97

5   Growing up between places of work and non-places of
    childhood: the uneasy relationship   99
    OLGA NIEUWENHUYS

6   Common neighbourhoods – diversified lives: growing up
     in urban Norway   119
     HILDE LIDÉN

7   Associationless children: inner-city sports and local society
     in Denmark   138
     SALLY ANDERSON

8   Changing place, changing position: orphans' movements in a
     community with high HIV/AIDS prevalence in western Kenya   162
     ERICK OTIENO NYAMBEDHA AND JENS AAGAARD-HANSEN

PART III
Place as a source of belonging: local communities,
national identities, global relations   177

9   Sweet and bitter places: the politics of schoolchildren's
     orientation in rural Uganda   179
     LOTTE MEINERT

10 'Imagined communities': the local community as a place
     for 'children's culture' and social participation in Norway   197
     ANNE TRINE KJØRHOLT

11 Children's places of belonging in immigrant families of
     Caribbean background   217
     KAREN FOG OLWIG

     Epilogue: children's places   236
     VERED AMIT

     Index   247

Illustrations

Figures

3.1 A selected representation of the Smith family   59
3.2 Map of Southeast Cape York   60
6.1 Maria's household   123
6.2 Oliver's households   124
6.3 Tieko's household   125
6.4 Nadja's household   125

Tables

5.1 Qualities of place: comparison between place of work
     (fishing place) and the government school in Poomkara   107
5.2 Qualities of place: NGO project sites in Addis Ababa   111

Contributors

Jens Aagaard-Hansen is a Senior Researcher at the Danish Bilharziasis Laboratory, Denmark.

Vered Amit is Professor at the Department of Sociology and Anthropology, Concordia University, Montreal, Canada.

Sally Anderson is a Research Fellow at the Institute of Anthropology, University of Copenhagen, Denmark.

Laura Gilliam is a PhD student at the Department of Educational Anthropology, the Danish University of Education, Copenhagen.

Eva Gulløv is a Senior Lecturer at the Danish University of Education, Copenhagen.

Laura Hammond is an Assistant Professor at Clark University, USA.

Anne Trine Kjørholt is Acting Director at the Norwegian Centre for Child Research, Trondheim, Norway.

Hilde Lidén is a Senior Researcher at Institute for Social Research, Oslo, Norway

Francine Lorimer is a Lecturer at the Institute of Anthropology, University of Copenhagen, Denmark.

Lotte Meinert is a Lecturer at the Department of Ethnography and Anthropology, University of Aarhus, Denmark.

Olga Nieuwenhuys is a Professor at Amsterdam Research School on Global Issues and Development Studies (AGIDS), University of Amsterdam.

Erick Otieno Nyambedha is a Researcher associated with the Danish Bilharziasis Laboratory, Denmark.

Karen Fog Olwig is a Senior Lecturer at the Institute of Anthropology, University of Copenhagen, Denmark.

Towards an anthropology of children and place

Karen Fog Olwig and Eva Gulløv

Places for children

The focus of this book is the social and cultural construction of children's place in society, with its ever-changing set of inter-generational relationships. Using a cross-cultural approach, it investigates children in relation to the complex qualities of the concept of place as both social position and physical location. It thus examines the ways in which adults and children, from their different generational vantage points in society, negotiate 'proper' places for children. Through in-depth ethnographic studies based on field research in Europe, Africa, Asia, North America and Oceania, the contributors explore the kinds of places that are associated with children as they reflect their generational position. The authors discuss children's socialisation and emplacement in society, and their possibilities for developing new places for themselves that may lead to a reconfiguration of the places designated to them.

The complex meaning of the concept of place has been discussed by the geographer Yi-Fu Tuan in his seminal article 'Space and place: humanistic perspectives' from 1974, where he points to the two basic meanings of the term: 'one's position in society and spatial location'. He adds that 'clearly the two meanings overlap to a large degree: one seems to be a metaphor for the other'. However, he concludes that

> the primary meaning of 'place' is one's position in society rather than the more abstract understanding of location in space. Spatial location derives from position in society rather than vice versa. . . . Place, however, is more than location and more than the spatial index of socio-economic status. It is a unique ensemble of traits that merits study in its own right.
>
> (Tuan 1974: 233–4)

From an anthropological perspective, the concept of place points to the existence of a close interrelationship between the physical, social and cultural conditions of life. When used in relation to children, the concept of place becomes somewhat double-edged. It may refer both to established places allocated to children by others and to informal, potentially 'subversive' places created by children as they engage in various kinds of intra- and inter-generational relationships. Children's place thus becomes, to a great extent, a matter of their relative status in the generational order of socio-cultural transmission in which they, as juniors, are incorporated into the society under the guidance of various senior carers or educators. And here we can detect a certain ambiguity concerning children in modern welfare society. A number of studies have shown that children tend to be set aside in places separated from the rest of the society – homes or various institutions – where their incorporation is closely supervised by adults. If this fails, they seem to be left to roam on their own in public spaces, outside adult control. Thus in these societies, adults attempt to keep children under their supervision in 'safe' educational institutions that impart social values to children.

These child-safe zones contrast markedly with the society beyond them, where increasingly massive urban agglomerations with large populations of strangers, traffic, pollution and a lack of green areas make for environments that are very difficult for children to negotiate on their own (Olwig 1990; Ennew 1994: 125; James et al. 1998; Jensen 2000; O'Brien et al. 2000). The problems of unsafe environments for children have also attracted attention in studies of cities in the developing world, where growing numbers of children spend most of their lives fending for themselves (Blanc et al. 1996; Aptekar and Abebe 1997; Glauser 1997). This development reflects the increasing social marginalisation of children, because adults regard them as out of place in the wider society where they live. Yet as future adults, they are on their way to assuming a place in this very society.

While there may be many good reasons to be critical of places designated for children in modern society, one suspects that many of the studies that critique children's place reflect an adult's idealised view of children. In a discussion of Norwegian life stories, the anthropologist Marianne Gullestad has noted that 'the place of childhood is often a metaphor for childhood, and childhood itself is another central category of belonging' (Gullestad 1996: 293). Along similar lines, Yi-Fu Tuan (1980) has suggested that adults associate childhood with stability and rootedness as a reflection of their wish to root themselves in the temporally and spatially distant place of innocent and peaceful childhood, before the many contradictory and pressing responsibilities of adulthood have wrought havoc in their lives. If childhood bears this heavy burden of providing a source of identification and rootedness for adults, it is no wonder that they have little regard for childhoods localised in safe but unadventurous institutions and homes, or alternatively in potentially exciting but also dangerous city streets.

The notion of proper places for children does not just refer back to idealised pasts with which adults can identify, but also forward to equally idealised futures that, it is hoped, are in store for children as future adults. Thus, the kinds of places that society allows to children will, to a great extent, influence their ability to develop new social and cultural contexts of life that do not just reflect the existing social order of which they are part, but rather carry the potential to modify this order. The safe welfare institutions and family homes can be said to keep children rather firmly in their place in the generational order as recipients of the transmission of socio-cultural values by adults. The relatively unsafe, uncontrolled open environments of urban areas, on the other hand, give considerably more leeway for children to develop social relations and cultural values that mainstream society does not necessarily either share or appreciate. Places for children, in other words, are defined by adult moral values about a cherished past and a desirable future, clothed in commonsense notions about children's best interests.

The impact of adult moral values on studies of children's childhoods has been brought out in recent child research, in which some authors have warned against accepting commonsense notions about what is good for children. It has been suggested that the urban arena may, indeed, offer a possibility for children to develop their social and economic agency independently of adults (James *et al.* 1998: 47–52; O'Brien *et al.* 2000). Similarly, some scholars have called for more nuanced studies of street children in the Third World, which can also acknowledge the positive aspects of their life, in particular the inventive and resourceful ways in which they cope under adverse conditions (Blanc *et al.* 1996; Aptekar and Abebe 1997; Glauser 1997; Valentin 1998). At the same time, careful ethnographies of institutions for children, such as childcare centres and schools, have called attention to the ways in which children may seek to turn these localities into places of their own (Ehn 1983; Amit-Talai 1995; Gulløv 1999; Anderson 2000). The potential of such institutions as places of cultural change and social transformation has also been apparent in the Third World, where these institutions represent new arenas where children may interact among peers outside the generational order of the family and traditional society (Nieuwenhuys 1993).

This book contributes to the study of children and place by developing a cross-cultural (and cross-societal) approach to the study of children that explores, through careful ethnographic case studies, the relationship between children, generation and place. Though it seeks to further under-standing of the physical and social emplacement and displacement of 'childhood', it does so as part of a broader investigation of children's places in a variety of socio-cultural contexts in which children may not necessarily be conceptualised as a specific group of people associated with the well-defined category of 'childhood'. An important aim is therefore to explore the mechanisms of social inclusion and exclusion that are set in motion when children are marked in different ways within various generational orders, and the sort of places that are constructed for and by children in these processes.

The recent interest in children's places within the new sociological/ anthropological field of research on children is noteworthy because place has not hitherto been of significant concern in sociology or anthropology. Clifford Geertz (1996: 259) has noted that, whereas such topics as 'Family', 'Kinship', 'Community', 'Economy', etc. have comprised important headings in the indexes of anthropological monographs, 'place' has hardly figured. Geertz speculates that this may be because place is everywhere and therefore not something that is studied in its own right. Life simply unfolds somewhere that we may call place. Besides, he argues, place is entirely embedded in its 'materialisations' and is therefore of little use as an analytical abstraction. We do not agree with Geertz on this latter point, believing instead that place has played an important but unexamined role in anthropological theory and method. This role is finally gaining recognition in anthropological theory, as anthropologists become increasingly aware of the culturally constructed nature of place and its implications for social life. This awareness has emerged as anthropologists have critically re-examined ethnographic descriptions of field sites as places defined by, and defining, a particular concept of culture. They have thus questioned the ways in which notions of place have shaped anthropological theory and practice. This re-examination of ethnographic method and theory, and the critical light that it sheds on place as a socio-cultural construction, has important implications for research on children and the place that is made for children in this research. The critique of the emplacement of the anthropological object in ethnographic field sites (see especially Gupta and Ferguson 1997) may therefore serve as a useful point of departure for re-examining the significance of place in recent studies of children and its influence on child research.

Place in anthropological theory and method

Place has played a central role in the development of anthropology as a scholarly discipline because the two fundamental pillars of modern anthropology, the concept of culture and the research method of fieldwork, are both defined in relation to place. The modern discipline of anthropology emerged as a field science, and it is a central aspect of anthropologists' self-image that it is necessary to leave the comfortable armchairs of the civilised library and the controlled experiments of high-tech laboratories in order to study at first hand how life unfolds in different parts of the world. Students learn that an important theoretical and analytical basis of anthropology was laid in the nineteenth century, when the notion of culture was conceptualised as a complex whole that could be studied through both in-depth research on a particular culture and the comparative analysis of a range of cultures (see, for example, Wicker 1997).

For anthropologists, fieldwork has essentially meant immersing oneself in a new place, getting acquainted with the people living there, learning about their ways of acting and thinking, and writing it all down in copious field notes that will make it possible to write an ethnographic monograph about these people upon return. Different places, in other words, have provided the framework for ethnographic fieldwork practice, but anthropologists have typically not examined how fieldwork as local practice has influenced the kinds of data that they bring back from the field. As Gupta and Ferguson note in their critical discussion of the localising practices involved in doing research in a field site, the 'idea of "the field," although central to our intellectual and professional identities, remains a largely unexamined one in contemporary anthropology' (1997: 2). Ethnographic fieldwork has not been regarded as the study of a particular place, but as 'a form of dwelling that legitimizes knowledge production by the familiarity that the fieldworker gains with the ways of life of a group of people' (ibid.: 31).

This lack of attention to the relationship between place and fieldwork practice is due to the fact that anthropologists have not been conscious of the fact that fieldwork is, to a great extent, defined – and thus confined – by the particular places where it is carried out. Rather, as the above quote illustrates, fieldwork has been regarded as closely linked to the study of particular localised 'groups of people' defined and distinguished by their adherence to a specific culture that distinguishes them from other groups of people. Anthropologists, in other words, have studied peoples and cultures, not places. As several critics have pointed out over the last decade, the problem with this kind of thinking is the undisputed relationship between place and culture, and the idea of culture as a distinct and locally circumscribed entity (Gupta and Ferguson 1992; Hastrup and Olwig 1997). From this perspective, culture has been conceptualised as a 'whole' that must be studied in its totality by delineating the patterned ways in which various elements fit into a complex, unique socio-cultural entity that gives a special sense of purpose and meaning to the people who are part of this culture (Wicker 1997). The most important task for the ethnographic fieldworker has therefore been to gather in-depth data on the many different elements of life that go into this whole, as well as to uncover the overall systemic structure whereby these elements are organised into a unique combination that can be called a culture and located on the map. Anthropologists, in other words, have developed an image of the world as made up of a large number of different cultures located next to one another on the ethnographic atlas. A central aspect of the discipline has therefore been the documenting and analysing of these cultures through ethnographic fieldwork, as reflected in the many fine ethnographic monographs that constitute the vital core of anthropological literature.

Many anthropological monographs, from their holistic perspective, have devoted considerable attention to children's place, especially their position in the kinship system and their movement through the various rites of passage whereby they gradually became incorporated as full members of society.[1] Since most societies studied by anthropologists were based on kinship, children have been regarded as an integral part of a generational order based on mutual relations of rights and obligations between junior and senior relatives. Children were therefore conceptualised in terms of their position in a system of intra- and inter-generational relationships that gradually changed as they grew up, matured and assumed a position of increased responsibility and power in society. The successful socialisation of children into these wholes was therefore regarded as an essential aspect of the continued existence of the cultural wholes. Because these were treated by anthropologists as reified entities – rather than as subjectively experienced and generated cultural contexts of life that might assume different form and meaning, depending on the position of particular people – anthropologists showed little interest in the children's perspectives. For this reason, children's lives as children, their understanding and experience of their socialisation and their development of a sense of place, received relatively little attention in these monographs.

The image of anthropology as the study of distant exotic peoples and cultures has long been challenged from within the field, and throughout the twentieth century anthropologists have gradually begun to include their Western home environments within the scope of ethnographic investigation. Anthropologists have, as it were, conquered the West from the periphery, beginning with small communities located in the geographic fringes of society; moving on to urban neighbourhoods inhabited by socially and economically marginalised groups, including ethnic minorities; continuing with studies in institutions and other officially demarcated places that are associated with various groups of people defined by such distinguishing features as their occupation, state of health, age, special ability or disability; and finally, moving into centres of power, such as bureaucratic structures, parliaments and private industry. As fieldworkers began to focus on places devoted to particular social concerns, the idea of culture as a distinct place lost its analytic potential. Now, the professional interest is focused instead on the meanings that people generate as they interact and interpret one another. In this new wave of anthropology, places of childhood and children's varying perspectives have emerged as topics of special interest.

Most will easily see that the notion of the well-defined, clearly demarcated field site corresponding to a particular group of people has had an important impact on child research. Thus a great number of studies, as noted above, have been located in particular places set aside for children, such as kindergartens, schools and clubs. Many of these studies have taken a critical stance towards these places because they see them as relegating children to particular institutions that restrict their potentiality as social actors. These studies show that there is a close connection between the emergence of the concept of childhood, the demarcation of a special segment of the population as children and the construction of particular places for these children. This critique of the social and physical marginalisation of children, coinciding with the historical emergence of the modern notion of childhood, pinpoints a significant social concern associated initially with the developed West and increasingly also with the developing world, as Western institutional structures penetrate the globe.

It is important, however, not to equate institutions intended as places for children with children's places. Places constructed for children do constitute important frameworks of life for children. They do not, however, determine children's lives, nor do they preclude the existence of other kinds of places that may be of central importance to children. By focusing on institutions for children, one runs the risk of tautologically reproducing a folk model of children and childhood because these institutions are founded on exactly these models. We suggest that one of the reasons why students of childhood have attached such significance to officially designated places for children may be that these constitute the most readily apparent sites of investigation. If we wish to broaden our research to include places for children that may be created by children as well as adults, it is necessary to go beyond the well-defined places of childhood and look for other field positions from which to examine children. In this endeavour we may draw inspiration from new anthropological approaches to place.

One of the important lessons of the prolonged critique of the classical fieldwork tradition in anthropology has been the realisation that places do not exist in and of themselves. Rather, places are cultural constructions that emerge in the course of social life as human beings attribute meaning to their surroundings and thus turn them into places of special value (see, for example, Appadurai 1996; Gupta and Ferguson 1997). From this point of view, one might argue that there may be many places within a particular community of people that reflect their different levels of experience, varying forms of identification and individual understandings of self and other (for a case study, see Kahn 1996). Furthermore, it is apparent that conceptions of place are continuously negotiated and reformulated in the context of ongoing social life and from different social positions, in the light of the exposure to and intrusions from the wider world that particular people experience. As Gupta and Ferguson note, ethnography therefore involves 'an attentiveness to the different forms of knowledge available from different social and political locations' (ibid.: 37). This obviously has great relevance for the study of children's perception and use of place.

Investigating children and place

If the meaning of place varies, a central issue in understanding the social dimensions of place becomes that of recognising the impact of social power and contestation, that is the uneven distribution of influence and status reflected in different conceptions and uses of places. The meaning of place both reflects and signifies social divisions and variations in influence and power.

In most societies, there are places for children and places where children will rarely be seen. Analysing the social implications of being and not being at a given location can therefore reveal the range of relationships that is within reach of children. Places frame different kinds of social meetings and opportunities, and children's movements and varying uses of places have consequences for their social experiences, as well as for the spheres in which they may engage. In some cases, children will have far more contact with different sections of society than their parents will; in others, they are severely restricted. Analysing children's uses of places gives insight into patterns of relations, social opportunities and varying forms of agency. Relations thought to be dangerous express the moral and social order in a society. Restrictions in movements and the division of space into go and no-go areas mirror hierarchies and symmetries in the relations between different parts of society. Ideas and practices about dangerous areas and bad influence relate to social division, separations and demarcations that children come to learn as they grow up in particular social and moral environments. Exploring where children are allowed to be and what kind of meanings both children and adults attach to these specific places can point to a better understanding of how children and childhood are conceptualised in a particular society. It can also indicate children's degree of influence and position in the generational order and in society at large. The places where children are to be found are physical sites and, at the same time, agents' symbolic expressions of social positions and views of the future. Contestations over what kinds of places are proper for children are therefore about the power to assert particular views on social life, as well as about safeguarding children's well-being and safety in a particular society, these two aspects of place-making being closely interrelated. By using place as an analytical tool to explore the lives of children, we are therefore attempting to investigate children's everyday practices and move-ments, at the same time examining more general principles of social relations, moral judgments and processes of change. Attributing meaning to places can be seen as a positive effort to organise the environment, to re-order interpretations of the physical as well as the social surroundings. As will be evident from the case studies in this volume, the interpretations of where children can go, where they ought to be, and where they are 'matter out of place' (Douglas 1966) differ from one cultural setting to another, reflecting the social order, cultural values and different interpretations of social changes.

By presenting a comparative approach to children and place, this book seeks to challenge prevailing notions of childhood that are often bound to Western commonsense perceptions of children. It does so by presenting rich ethnographic descriptions of places for children and children's places in widely different parts of the world, while pointing to some of the commonalities that emerge in these case studies across this cultural variability. This study of children and place therefore entails two different foci. The first is careful investigation of the everyday lives of specific children, their relationships, communications, beliefs and aspirations in certain cultural settings. By studying the micro-geographies of particular children, therefore, it becomes possible to understand different ways of being a child. This means examining different ways of incorporating and transforming cultural values and practices through encounters with others in relation to culturally constructed notions of children and childhood. The other focus concerns the investigation of the social organization and social institutions of children and childhood. This involves studying children's place in the generational order, both the established social structure that seeks to maintain children in a particular place, and the emerging social relations that lead to processes of change.

This book is organised into three different sections, each focusing on a salient theme in current discussions on children within the social sciences.[2] These themes represent three different dimensions of place that are of central importance when studying children. They are: (i) place as a site of opportunity and control, (ii) place as a site in the field of generational relations, and (iii) place as a source of belonging: local communities, national identities, global relations. Through in-depth analyses of particular practices and conceptions in relation to place in different parts of the world, the authors are seeking to develop a cross-cultural perspective on children and childhood that can help both broaden and refine theoretical and methodological approaches within the field of children's studies.

Place as a site of opportunity and control

Several studies of children's spaces and places point to control as a major theme in understanding children's movements and mobility in society (Rose 1989; James *et al.* 1998; Philo 2000; Hultqvist and Dahlberg 2001). James *et al.* describe childhood space as follows:

> Physical, conceptual and moral boundaries circumscribe the extent of children's wanderings. From the closed arenas of domestic space to the infinite horizons of cyberspace, boundaries forestall and contain the child's movement. Erected by a gerontocratic hegemony and policed by

discipline, the boundaries are legitimized through ideologies of care, protection and privacy.

(James *et al*. 1998: 38)

In their discussion of the relationship between the placement of children and modes of control, they draw a general picture of the Western child as restricted in movement and under constant surveillance by adults. This way of understanding children's lives as circumscribed by physical, conceptual and moral boundaries gives insight into aspects of those lives, as well as of social priorities. It reveals aspects of power and panoptic observation as central in the general relationship between children and society. This perspective draws on Nicolas Rose's description of modern childhood as the most intensively governed sector of personal existence (Rose 1989). He suggests that governance works through the autonomy of the child, through a kind of self-guidance where the child regulates itself (ibid.: 120–2). From this perspective, the child's freedom to move around and define places for itself is embedded in new forms of power–knowledge relations, where children are at once being controlled by others and enjoined to regulate their own behaviours (James *et al*. 1998: 8).

Using place as an analytical tool to understand the social life of children points to questions not only of control and discipline, but also of opportunities, agency, and the production and reproduction of generational structures. The case studies in this volume show that throughout the world children are subjected to certain demands on where they can be at what time, reflecting adult visions of the proper behaviour and social classifications of people. Children are sited and their movements restricted on the basis of personal and social as well as political considerations. There are places for children and places that are not suitable for children, and failure to accept this conceptualisation of space may have important consequences for the moral reputation of the children and their families. Thus places are a means of classifying people into different sorts, symbolising the social and moral order. However, while the theme of control is highly relevant in these studies, it must be stressed that control and discipline are not necessarily the most important issues in understanding the lives of children everywhere. This is apparent in several of the studies in this book.

In the first chapter in this section, Eva Gulløv discusses Danish perceptions and practices in relation to kindergartens. She shows that these places for young children are characterised by considerable ambiguity, reflecting the complex and contradictory ways in which societies may define and practise places for children. At one and the same time there exists an explicit discourse of the child as a self-managing individual, in need of a place to realise opportunities and inbuilt potentials, and an institutional logic that, in practice, leaves the children with very little influence on where to be and what to do. Placed as they are in circumscribed day-care centres for many hours a day, pre-schoolers are encouraged to take their own decisions and articulate their feelings and wishes. Thus in this para-doxical setting, self-realisation and restriction, opportunities and control, co-exist and express ambivalent perceptions of children's social position.

The only study where the control of children's spatial movements is clearly of overriding importance is Laura Gilliam's case from Northern Ireland. She shows how, in the conflict between Catholics and Protestants, children in Belfast are strictly controlled by the local sectarian community to which they belong. The city is divided into sectarian areas, and children are kept within the zone associated with their religion. They therefore stay in their close neighbourhood and attend schools and day-care institutions identified with their particular religion. Through this restriction to the local area the children are also restricted to the local group and its conflict discourse, including the negative experiences of the other group that it produces. At the same time the children are exposed to a range of cultural practices that ensure the avoidance of conflict, and they therefore develop completely negative stereotypes of 'the others' and a conflict identity that motivates them to become involved in the conflict. Thus the restriction to the local area severely limits children's agency, and they gradually inter-nalise and reproduce the conflict. This Northern Irish case is an extreme one, however, and other cases show that there is considerable cross-cultural variability in children's opportunity to explore the world through their own movements and constructions of different places.

Among Australian Aboriginal Kuku-Yalanji, a setting analysed by Francine Lorimer, children exercise considerable freedom of choice as they extend their movements, by way of their kinship network, into new places. In the process they create place for themselves, as they get to know various natural, social and spiritual environments and the institutions and relations connected with them. Lorimer presents a cultural mode of behaviour where children are rather free to choose where to stay, where to go and whom they are together with. It seems that it is up to the children to decide for themselves whether they will go to school and which school they will attend. Thus, these children are able to explore a range of places and opportunities, thereby becoming part of Aboriginal society. At the same time, however, they miss the kind of education, associated with localised Western institutions of learning, necessary to improve the social and economic position of Aboriginal people in Australian society. Lorimer points out that Aboriginal children's schooling would undoubtedly improve considerably if the school system recognised and worked creatively with Aboriginal children's place-making activities, rather than dismissing them as unruly, irrelevant or unreasonable.

Laura Hammond's study of a returnee settlement in Ethiopia for refugees also depicts a relatively open system. Children are freer to move around and choose where to be in the physical locality than are either adult men or women. As they are not bound to any place in particular, they have the freedom to experience all places. This freedom is closely related to their position of not yet having become entirely socialised into the social and cultural order of the settlement, and to the fact that this order has not been completely established due to the recent relocation of its inhabitants. There is therefore still a certain leeway for negotiation concerning children's proper social place and the ways in which this is reflected in places for children in the physical environment. Furthermore, perhaps due to the harsh conditions under which the resettled refugees live and the resulting high rates of illness and mortality, adults attempt to control their children's well-being by applying various practices to their bodies, such as circumcision, scarring and different forms of healing. Rather than controlling the movements and places of children, adults inscribe social belonging on to the corpus of the child.

These studies show that the issue of control over places for children varies across ethnographic settings. As Michel Foucault pointed out in *Discipline and Punish*, his work on surveillance (Foucault 1977), the shift from external punishment and public control to the individual subject being responsible for the regulation of the private self is a process formed by the specific development of Western modernity. The construction of the child as a subjective being cannot be held as a universal idea, no more than new technologies of governing and regulating child behaviour can be seen as a general characterisation of contemporary childhood. We have to examine the various ways of conceptualising childhood and children's local practices and relationships before we know the relevance and meanings of place as a source of control or opportunity. The contributions in the following section do this by examining children's place in the generational order. They show that both within and outside the Western world, there is considerable variation in the conceptualisations and practices of children and childhood, and the places that are created for and by children.

Place as a site in the field of generational relations

One of the aspects of research on children most taken for granted is the categorisation of populations into children and adults. This is often put forward as an ever-relevant distinction in the analysis of children's lives, an instrument of thinking and organising ethnographic studies of children. However, as several of the articles in this book show, the distinction between adults and children is not necessarily central for understanding the particular way that social life is organised, especially if it is presented as a general polarisation between dominators and dominated. The empirical investigations of the various kinds of place that are formed both by adults for children and by children themselves show that the separation of children and adults so often described in the literature on Western children

(Ennew 1994; Strandell 1994; Qvortrup 1995) is not a general characteristic of life everywhere in the world. Children are not necessarily marked as a distinct group defined in contrast to adults, and we therefore need to examine closely the nature of relationships between people of varying ages in different cultural settings.

From this theoretical point of view, a focal point of research on children and place will be the impact of generational orders, however variously they may be organised in different societies, on children's lives and the sort of places that are constructed by and for children in particular societies. In so far as children's position in the generational order changes through time as they grow up and mature, we should expect this to be reflected in the sort of place-making in which they are involved. From this processual perspective, an important task therefore becomes that of examining the various positions from which children seek to develop a place for themselves in society through time. This perspective requires careful research on how children gradually learn, through reciprocal relationships, to take inter-subjective action that is meaningful in relation to their physical surroundings and the wider society of which they are part.

Places are defined through social interaction, but interactions are defined by relationships, aims and conceptions of place. This perspective challenges the adult–child relationship as a dichotomy that is always relevant and points out that we have to look at the ways in which children are spread over different places – the differences among them, as well as their relation to other generations. By taking our point of departure in social relatedness and the possibilities and restrictions inherent in different places, we aim to elucidate children's generational positions, thus pointing to children's participation in the production and reproduction of socio-cultural systems.

The first chapter in this section, by Olga Nieuwenhuys, presents a comparative analysis of children in a South Indian village and street children in Addis Ababa, Ethiopia. She criticises the way child researchers base their studies on unreflective notions of childhood. Childhood is predicated upon the spatial separation of children, which means that the places children occupy are often as inconspicuous as their status in the generational order of their society. Nieuwenhuys argues that this juxta-position of physical space and social place has led researchers to investigate only places defined for children, though such places quite simply may not exist in many non-Western societies. She argues that children can be embedded in society without necessarily being in 'places of childhood', and that too much focus on child-specific places reflects an ethnocentric idea of children and childhood. Thus, childhood works as a tool of spatial segregation, stressing the distinction between children and adults.

In modern, complex societies, there will be great variability in the kinds of generational structures to which children are subject, as a variety of social, economic and cultural factors come into play in children's lives.

While a generational approach is essential in understanding children's place in society, it should therefore not be presented as an all-too-rigid categorisation of children's lives, but as a point of departure for empirical investigations. In her study of children in a suburban neighbourhood of Oslo, Norway, Hilde Lidén shows that there are key differences in children's ways of moving around and use of their neighbourhoods and public spaces in general, and that these differences are connected with a complex set of factors involving age, gender, ethnicity, family relations and varying cultural values concerning nature and local communities. All these combine to result in different patterns of mobility among children in the local neighbourhood (cf. Philo 2000). Lidén details how children use their physical environment as they interpret the neighbourhood in accordance with the social relations, cultural values and perceptions of belonging that they learn through their family's system of intergenerational relations. Since children are integrated into the neighbourhood in different ways and to varying degrees, children living in the same area, who are classmates in the school, may never meet in the street or play together, as their use of places in the neighbourhood reflects their belonging to different social groups. Gender and ethnicity are particularly important factors in this varying exploitation of the neighbourhood.

Like Lidén, Sally Anderson looks at how children with different backgrounds may use the local community and its institutions in different ways. She argues that there are dominant notions of sociality that presuppose that children have a particular place in the generational order. Failure to understand this may limit children's ability to engage in society, even when society intends to engage them as active participants in social life. In her study of a sports centre in central Copenhagen, she shows that children are incorporated into Danish society through a network of exchange relations that involve, on the one hand, child-givers, represented by parents in the private, domestic sphere, and, on the other hand, child-receivers, represented by various carers and educators employed in public institutions. Children's ability to take part in social activities therefore depends on the development of a proper exchange relationship, where the partners involved understand the rights and obligations entailed by this exchange of the children. Even though most children were perfectly capable of interacting, and indeed enjoyed the wide variety of games and tumbling opportunities offered by the open-house programme, organisers chose to close the activity to children who were not members of local children's clubs. In doing so, project organisers criticised parents, especially immigrant parents, who did not master the Danish rules of exchange that would allow their children to take part in the activity in its new club form. The failure of the project coordinators to incorporate children (and parents) who held different notions of social relations becomes an image of the more general failure to integrate certain population groups into Danish society.

The last contribution in this section, by Erick Otieno Nyambedha and Jens Aagaard-Hansen, explores children's position in a system of generational relations that is seriously threatened by the AIDS pandemic. On the basis of extended research on orphans among the Luo in Kenya, they show how the places of child-rearing in the family compound associated with the patriline have disappeared as the parental generation has died out and the network of kin relations being built around the patriline has disintegrated. As a result, many children begin to explore places of opportunities outside the area controlled by their kin group. This exposes children to the risk of exploitation, but it also introduces them to new social and economic opportunities that they might not have experienced if they had been subject to the sort of control exercised in kin groups where the generational order is still intact. While children do have generation-specific experiences, their experience of place can therefore vary a great deal, depending on their social and economic position in society.

Place as a source of belonging: local communities, national identities, global relations

Several of the contributions discussed so far have shown that children's places may exist at different levels, ranging from the private home or family compound to the local neighbourhood and to more distant areas visited by children. These places become children's entry points into the wider society – indeed, many of these entry points, such as schools, clubs and day-care institutions, are organised and structured by the state, or in some cases by global organisations. The last three studies, from different parts of the world, discuss children's relationships with their local community in the light of global relations and national strategies pursued on behalf of children.

At a general level, Gupta and Ferguson (1992) argue from a world system approach that there has long been a global network of political, economic and social ties extending to every corner of the earth, and that all human beings are therefore part of this worldwide mesh of relations, though at varying levels of intensity. This means that the world is basically characterised by a contiguous space of relations and interconnectedness, rather than by separate places of distinct units of belonging. This does not imply, however, that there are no places, because places emerge in the course of locally lived everyday lives, as particular sets of relations become constituted as communities of special meaning anchored in specific localities. In his study of modernity, however, Appadurai (1996) argues that in the present era of globalisation many people will experience their local communities as full of constraints in relation to the wealth of social and economic opportunities offered on the global arena. This may lead them to 'seek to annex the global into their own practices of the modern'

(1996: 4), changing the local community in the process. From this broad perspective, the construction of place therefore necessarily occurs within a wider framework of non-local relations. Indeed, it may be argued that the very notion of place only makes sense when seen within a larger context of emplacement that occurs in a wider space of global relations.

The first chapter in this section, by Lotte Meinert, is based on fieldwork in a village in Uganda. It describes children's desires and strategies to have a life in town away from the poverty and remote existence of the village. The dream of moving is connected to the educational system: thus it is believed that schooling gives one an opportunity to improve an inferior socio-economic situation through social and physical mobility. These aspirations on the part of the children and young people of the village are confronted by state policies that are aimed at preventing rural immigration. The schools are used to persuade people to stay in the countryside by stressing a curriculum relevant to the establishment of a prosperous local society. The school therefore turns into a battlefield in the tension between children's longing for other places and national endeavours to build up a strong relationship between people, place, culture and identity.

A similar effort to revitalise local society through the children can be seen in the Norwegian 'Try Yourself', project, examined by Anne Trine Kjørholt. This project, directed primarily at children living in rural communities, encouraged children to become active, independent participants in public life. The local authorities hoped that by offering children public grants for various projects of their own making, they might reinforce their participation in society, democratic awareness and sense of local community. Rather than helping the children to assert themselves as actors in society, however, the adults in charge of the project insisted on encouraging the children to engage in projects corresponding to their own, very adult notions of children and childhood in society. Thus, the state-funded project attempted, through children's engagement, to realise communities of egalitarian relations associated by adults with local communities and children's culture. In this vision there was little room for adult participation, even when the children requested adult involvement in their projects.

The last case study, by Karen Fog Olwig, looks at children's place in immigrant societies in the Western world, where multicultural policies and ethnic politics have become important. In such societies, the second- and third-generation children of immigrants are expected to develop a tie to their ancestral place of origin, which is often located in a distant and unfamiliar country in the developing world. The study shows how some children develop a pragmatic approach to their public identity by adopting one of the ethnic identities matching their family background and appearance, whereas others entirely reject the multicultural project and the ethnic identities it promotes. More importantly, in the course of their everyday lives, the children develop various local, regional, national and global ties that they interweave into complex identity structures that defy easy classification in society. By failing to take into consideration the multifaceted social contexts within which children develop their sources of identification, multicultural national strategies may therefore have the inadvertent effect of displacing children from the local communities where they live.

In the epilogue, Vered Amit addresses the themes of agency and social reproduction emerging from the volume. She argues that the challenge for further anthropological child studies is neither to reduce our investigations to questions of futurity or systems of tutelage nor to overemphasise the impact of children's own agency and cultural production. Amit notes that many studies of children and youth have tended to take their point of departure in pre-defined categories of social actors that generate particular kinds of moralities and value judgements. With its detailed ethnographic case studies and its focus on the 'interaction between generation and place,' this book avoids such categorising and opens up for critical investigation of 'the kinds of social identities and moral evaluation which are mobilised in the cultural construction of historical progression'. This leads to further questions concerning the role of children and youth in historical change and structual transformations that need to be addressed in future reseach.

Notes

1 A few examples from the anthropological classics must suffice here. *The Sexual Life of Savages* by Bronislaw Malinowski (1929) makes numerous references to children and includes a description of 'The sexual life of children' (1929: 52–9); *We, the Tikopia* by Raymond Firth (1968[1936]) includes a chapter on 'Personal Relations in the Family Circle' that focuses on children (1968: 125–85); *The Forest of Symbols* by Victor Turner (1989 [1967]) describes and analyses Ndembu rituals, including several important rites of passage for children and young people.

2 This book is the outcome of a research seminar held at the University of Copenhagen in May, 2001, by the Danish Network for Cross-Cultural Child Research. The network was funded by a grant from the Social Science Research Council in Denmark. We gratefully acknowledge this economic assistance, as well as the support we received from the Institute of Anthropology, University of Copenhagen, which hosted the network. The title of the seminar was 'Children, Generation and Place', and a central aim of the discussions at the seminar was to examine the advantages of a cross-cultural approach able to explore the ways children are positioned and position themselves in the generational orders of different societies.

References

Amit-Talai, V. (1995) 'The waltz of sociability: Intimacy, dislocation and friendship in a Quebec high school', in V. Amit-Talai and H. Wulff (eds) *Youth Cultures: A Cross-cultural Perspective*. London: Routledge, pp. 144–65.

Anderson, S. (2000) *I en klasse for sig.* Copenhagen: Gyldendal, Socialpædagogiske Bibliotek.

Appadurai, A. (1996) *Modernity at Large: Cultural Dimensions of Globalization.* Minneapolis: University of Minnesota Press.

Aptekar, L. and B. Abebe (1997) 'Conflict in the neighborhood: Street and working children in the public space', *Childhood* 4(4): 477–90.

Augé, M. (1995 [1992]) *Non-Places: Introduction to an Anthropology of Supermodernity.* London: Verso.

Blanc, C. S., E. Porio, P. Mehta and W. Moura (1996) 'Life paths of urban children and youth in comparative perspective', *Childhood* 3(3): 375–402.

Douglas, M. (1966) *Purity and Danger.* London: Routledge & Kegan Paul.

Ehn, B. (1983) *Skal vi leka tiger? Daghemsliv ur kulturell synsvinkel.* Stockholm: Liber Forlag.

Ennew, J. (1994) 'Time for children or time for adults?' in J. Qvortrup (ed.) *Childhood Matters: Social Theory, Practice and Politics.* Aldershot: Avebury, pp. 125–43.

Feld, S. and K. H. Basso (1996) 'Introduction', in S. Feld and K. H. Basso (eds) *Senses of Place.* Santa Fe, NM: School of American Research Advanced Seminar Series, pp. 3–11.

Firth, R. (1968[1936]) *We, the Tikopia: Kinship in Primitive Polynesia.* Boston: Beacon Press.

Foucault, M. (1977) *Discipline and Punishment.* London: Penguin.

Geertz, C. (1996) 'Afterword', in S. Feld and K. H. Basso (eds) *Senses of Place.* Santa Fe, NM: School of American Research Advanced Seminar Series, pp. 259–62.

Glauser, B. (1997) 'Street children: Deconstructing a construct', in A. James and A. Prout (eds) *Constructing and Reconstructing Childhood.* London: Falmer Press, pp. 145–64.

Gullestad, M. (1996) *Everyday Life Philosophers: Modernity, Morality, and Autobiography in Norway.* Oslo: Scandinavian University Press.

Gulløv, E. (1999) *Betydningsdannelse blandt børn.* Copenhagen: Gyldendal, Socialpædagogiske Bibliotek.

Gupta, A. and J. Ferguson (1992) 'Beyond "Culture": Space, identity, and the politics of difference', *Cultural Anthropology* 7: 6–23.

—— (1997) 'Discipline and practice: "The field" as site, method, and location in anthropology', in A. Gupta and J. Ferguson (eds) *Anthropological Locations: Boundaries and Grounds of a Field Science.* Berkeley: University of California Press, pp. 1–46.

Handler, R. (1985) 'On dialogue and destructive analysis: Problems in narrating nationalism and ethnicity', *Journal of Anthropological Research* 41(2): 171–82.

Hastrup, K. and K. F. Olwig (1997) 'Introduction', in K. F. Olwig and K. Hastrup (eds) *Siting Culture.* London: Routledge.

Hultqvist, K. and G. Dahlberg (2001) *Governing the Child in the New Millennium.* New York and London: Routledge Falmer.

James, A., C. Jenks and A. Prout (1998) *Theorising Childhood.* Cambridge: Polity Press.

Jensen, T. A. (2000) 'Bystruktur og børns hverdagsliv', *Barn* 18(3 & 4): 57–69.

Kahn, J. (1989) 'Culture: Demise or resurrection?' *Critique of Anthropology* 9(2): 5–25.

Kahn, M. (1996) 'Your place and mine: Sharing emotional landscapes in Wamira, New Guinea', in S. Feld and K. H. Basso (eds) *Senses of Place*. Santa Fe, NM: School of American Research Advanced Seminar Series, pp. 167–96.

Malinowski, B. (1929) *The Sexual Life of Savages in North-Western Melanesia*. New York: A Harvest Book, Harcourt, Brace & World, Inc.

Malkki, L. (1992) 'National Geographic: The rooting of peoples and the territorialization of national identity among scholars and refugees', *Cultural Anthropology* 7: 24–44.

Nieuwenhuys, O. (1993) 'To read and not to eat: South Indian children between secondary school and work', *Childhood* 1(2): 100–9.

O'Brien, M., D. Jones, D. Sloan and M. Rustin (2000) 'Children's independent mobility in the urban public realm', *Childhood* 7(3): 257–77.

Olwig, K. R. (1990) 'Designs upon children's special places?', *Children's Environments Quarterly* 7(4): 47–53.

Philo, C. (2000) 'The intimate geographies of childhood', *Childhood* 7(3): 245–56.

Qvortrup, J. (1995) 'Childhood in Europe: A new field of social research', in L. Crisholm, P. Büchner, H. Krüger, M. du Bois-Reymond (eds) *Growing up in Europe*. Berlin: Walter de Gruyter, pp. 7–21.

Rose, N. (1989) *Governing the Soul: The Shaping of the Private Self*. London. Routledge.

Strandell, H. (1994) *Sociala möteplatser för barn. Aktivitetsprofiler och förhandlingskulturer på daghem*. Helsinki: Gaudemus.

Turner, V. (1989[1967]) *The Forest of Symbols: Aspects of Ndembu Ritual*. Ithaca, NY: Cornell University Press.

Tuan, Y.-F. (1974) 'Space and place: Humanistic perspectives', *Progress in Geography* 6: 211–52.

—— (1980) 'Rootedness versus sense of place', *Landscape* 24: 3–8.

Valentin, K. (1998) 'Storbyens børn. En risiko?', *Tidsskriftet Antropologi* 38: 55–64.

Wicker, H.-R. (1997) 'From complex culture to cultural complexity', in P. Werbner and T. Modood (eds) *Debating Cultural Hybridity: Multi-Cultural Identities and the Politics of Anti-Racism*. London: Zed Books, pp. 29–45.

Part I

Place as a site of opportunity and control

Creating a natural place for children

An ethnographic study of Danish kindergartens

Eva Gulløv

In 1993 the Social-Democrat government in Denmark announced that every child in the country must be offered a place in the public day-care system at the age of one (at the latest).[1] This policy was called 'a guaranteed place', and it reflected the difficulties of returning to the labour market following parental leave. It gave rise to a heated debate concerning how to reach this goal, the quality of day-care institutions and, at a more general level, the right place for the youngest children.

A few years later another political issue relating to childcare was debated, namely the role of day-care in integrating the children of immigrant parents.[2] Discussion focused on whether it should be mandatory for these parents to send their pre-school children to public day-care centres in order to improve their language skills and ensure their cultural integration into Danish society.[3] This debate continues with increasing attention, but the requirement that immigrant children be enrolled in day-care centres has not yet been implemented officially. Nevertheless the issue indicates the socialising forces that are attributed to the public care system and illustrates that discussions of where to place the youngest children touch upon a broad range of cultural values.

This chapter analyses the politics of placing children in a modern welfare society in which most pre-school children spend their days in public care.[4] I use the notion of policy in a very broad sense as 'a complex social practice, an ongoing process of normative cultural production constituted by diverse actors across diverse social and institutional contexts' (Sutton and Levinson 2001: 1). In using this approach, my intention is to stress that childcare arrangements must be seen as a complex social practice, including the production and negotiation of cultural values. This means that the question of where to place the youngest members of society is related to the individual parent's life situation, choices and possibilities, as well as more general normative assumptions. Considering discussions of and practical arrangements for children's everyday lives, I argue that the choice to send children to day-care institutions cannot be explained by the demands of the labour market alone. The placing of children in day-care is a social practice invested with moral and social meanings that have implications for the standing of both parents and children in the community, as well as for cultural assumptions regarding childhood and socialisation more generally.

Using various sources of information, including fieldwork in a kindergarten, visits to about forty day-care institutions, a questionnaire administered to kindergarten parents, interviews with pre-school teachers and debates in the media, I discuss the ambiguities and discrepancies reflected in the material concerning the right place of childhood. The most fascinating feature of existing day-care arrangements and the discussions associated with them is that they are packed with moral assumptions and understandings concerning individual autonomy, social coherence and conceptions of children and childhood. From the point of view of cultural analysis, the discussion of what is the best place for children reveals ambivalences and paradoxes reflecting, I will argue, a more profound cultural uncertainty about the role of children, citizenship and the welfare system in contemporary Danish society.

The aim is therefore to contribute to the theoretical discussion of children's place in a contemporary Western society. Several authors on children in welfare societies have stressed how children are controlled and, especially in educational institutions, enrolled in disciplinary discourses that construct the child as a subject (e.g. Fendler 2001; Rose 1989). In this chapter I will discuss how all notions of proper childhood are played out in institutional arrangements. While an important stated goal of day-care practice is to teach children to make decisions for themselves, their choices are restricted by the fact that they cannot place themselves, nor do they have any influence on adult ideas of what is a proper childhood. Children are controlled and protected, but at the same time regarded as self-managing individuals, a paradox that points to an unsolved conflict regarding children's social position. Thus to understand children's place in a welfare society, we need to go beyond the notion of control and look into both surveillance and self-management as co-existing features in the cultural formation of citizenship.

Children in the day-care system

During the last 25 years there has been an enormous expansion in the number of pre-school children enrolled in the Danish day-care system. Today most children spend their days in institutional settings where they are looked after by professionals. Two-thirds of all children between 1 and 3 years are in day-care, and 91 per cent of all children between 3 and 5, compared to 34 per cent in 1975 (Winther 2001). Most children therefore spend between 5 and 11 hours a day in public day-care while their parents are working. As a result day-care institutions have become an integral part of Danish society, accounting for an increasing proportion of municipal budgets, and placing a high political priority on the public care of the youngest children. In other words, daily care is a fundamental part of the lives of almost all pre-school children in Denmark today.

The expansion in the number of pre-school children being looked after in the public day-care system is closely related to the political agenda concerning children and childhood. This means that public debates concerning the social position and well-being of children have focused mainly on institutional practices and conditions, the number of children per teacher and the quality of care. The issue of 'a guaranteed place', mentioned above, exemplifies the high political priority placed on finding places for all children in day-care institutions, and it illustrates the way childhood reflects the organisation and priorities of the welfare society. Thus, not only has the care system become a condition of modern childhood and a civil right for parents, it also provides the framework for discussions of contemporary childhood.

An important public debate in the mid-1990s concerned the question of whether the children of the unemployed have the same right to a place as the children of employed parents, and whether the two groups of children should be included on the same waiting list. By 1 July 1998, the law was insisting that the children of the unemployed have the same right to be enrolled in day-care institutions, though their place on the list can be bypassed twice by employed parents needing a place for their children.[5] The aim of the law was to make the two groups of children equal and to confirm that a place in a day-care centre does not depend on the parental connection to the labour market. This aim was backed up by several child researchers, who argued that a place in the institutional system is important for the well-being of a child and thus should not be related to the demands of the labour market alone. In a society where almost all children enter the day-care system, they argued, children hardly encounter any other children outside this particular institutional setting during the daytime. Consequently, it is in the nurseries and kindergartens that children develop social skills and experience themselves as autonomous beings (see, for example, Hviid and Thyssen in *Aktuelt* 14 August 1998).

Of course, the rationale behind the vigorous political attempts to find places for all children in the institutional system has to do with labour market conditions and the attempt to avoid a decline in the labour force, as well as pressure from parents who cannot look after their young children while they are working. Nevertheless, as the debate about the children of unemployed parents shows, the importance of the institutional system must be seen in a wider perspective, for the politics of placing children is an integral part of the cultural understanding of the social development and formation of tomorrow's citizens. As the debate on where to place immigrant children shows, the day-care system is considered to be a prerequisite for societal integration. In a sense the cultural production of the members of society occurs through institutional enculturation, which means that institutions are significant loci of cultural transmission and the articulation of values. It is therefore paradoxical that although the care-system actually frames the everyday lives of almost all pre-schoolers and is debated in terms of cultural integration and socialisation, the social aims of the day-care system are not clearly expressed in either law texts or institutional practices.

Nevertheless, the institutions are loaded with cultural meanings and political ambitions. If one looks a little closer at social practices concerning pre-school children, one striking feature is the many incompatibilities in assumptions and attitudes. On the one hand, the political discourses, the creation of a large number of institutions over the last ten to twenty years and the explosion in demand for a place in the day-care system all point to overwhelming cultural support for professional care for pre-school children. Seen from this very functional perspective, there seems to be a general agreement on where to place children. On the other hand, the heated and recurrent debates, the vague political definitions of the educational content of the day-care institutions and the variations in institutional arrangements indicate that placing children in professional day-care does not reflect a cultural consensus on the treatment of children. The politics of placing children cannot be understood from a top-down perspective, but must be seen more broadly as a practice in a social field in which parents and professionals, experts and, to some extent, children themselves negotiate and evaluate the well-being of the individual child as well as childhood in general. These negotiations illustrate that childhood, as a social pheno-menon, is the locus of discussion pointing to a more general disagreement or cultural uncertainty of the role of welfare institutions, processes of enculturation and social responsibility.

Looking more closely at day-care centres in Denmark today, one is confronted with a wide range of perceptions of how pre-schoolers should spend their time. Some institutions, built with the aim of accommodating a lot of children, are designed with a panoptic centre from where the teacher can overlook the different sections and look further out of the windows to the playground outside. Other kinds of institutions are located in old houses or apartments with lots of different rooms and possibilities for escaping this pedagogical monitoring. There are forest kindergartens and nurseries, where city children are transported out to the woods every morning and returned every afternoon; bus kindergartens, where the children are based in a bus and are driven to a new playground every day; institutions emphasising special activities like theatre or sport, which are meant to provide children with alternatives to the more academic learning at the school they soon will enter; night kindergartens to take care of children whose parents work at night; and institutions organised according to various pedagogical ideologies resulting in differences in structure, architecture, schedule and especially in the relationships between children and staff.

These different ways of arranging the institutional life of pre-school children indicate the many co-existing conceptions of children and childhood, and express a variety of attitudes to children's social position and the purpose of institutions. In what follows, I shall examine ambiguities in practices concerning children in institutional settings. I shall argue that children today do not have a fixed place in either society or the generational order. The many dilemmas and discussions concerning the right place of children reveal a conflict between the perception of children as products of nature on the one hand, and as modern individuals, as self-responsible agents or social citizens related to the national or global community on the other. Within these conflicts lie several other dilemmas concerning the nature of children, the role of the family, the private and the public spheres, and what it means in contemporary society to be a responsible citizen. The creation of places for children reflects, I shall argue, visions for society, as children become symbols of the time to come. Children's places are at once concrete, material loci, and symbolic expressions of social positions and expectations for the future.

Children of the past

Despite the overwhelming social acceptance of institutionalisation as a condition of modern childhood, there is a touch of nostalgia in many of the institutional arrangements that are made for children. An example of this is the forest kindergarten, a much sought after institution, where the children are transported to small houses located in the forest in order to spend their day close to nature. This was the kind of kindergarten where I carried out fieldwork over seven months in 1994–5 (Gulløv 1999). Every day a bus brings the children out to a small wooden cottage that is a far cry from ordinary institutional buildings in terms of heating, hygiene and safety. There is an expressed desire for spartanism and for not bringing too many toys to the cottage, so that the children may have a chance to experience the more 'authentic' life of the forest and to create things to play with themselves. The materialism of the modern child is supposed to be countered by the possibilities offered by nature and the activities of the adults, who spend their time building fires, making jam from wild berries, building small huts out of twigs and so on, usually but not necessarily with the help of some children.

This particular kindergarten, and similar forest institutions, are extremely popular, especially with middle-class parents. There are long waiting lists, and strong pressure from parents wishing to obtain a place here for their children. But although parents actively choose this kind of institution and support its values and pedagogical aims, it is not unusual to hear the children themselves complain about the cold, the discomfort and the lack of toys. Such complaints are met with indulgent smiles and knowing looks between the adults: these are not the kind of complaints that parents are concerned about. There seems to be no doubt that this is a healthy way to spend one's childhood.

The increasing number of forest kindergartens is an urban phenomenon. The explicit ambition is to expand the experiences of urban children, offering alternatives to what they can learn on the streets and playgrounds of the city. At the same time, the forest kindergartens can be seen as a symbol of the marginalisation and protection of childhood of today (Ennew 1994: 125; Strandell 1994: 8). Forest kindergartens offer an alternative kind of everyday life, in contrast to the materialism of modern city life. From this perspective, children are separated from their parents, separated from adult life in general, separated from city life and bussed out to another societal vision.

The interesting point is that the pedagogical aim is not directed towards preparing the children for school or for their lives as future adults. On the contrary, this particular institutional practice is built on anti-middle-class symbols (e.g. no comfortable furniture, no central heating, food cooked on an open fire or based on berries and fruits from the trees), with an explicit effort to contrast and oppose exactly the kind of society that produces the need for day-care institutions. It seems that the cultural differences between children and the rest of society are further underlined by an institutional arrangement based on explicit non-industrial values. The meta-communicative framework of this kind of kindergarten appears to suggest that this is not a modern society, and that children are neither materialists nor city-dwellers. Children belong to another kind of society.

This kind of symbolic expression and opposition to the existing society can be identified as a more general feature of contemporary institutional practices in Danish day-care centres. Many kindergarten institutions have mythological or poetic names like 'Valhalla', 'Rivendell', 'The Planet', 'Saturn', 'The Rose of the King', 'The Apple-Farm', 'The Dandelion', 'The Anthill', all indicating another time or life style far from the time-regimented order of modern society. Chickens and rabbits are common features, as are fireplaces and bowers. Institutional playgrounds often have nature-like components like fruit trees and beds with vegetables, trees for climbing, small areas with water and hilly formations – not least in urban institutions privileged with their own playground. The connection with nature, the association with other kinds of societies tied more closely to earlier forms of livelihood production, can be interpreted as a way of negating the conditions of childhood today, not as some kind of repression but as a political standpoint, an active voice in the discussion of where to place small children. Carried to its extreme, children should be in childhood, and childhood has no place in modern society.

In his analysis of transformations in Swedish educational discourse, Kenneth Hultqvist (2001) describes the ideologies of the pioneers of kindergartens at the beginning of the twentieth century as being based on a notion of an ideal way of living with the sort of intimate relationships supposed to prevail between people in small communities. The 'garden' expressed metaphorically both the protected ground of a community and the humanistic soil in which the new crops should be cultivated (ibid.: 144 –5). As Hultqvist argues, the ideology changed during the 1930s and 1940s: 'the garden image of community and the child was "industrialised" and technology, formally opposed to nature, became the natural means to realise the nation's resources, material as well as human' (ibid.: 145). Looking at the institutional practices of kindergartens today, one could argue that they reflect the reappearance of an image of the child as a more natural, humanistic subject, and of visions of the kindergarten as a humanistic place for social upbringing. However, instead of reappearance, I would suggest that the practices should be understood rather as reflecting cultural uncertainty in conceptualising the child and the outcome of upbringing. The stress on nature in contemporary childcare institutions could thus be seen as a reaction to a certain way of life in urban middle-class milieus. From this perspective, the nature element does not represent a new vision for socialisation, but should be interpreted in terms of a much more modest aim of counterbalancing the inputs received by children in order to influence their values and knowledge. Different images of children co-exist today, and I do not wish to draw a picture of a general symbolic opposition to society or to the ways children are treated. Rather I wish to draw attention to some of the cultural ambiguities and negotiations that can be found in current institutional practices. These ambiguities represent different perspectives on the social status of childhood and the role of citizenship in a modern welfare state. It seems to me that the nature-like components in institutional arrangements constitute a political statement expressing a vision of the child as organically related to nature rather than to the surrounding society. There is an element of protest in the 'altmodish' arrangements of some of today's institutions.

Parents and the professional authorities

On the basis of a questionnaire[6] that I carried out among the parents in a Copenhagen kindergarten accommodating sixty-six children and interviews with pre-school teachers there, I now turn to a discussion of parents' role in kindergartens. The parents' answers reveal a deep uncertainty of their role in the institutional setting, despite the fact that parents have a formal say in the organisation, administration and pedagogical aims and everyday practices of the kindergarten. By law the parents have considerable influence, and in this institution (as well as in most others) the teachers have encouraged parents to engage in social events and daily activities. Nevertheless, the parents' answers reveal a widespread feeling of discomfort and uncertainty concerning their own role in the institutional setting and the division of authority in relation to the child. A double-bind form of communication seems to be experienced (Bateson 1987). The explicit message is that children belong to their parents, but also that the teachers in the day-care centre are very interested in cooperating with families with respect for the well-being of the individual child. The meta-communicative message is that this is a place of work organised by professional authorities, and the presence of parents disturbs the institutional logic.

Two themes were salient in the questionnaire answers. The first concerns the amount of time children spend in the institution. Many parents seem to be worried that their children spend too much time in the institution, since they fear that they will lose contact and that the separation will have consequences for the emotional development of the child. At the same time, the few non-working parents in the group I investigated answered that they do not pick their children up from the centre too early, in case this could hinder the child in developing social relations. Thus, the amount of time a child spends in day-care seems to function as a key to interpreting social relations, and especially to assessing parents' emotional concern for their children. One pre-school teacher ended an interview on her opinions on contemporary kindergarten institutions by saying, 'I am sorry I have to interrupt the interview, but I don't want to be too late in picking up Isabella. You know, a good teacher never picks up her *own* child too late.' The social logic of time points to an awareness that if the child stays too long (more than eight hours a day), this might be interpreted as a lack of parental care, as a kind of neglect. If, on the other hand, a child spends only a few hours a day in the institution and has days off on a regular basis, this unusual practice may generate suspicions of too close a bonding between the parent and child concerned, with a risk that the child will be hindered in its normal social development. In this way the amount of time children spend in an institutional setting is read as indicative of their social relationships and degree of emotional bonding, but also of parental respect for professional work with children. Being in day-care is so much part of the normal trajectory of a child that not fulfilling the expectations of this environment is interpreted as potentially damaging to its development.

The second theme concerns parents' worries about their own relationships with their child. The decision to place a child in a kindergarten institution contains more complex feelings than can be seen from the statistical figures of the number of children enrolled in the child-care system. In particular, starting in a new institution seems to be experienced as a difficult time for both children and parents, a period where the child must get used to daily life at the new institution, and the parents must learn how to behave in a proper way in order to become respected day-care parents. This initiation period not only involves the relationship of the child to its parents, it can also be seen as a transition into a certain moral environment, where parents and pre-school teachers judge one another's caring skills. Some parents express uncertainties as to how *they* are looked upon and anxieties that the teachers are not caring for *their* child. They express emotional discomfort in communicating with the staff over the daily life of their child, and doubts as to their own roles and their right to know everything about their child. As the child now is an actor on a public stage, the parents' right to know about its secrets, acts and social inter-actions can be questioned.

This points to a more profound uncertainty concerning the relationship between professional and parental roles and authorities in relation to the institutional framework. Despite the fact that parents are in some ways the institutional customers, they are not part of the institutional setting, and although they are very much encouraged to participate in practical arrangements and the daily lives of their children, in practice they are often not very welcome. From interviews with some of the teachers, it seems that the parents' feelings of discomfort are well founded. The teachers complain that parents hinder their work and disturb the rhythm of the day, are too demanding, and have difficulties in respecting the institutional logic, especially when it comes to their own child. It is often said that parents are concerned only with their own child and are not concerned with the social dynamics of the whole group of children. As a result, it is argued, children today are more protected and selfish.

Thus parents seem to be 'matter out of place' in terms of institutional practice. I suggest that this ambivalence towards parents' place in day-care centres has to do with the character of the institution. At one and the same time it is a public, a personal and an intimate place. For the staff it is a public place of wage employment with professional challenges. For the children the institutional setting is a place for personal relations and sometimes very intimate friendships. The parents hand over the child, the symbol of the family, to professionals, thus publicly exposing their own private lives and their parental competences. As Ehn points out (1983), parents, professionals and children are constantly negotiating over what kind of social setting a day-care centre is, and what kind of relationships and forms of authority can occur within this setting. Some of the most dramatic media discussions of day-care in recent years concern exactly the blurred boundaries between the intimate, the private and the public in relation to communion with children. Negotiations over the nature of relations, the question of authority and the degree of intimacy between adults and children are a constant part of the day-care setting, pointing, I argue, to a general cultural negotiation of the generational order and social status of childhood.

Being at home

Organisations have purposes and cultural meanings that can be more or less well defined or articulated (Barth 1994: 90–1). Day-care institutions have, of course, the explicit purpose of taking care of small children while their parents are at work, but they also have more implicit meanings and intentions that are built into the daily routines and interactions between teachers and children. Institutions are filled with non-verbalised ideologies and cultural perceptions that are kept alive through the unreflected repetition of everyday life. Examining more closely the organisational arrangements of day-care centres, it seems that one of the central ideologies of the daily encounters is that children need to be in families and that families are placed in homes. Thus the notion of 'home' stands out as an interesting and paradoxical symbol of a culturally ambivalent perception of where small children ought to be.

Just as day-care structurally influences family life, kindergartens are influenced by ideas of home (Winther unpubl. paper 2001). Teachers express concerns that children do not have the necessary parental care, and posters on the wall explicitly declare that children are in need of parental contact and need to have breaks from the institution, for example, at holiday time. A commonly seen poster in kindergartens asks: 'Have you spoken to your child today?' Apart from this explicit and somewhat patronising stress on a child's need for its parents, a more implicit reference to the ideology of families and homes is to be found in the interior and organisation of the pedagogical environment. It is not that day-care centres actually look like homes or, in fact, have family-like relations. In reality there are far too many practical functions, varying activities, and individuals with different interests and relationships being played out at the same time for the institution to be home-like. But symbols referring to home seem to be inevitable in the arrangement of appropriate environments for children. Generally speaking, day-care institutions in Denmark are usually divided into different sections referred to as 'stuer' or 'living-rooms'. The interior is often characterised by a gentle and light atmosphere, with candles, dining tables, comfortable sofas with matching cushions, and photographs of active children smiling from the walls. All this suggests that this is a decent place, neat and open, a place of positive values and recreational activities, of content and active people. The style is at once personal and totally uniform, but significantly it defines itself in opposition to the clinical atmosphere of institutions in the past and the authoritative relationships between teachers and children that formerly characterised institutional life (Kjær 2001).

In pedagogical discourse, the intimacy and knowledge of the individual child is highly stressed, even though the number of children per adult makes this kind of ideal very difficult to implement in practice.[7] Despite the well-established institutionalisation of children, organised with many children, few teachers and a lot of co-existing activities, it seems that it is still the home and the family, the intimacy and dyadic relationship, continuity in place and social relations, that works as the ideal for childhood of today (cf. James *et al.* 1998: 53).

Analysing Swedish kindergartens at the beginning of the 1980s, Ehn (1983) describes how the kindergarten institution is full of contrasts. It is both human and standardised, individual and collective, child-focused and bureaucratic, solicitous and disengaged. The day-care institution displays intimacy, homeliness and respect for the individual child, while, at the same time, being instrumental, formal and totally impersonal. These paradoxes are highly recognisable in the Danish context today, despite the fact that institutions have been a part of childhood for decades. The many incongruities reflect a discrepancy between the actual conditions in the institutional setting and a cultural perception of the child as being bound to the family and the home. The organisation of the pedagogical environment and the articulations of children's needs reveal a perception of the child as vulnerable and psychologically attached to its parents.[8] There exists, I suggest, a cultural norm of the home as being the right place for small children, a perception that gives rise to the symbolic ambiguities that can be identified in the institutional arrangements. The discrepancy between the actual everyday life of children and family-based ideals reveals a profound cultural uncertainty about the relationships between the generations and what kind of caring, dependence or independence and individual autonomy a small child needs.

The self-managing child

This leads me to the last theme I shall take up before reflecting on how one can interpret these incongruities concerning the cultural place of young children. During the last ten years – and very much in line with both the UN Convention on the Rights of the Child and the scientific emphasis on children as social actors – the pedagogical focus of pre-school teachers and parents has been on children's skills and abilities to make decisions. The legal texts on kindergartens underline the child's right to have an influence and state that every child should be heard in matters concerning daily activities, as well as more general aspects of their lives (Lov om social service [Law on Social Service] LBK no. 844 24.09.01, ch. 4. §8). The official statement is thus that children are persons with viewpoints and specific interests that should be taken into account in the planning of kindergarten activities.

Many kindergartens today make an effort to promote an anti-authoritarian relationship between children and adults. In the kindergarten where I carried out my fieldwork, the idea of the child as a competent and responsible being is expressed in several ways. There is almost no schedule during the day except for the set time for the bus to depart, and no common meals except for a brief meal in the afternoon to ensure that every child has had something to eat. The children decide for themselves where they want to be, what they want to do, when they will eat their packed lunch, and whom they want to be with.

The adults function as observers and promoters of different activities such as baking, making a fire, singing songs with a guitar and reading books, but there is no attempt to persuade the children to participate, nor are any ideas expressed of the educational outcome of the activities. The pedagogical aim is to teach the child to take its own decisions and take responsibility for its own actions. This kind of institutional practice is by no means exceptional, although naturally different institutions have different practices. But the stress on children's choices and self-management is a widespread phenomenon in Danish kindergartens these days. There is an interesting paradox here. Today pre-school children are placed in institutional settings by their parents, because it is not considered safe or conducive to their well-being to be left alone in the home. Thus the individual child has no influence over where to be, no ability to choose to be alone, no opportunity to place itself. There is in general considerable emphasis on safety and adult responsibility so that the children will not be harmed or placed at any kind of risk. At the same time – or perhaps as a consequence – there is considerable emphasis in pedagogical discussions and practices on children's self-management.[9] As I have tried to show, children are encouraged to create places for themselves within the framework of the institutional setting. On the one hand, there is an overwhelming symbolic stress on the child as a self-managing, competent individual and on the relationship between children and adults[10] as antiauthoritarian and based on mutual respect. On the other hand, there is a very distinctive power relation expressed in the ways children are placed in child-care institutions, with no influence over their inferior structural positions. In other words, on the one hand, there exists a very explicit discourse on the child as an individual in modern society. Here the nature of children's citizenship has been a topic of debate, especially in relation to questions of legal responsibility. On the other hand, in practice the possibility for young children to take decisions and realise their own wishes is restricted to certain well-defined areas. Their movements are controlled and confined to specific institutions designed for looking after children. Despite the rhetoric of the competent child, in many ways children are excluded from citizenship (Cockburn 1998).

Conclusion

I have argued in this chapter that the various practices and ideologies of kindergartens reveal different ways of imaging and reasoning about children and childhood. According to one line of thought, children belong to the family, the home standing as the symbol of a safe and optimal development, even when children are placed outside the home. Another point of view is that children are connected to nature and should be protected from the scheduled and de-humanised logic of contemporary society. A third image represents children as autonomous beings with a right to a participative voice in their own lives, as well as in society more generally (cf. James *et al.* 1998: 134). These images to some extent contradict one another, reflecting, I argue, uncertainties concerning the place of children in the societal order.

The ambiguities presented in this chapter therefore point to profound cultural dilemmas concerning what kind of being a child is, that is, how much autonomy, responsibility and social consciousness one can attribute to a child. Is it responsible for its own behaviour; is it under its parents' protection? Is it under society's jurisdiction? Is it a citizen *in spe*, or already a member of society? Or what exactly are the criteria for cultural membership?

I have argued that such questions lie behind the ambiguous institutional practices and debates on the right place for small children. Placing children is never a neutral practice, nor are the circumstances under which children are looked after. Sending one's child to a public day-care centre must be seen as a deliberate act of rational choice, motivated by an analysis of the social costs and benefits and cultural values concerning perceptions of children, social coherence and social order. The fact that children today spend their days in day-care settings points to a change in the social order of the generations. The authority of the parents is challenged by divisions between parents and professionals, and by considerations concerning at what point a person becomes able to manage him- or herself. The placing of children in day-care is, despite the overwhelming statistical support, a deeply challenging practice with profound consequences for the cultural formation of a person, social authorities and citizenship. In a society that is being transformed by global processes as well as by new liberal challenges to the welfare state, discussions on the right place for children reflect the many co-existing cultural perceptions of individual autonomy, social responsibility, citizenship and the character of public services.

Discussing technologies of power in contemporary society and the ways individuals are governed and govern themselves, Hultqvist points to a shift in the ways citizens are perceived in Sweden today, compared to the early twentieth century. The 'citizen of the social' is replaced by what he calls 'the cultural citizen'. In other words, where citizenship was formerly defined by social relations and obligations, the cultural citizen is an independent individual responsible for his or her own risks (Hultqvist 2001: 155). Hultqvist argues that this shift in the cultural perception of the citizen has consequences for loyalties and feelings of relatedness. 'In such a scenario, society and the national community assume less importance. Community is something one chooses and not something to which one is under obligation, as was the case earlier' (Hultqvist 2001, with reference to Nicolas Rose).

Inspired by this line of thought, one could interpret some of the issues involved when places for children are being discussed or created as more fundamental uncertainties on the nature of citizenship in contemporary society. There is a conflict between the perception of the individual as a cultural citizen responsible for his or her own well-being, and the idea of the social citizen being related to the national community. The welfare institutions can be seen as a battlefield, as the locus of tensions in the different perceptions of social responsibility and individual autonomy. Analysed from this angle, the politics of placing children offers insights into important issues and changes in the modern welfare state. There is more to politics than the 'guaranteed place', the public caring for immigrant children and children of the unemployed. Political debates, as well as the practice of every individual family, relate to vital societal questions of membership and citizenship, of individual autonomy and the relationship between the private and the public spheres. The various practices can be interpreted as different perceptions of childhood and caring that give voice to different societal visions.

In this chapter I have drawn attention to cultural themes expressed in the form of dilemmas in relation to day-care practice. My intention has been to show that the politics of placing children contains a complexity of cultural values and ambiguities that can easily be overlooked by too great a focus on the practical functions of placing children. The fact that a majority of parents choose public day-care does not reveal the inbuilt cultural ambiguities and negotiations. Children are controlled and protected, but at the same time considered as self-managing individuals, a paradox that points to a cultural uncertainty about children and childhood. Thus, to understand children's place in this welfare society, we need to accept that surveillance and self-management co-exist in day-care practices, as do several conflicting images of children. Children are placed and therefore confined to creating places for themselves within sites designed by adults. Thus in this kind of society, the cultural formation of citizenship is somehow designed through the places made for children. But as is the case with all politics, the politics of placing children is filled with paradoxes, ambiguities and negotiations.

Notes

1   Poul Nyrup Rasmussen, opening speech to Parliament 5 October 1993.
2   See articles in *Aktuelt* 31 July 1997; *Information* 6 November 1997; *Aktuelt* 20 October 1999; *Jyllandsposten* 19 November 1999; *Information* 26 January

2000; *Politiken* 9 March 2000; *Nyhedsmagasinet Danske Kommuner* 18 May 2000; *Jyllands-Posten* 2 February 2001.

3 In 1998 the law was interpreted as enabling the children of immigrants to jump the queue of children waiting for a place in day-care under certain circumstances, in order to ensure 'appropriate integration' (Vejledning (guidance) nr. 53 of 6.3.98 to Law on Social Service ch. 4, §12 stk. 3).

4 Children in Denmark enter school in the year they reach the age of 7. Before school they spend their days in nurseries in the case of children from 6 months to 3 years of age, and in kindergartens in the case of children from 3 to 7. Though compulsory school attendance begins with the first grade, most parents today send their children to a kindergarten class a year before official school enrolment, that is, a voluntary introductory year intended to prepare children for the demands of school.

5 Lov om social service (Law on Social Service). Vejledning (guidance) no. 53, 6.3.1998, ch. 4, §12, stk. 4.

6 The questionnaire contained 40 open questions concerning parents' viewpoints on the pedagogical visions, practices and priorities, their interpretations of the social environment of the institution, communication among the children, between children and staff, and between parents and staff, and their own place in the institutional logic. Out of 66 questionnaires distributed, 42 were returned. As the answers were textual not numerical, I have not handled them statistically but have instead analysed them as other kinds of qualitative data identifying patterns in themes. The same kind of cultural analytical approach lies behind the six interviews I carried out with pre-school teachers in the same kindergarten.

7 The teacher–child ratio in nurseries (age 6 months to 3 years) is about 3 adults to 12 children. In kindergartens (3–6 years) the figure is about 3 adults per 20 to 23 children (Winther 1999).

8 Fx B. Bae and J. E. Waastad 1992; Ole Schouenborg 2001.

9 Jan Kampman provides a related argument in his analyses of the representation of the child in the UN Convention on the Rights of the Child. He shows that the convention presents two approaches, one seeing children as vulnerable and in need of protection, the other seeing children as reliable, responsible and rational and therefore with a right to be heard (Kampmann 2003).

10 'Adult' is the emic term for professionals. The term 'teacher' is never used for the kindergarten context, indicating the anti-authoritarian relationship between the two generational sets (Kjær 2001: 110).

References

Bae, B. and Waastad, J. E. (1992) *Erkjennelse og anerkjennelse – perspektiv på relationer*. Oslo: Universitetsforlaget.

Barth, F. (1994) *Manifastasjon og prosess*. Oslo: Universitetsforlaget.

Bateson, G. (1987) *Steps to an Ecology of Mind*. Northvale, NJ: Aronson.

Cockburn, T. (1998) 'Children and citizenship in Britain', *Childhood* 5(1): 99–118.

Ehn, B. (1983) *Ska vi leka tiger? Daghemsliv ur kulturell synvinkel*. Stockholm: Liber Forlag.

Ennew, J. (1994) 'Time for children or time for adults', in J. Qvortrup *et al.* (eds) *Childhood Matters: Social Theory, Practice and Politics*. Aldershot: Avebury.

Fendler, L. (2001) 'Educating flexible souls: The construction of subjectivity through developmentality and interaction', in K. Hultqvist and G. Dahlberg (eds) *Governing the Child in the New Millennium*. New York: RoutledgeFalmer.

Gulløv, E. (1999) *Betydningsdannelse blandt børn*. København: Gyldendal.

Hultqvist, K. (2001) 'Bringing the gods and the angels back?', in K. Hultqvist and G. Dahlberg (eds) *Governing the Child in the New Millennium*. New York: RoutledgeFalmer.

Hviid, P. and S. Thyssen in *Aktuelt* 14 August 1998.

James, A., C. Jenks and A. Prout (1998) *Theorising Childhood*. Cambridge: Polity Press.

Kampmann, J. (2003) 'At være sig etikken bevidst', in E. Gulløv and S. Højlund (eds) *Feltarbejde blandt børn*. København: Gyldendal.

Kjær, B. (2001) 'Barndom, voksendom, pædagogdom', unpublished Ph.D. Thesis, University of Southern Denmark.

Lov om social service (law on social service), LBK no. 844, 24.09.01.

Lov om social service (law on social service), vejledning no. 53, 6.3.98.

Rose, N. (1989) *Governing the Soul*. London: Routledge.

Schouenborg, O. (2001) *Velfærdsyngel: omsorg for småbørn og småbørnsfamilier*. København: Fremad.

Strandell, H. (1994) *Sociale möteplatser för barn. Aktivitetsprofiler och förhandlingskulturer på daghem*. Helsinki: Gaudemus.

Sutton, M. and B. A. Levinson (2001) *Policy as Practice: Towards a Comparative Sociocultural Analysis of Educational Policy*. Stamford, CT: Ablex.

Winther, I. W. (1999) *Småbørnsliv i Danmark – anno 2000*. København: Danmarks Pædagogiske Institut.

—— (2001) 'The photographed home', unpublished paper presented at Brunel University, International Conference: Children in their Places, June 2001.

Chapter 2

Restricted experiences in a conflict society

The local lives of Belfast children

Laura Gilliam

Place and experience

Once in a while, the international press is reminded of 'The Troubles' in Northern Ireland by some new act of terror or intransigence, and the world is taken aback by the persistence of the hatred between Catholics and Protestants in this old area of conflict. Generation after generation becomes involved in the strife, and the strength of the feelings involved does not seem to wear out over time. As is typical of children in such areas of conflict, children in Northern Ireland have been portrayed by the press and researchers either as victims of adult stupidity or as little devils showing distressing proof of the human capacity for evil. Since these children challenge our image of children's characteristics and appropriate lives, understanding their experiences of growing up in the midst of conflict is of great relevance to the study of children.

For this understanding, children's location in physical space is of central importance. In the working-class areas of Belfast where I did fieldwork in 1996–7, children are typically kept within their local area by their concerned parents. As I shall argue, the co-existence of this practice with a range of social and cultural practices relating to the conflict result in a restriction of children's experiences and understandings of the conflict. In this chapter, therefore, I shall describe the experiences and understandings of a group of Belfast children within their local area, and analyse the relationship between their social positions as children and the different conflict practices and discourses in Northern Ireland. In doing so, I shall demonstrate the consequences of children's restriction to specific places in a conflict situation and, through this description of an extreme case, illustrate the significance of location in physical place for children's experiences and understandings.

By illuminating this important aspect of children's relation to place, the present chapter will emphasise the point made by James, Jenks and Prout, that issues of spatiality should be integrated into the social theory of childhood, as has been done in general social and cultural theory (James *et al.* 1998: 40). Another point made by these authors is that the central issue of childhood space is the control and regulation of the child's body and mind (ibid.: 38). In line with this, I shall argue that, in many Western societies, the relationship of children to physical places is different from that of adults, due to the fact that they do not move about freely, but are often restricted physically by adults who have the authority to decide their location. Thus children in these societies are often kept within specific physical places in order to protect their highly treasured and presumably vulnerable hearts, bodies and minds. As James *et al.* put it:

> Physical, conceptual and moral boundaries circumscribe the extent of children's wanderings. From the closed arenas of domestic space to the infinite horizons of cyberspace, boundaries forestall and contain the child's movement. Erected by gerontocratic hegemony and policed by discipline, the boundaries are legitimized through ideologies of care, protection and privacy.
>
> (Ibid.: 38)

As such, a prevalent Western understanding of children's vulnerability, changeability and immaturity, combined with an even more widespread generational order of power that places children as a dominated group under the authority and control of their parents and other adults, tends to make adults restrict children to specific physical places for protection and control. Drawing on Bourdieu's theory of doxa and heterodoxy (Bourdieu 1977), I shall argue that such restrictions have important consequences for children's social outlook, their knowledge of the world and their agency. This is because their location in place structures their experiences and thus their understandings and behaviour, through their restriction to the practices, norms and discourses of the social groups that occupy these physical places. Thus this case study will demonstrate that physical, conceptual and moral boundaries not only circumscribe the extent of children's wanderings: when 'children's wanderings' are severely circumscribed, this may result in the maintenance of yet other physical, conceptual and moral boundaries, and thus of the political conflicts that these boundaries uphold.

Conflict explanations and conflict involvement

The purpose of my fieldwork in Belfast, Northern Ireland, was to study how children in this old area of conflict actually make sense of the violence and strife going on in their society. I studied two play centres in two poor working-class areas of Belfast: the Protestant area of Avoniel in East Belfast, and the Catholic area of New Lodge in North Belfast. These two areas are comparable in the sense that they are both poor working-class areas with high unemployment and poor living conditions. In addition they are both regarded as 'solid areas' typical of Belfast; that is, areas where all or most of the inhabitants belong to the same religion and are generally politically hardliners. As a consequence, the children attending the play centre in the Protestant Avoniel area were all Protestants, whereas those attending the play centre in the Catholic New Lodge area were all Catholics. In the play centres, I spent time with and observed the children, and interviewed 49 of them, all 7 to 11 years of age. I also interviewed parents, visited the children's schools and collected drawings from 180 pupils, and I participated in and interviewed the organisers of cross-community and reconciliation programmes, which a large proportion of the children had attended, were attending or were going to attend.

One of the first things that struck me when talking to Belfast children was the difference between their conceptions of the conflict and the usual explanations of adults. Northern Irish adults most often explain the conflict in their society by referring to the history and politics of the 400-year-old strife between Protestants and Catholics in Ireland and, since the partition of Ireland in 1920, in Northern Ireland. Though Protestants and Catholics in general understand the conflict very differently, the conflict discourses of the two groups characteristically explain the violent conflict and hatred between them with reference to historical and political causes. In this way the conflict and its duration and continuous existence, as well as people's current involvement in it, are explained by historical incidences, political struggles, economic inequalities, social injustices, deeply felt connections between identity and territory, and, as Vigh has argued, increasingly also cultural threats between the communities (Vigh 1998).

As the anthropologist Elizabeth Hughes has shown in her study from 1992 of 13–16-year-old youngsters in Belfast, even Belfast youth know and use the different political tales of oppression, nationalism, territorial rights, freedom and cultural pride that adults use to explain the conflict (Hughes 1992). But through my interviews with 7–11-year-old children, I learned that the different political, historical and social explanations of the conflict that Northern Irish adults give had little if any relevance to the children. The conflict was never explained in these terms, and the children were not interested in the political debate or in historical representations of the strife between the two groups. In addition, the drawings called *My Country*, which I collected from 180 7–11-year-olds attending local schools in the two areas of my study, show a parallel lack of concern with the territory of Northern Ireland. In drawing these pictures, only the oldest children showed any signs of feelings of identity connected to a wider area called Northern Ireland or Ireland (Gilliam 1998). These interviews and drawings show a similar tendency in the children of both religions in their understanding of *My Country*. With increasing age, the children seem to understand *My Country* as referring to a place of increasingly larger size and of decreasing 'homeliness', that is, of more and more abstracted connection with identity. As such, the youngest, aged 7–8, drew pictures of their house, whereas those a bit older, aged 8–9, typically drew a street. When asked about their country in the interviews the children of the same age group (aged 7–9) gave me their address. The 9–10-year-olds called their country Belfast and drew a city, typically Belfast or well-known sites in it. Only some of the oldest of both groups, the 10–11-year-olds, drew maps of Northern Ireland, Britain or Ireland, and a minority of these drew pictures with written tributes to these countries or national symbols, such as flags and, in the case of the Catholics, Celtic patterns, leprechauns and shamrocks, which are all Irish national symbols.

As their pictures hint and their interviews underline, the youngest of the children did not demonstrate any knowledge of or relationship to the territory of Northern Ireland, and were not aware of the strife over this territory. Some of the oldest boys knew bits and pieces of the conflict discourse of their own group. These boys treated the argument about the constitution of Northern Ireland as an argument about what this land shall be called, and a few of them described a conflict about who has the right to the territory. But in general, as this quote from two of the oldest and most anti-Catholic Protestant boys I interviewed demonstrates, constitutional questions did not concern the children seriously:

LG: Would you mind if Northern Ireland became part of Ireland?
D: No, I mean . . .
T: [As] long, long as we have . . . the bigger side.
LG: Yeah?
D: I mean, we would . . . but I wouldn't wonna move in that end . . . as far as they are, 'cos . . .
T: As long as we have shops and all.
D: That's all we want.
T: Big, big shops.
D: Shops, shop, shop, shop, shop, shop, sweet shop.
                    (Derek 10 years old, Thomas 11 years old, Protestants)

Like Derek and Thomas,[1] most children were satisfied with the fact that Protestants and Catholics live in different areas or, as many of them thought, that they occupy different countries (Gilliam 1998). Presumably as a conclusion drawn from the difference in Catholics' and Protestants' naming of the same territory, many expressed the idea that the groups live in separate countries, that is, that Catholics live in a country called Ireland and Protestants live in Northern Ireland or Britain. These, as I shall explain later, they often believed to be the local areas of their immediate surroundings, and they were not concerned with the territory of the others as long as the latter kept to themselves.

As such the various factors central to the conflict explanations of adults turned out not to be what motivated the children's interest in the conflict in

Northern Ireland. But what is remarkable is that, in spite of the fact that the political, historical and social explanations of the conflict did not make sense or have relevance for the children, most of the 49 children I interviewed were deeply and emotionally involved in the conflict and vested a great part of their identity in it. Many of these children took part in the recurring riots between the two communities, and most of them spoke of the other group with hatred. During my interviews, it became obvious that they were not just mechanically repeating the words of their parents, but rather trying to express their own anger and fears. Although it is a common explanation for children's involvement in conflict, these children were not just being indoctrinated into hatred and sectarian views. Instead, the antagonism towards the other group central to the local discourse of the conflict made sense to these children and was emotionally relevant to them, because of their own experiences of the conflict from the vantage point of their local area.

It is important to emphasise that a rather large group, constituting approximately a quarter of my informants, also expressed quite anti-sectarian views. In other words, they assured me that they liked 'the others' and did not want to fight them. I shall return to this issue of anti-sectarianism below. What I would like to stress here is that at least three-quarters of the children I interviewed were emotionally involved in the conflict, without knowing, and thus without being motivated by, the political explanations that adults and adolescents use. This suggests that, even before the political dimensions become important to them, children from the poor areas of Belfast are emotionally involved in the conflict and identify with one side in it. Consequently, if these children construct political understandings similar to those of the Northern Irish youngsters and their parents, the Northern Irish know the hatred before they know the political reasons for hating. Thus I argue that in an old society of conflict like Northern Ireland, the political dimensions and explanations have become secondary to the hatred between the two communities. In fact, it is the hate and fear of the other group that stems from experiences in a sectarian society that give these political issues resonance. Thus as the children grow older, political explanations gain great importance and fuel the strife between the two opposing groups, as well as legitimising involvement in the conflict.[2]

I shall now examine more closely how children get involved in the conflict, and explain why place plays such an important role in this process. This is closely related to the significance of place in Belfast city and in the everyday lives of the children.

The sectarian divide

Belfast is a divided city. Apart from mixed middle-class areas, which are mostly found in South Belfast, the town is a mosaic of small Catholic and

Protestant areas. In West Belfast Catholic areas predominate, while East Belfast is mainly Protestant with a few Catholic areas, and North Belfast a true jigsaw of purely Protestant and Catholic areas, together with some mixed areas. The city centre is supposedly neutral ground void of symbols, except for British flags on official buildings, but the streets leading out of the city towards the surrounding areas are understood as being the territory of the dominant group in those areas. Thus the direction from which one enters or leaves the city centre gives one's identity away, as does the number of the bus one takes to and from the city. This sectarian geography is partly a result of some eighty years of civil strife in Belfast, during which people have tended to choose neighbours of their own religion out of fear of trouble with the others. Every time the conflict has blossomed, the areas have become more purely Protestant or Catholic, as many people have voluntarily moved to a neighbourhood of their own group, and as residents and paramilitary groups have intimidated and still intimidate neighbours of the other religion until they move out of the area.

The sectarian divide is not only physical: it is social in the extreme. First of all, at the time of my fieldwork (as well as traditionally), only 2–5 per cent of Northern Irish marry a person of the other religion (Whyte 1990). In addition, two distinct school systems exist for Catholic and Protestant children, and people go to different pubs and shops and practise different sports. Although football is an interest common to both religious groups, the teams are divided into Catholic and Protestant clubs. Only workplaces are supposed to be mixed, as a fair employment programme tries to ensure that employers hire people from both groups. Nevertheless, as job applicants seem to prefer their own people as colleagues, there is a low rate of intermixing at work. As a result, very few places in Northern Ireland are neutral or mixed. Physical places are generally loaded with social meaning, but in Belfast places belong to one group or the other, and their division and symbolism is of vital significance. Symbols such as colours, flags and slogans are used to show what the Northern Irish call the 'colour' of the place, be it green (that is, Catholic) or orange (that is, Protestant).[3] And if these symbols are not present, people are keenly interested in knowing and decoding the place, as it determines their rights, belonging, security and comfort.

Restricted children

In the religiously pure and solidly working-class areas of Belfast, children are regarded as fragile and powerless, but also as potentially rebellious, and should therefore – ideally – be kept on a short rein and raised as God-fearing Christians, whether as Catholics or as Protestants. As in most other societies, their biological immaturity places them under the control of their parents. As such they are regarded as the possession and responsibility of the latter and, at least until they reach adolescence, their parents generally feel that they have a right to determine what they shall hear and experience.

For parents in these areas, one of the main ways of protecting and controlling their children is to ensure that they stay in their local neighbourhood. Due to the conflict and the understanding of children as being in need of protection, areas belonging to the other group are out of bounds. But in the local working-class area, children are actually very visible publicly, as many children are allowed to play on the streets of their neighbourhood until dusk, and sometimes long after. In the local area the children have their family and neighbours; it is here that they go to school and spend their leisure time playing outside or in play centres similar to those where I conducted my fieldwork. As a result, the only first-hand experiences of the world outside the area that most of the children I interviewed had came from trips to family and friends of the family in areas of the same religion, shopping trips to the neutral city centre and shopping malls, and possibly rare holiday trips to Ireland, England or Scotland.

Children's place in the generational order of power, as well as the understanding of children as vulnerable and potentially rebellious, thus has the consequence that many children in Belfast are restricted to a local place. Parents and other adults in charge of the children actively use restriction to physical places to protect children against physical harm as well as unwanted influences. Presumably, this is no different from other societies, where adults also place their children in physical places that correspond to the social and discursive spheres matching their adult convictions. In Britain children are typically kept away from the street, within private homes and in specific designated institutions for children (James *et al.* 1998). In these places children are thought to be subject to good influences, which most often means the practices and discourses that their parents consider culturally legitimate. Conversely, they are kept away from places representing practices and discourses that their parents regard as bad and dangerous to their minds and bodies. But in a deeply divided society like Belfast, this restriction has more serious consequences for the experiences and understandings of the children than it does for those growing up in more peaceful and mixed societies.

The violent others

Their restriction to the local area means that children in Belfast are part of the division of the society. They are kept within a specific social group, namely the local community belonging to the same religion and predominantly also the same social class as their parents. This also restricts them to the highly homogeneous conflict discourse of this community. And significantly this also means that they only have a few experiences that might challenge this discourse, as most of their experiences in this local place actually support the local conflict discourse and its interpretation. The children therefore only hear about the other group in the discourse of their own community, and only meet members of the other group in the violent clashes that take place on the borders between their own area and the neighbouring areas of the other group. Actually some will unavoidably meet members of the other group in neutral, peaceful contexts such as the city centre, shopping malls and cross-community projects, but, as I shall explain shortly, here a complex of facts and practices leads them either never to realise that these people are of the opposite religion, or to regard the situation not as peaceful but as potentially dangerous.

What the children in New Lodge and Avoniel seemed to conclude from their experiences was that the only possible and indeed socially sanctioned form of interaction with the other group involved violence or verbal abuse. As children tend to draw conclusions from the regularities of their experiences, such as the structures and repeated events that they experience (Bourdieu 1977: 72, 88), they inferred from this that the other group is dangerous, violent and opposed to them. In the same way they told me that the walls between the Catholic and Protestant areas were built to protect them against the evil people, and similarly, they understood the separation of the lives of Catholics and Protestants as proof of how potentially dangerous interaction between these groups is. The conflict discourse of their local community supports this understanding, making the children's experiences resemble what Bourdieu called doxa. This is an experience of perfect correspondence between the objective order (what the children experience) and the subjective principles of organisation (how the child is taught to organise his experiences), as well as a lack of acknowledgment of the fact that alternative orders exist (ibid.: 164). Belfast children are as active and imaginative as any other children, but up to a certain age their experiences of the conflict, their own people and the others are restricted, to the extent that they rarely have experiences that challenge their understandings. Furthermore, they never encounter alternative understandings of the two groups or of the conflict, and therefore never realise that their understandings and practices can be questioned.

Being kept within the physical, social and discursive place of the local area, Belfast children never acquire any peaceful or positive experiences of the others. To the children I interviewed, this merely emphasised that the only characteristic of the others is that they are violent, evil people. Here one Protestant and one Catholic child express this exclusively violent image of the others. One should note that these are mirror images of one another, painting equally grim pictures of 'the others' – a fact that testifies to the similarity of the children's lives, experiences and interpretations of the conflict discourse of their group, in spite of their separated lives:

Have you ever seen one?
Yeah.
How could you see that it was a Fenian?[4]
Don't know, because you can hardly recognise one!
Can you hardly recognise one? But how did you know that it was a
    Fenian, then, did anyone tell you or . . .?
No – they threw a bottle at me.

(William, 10 years old, Protestant)

Could you recognise an Orangie[5] if you met one?
[She nods]
How can you recognise him?
If he's running to your . . ., if he's running . . . he comes and does your
    house in.

(Kerry Lee, 7 years old, Catholic)

Through many years of living in a purely sectarian area within a divided
society at conflict, these children know of no other way to understand the
other group than through this obviously negative and violent stereotype.
Although violent stereotypes of other ethnic groups also thrive in ethnically
mixed areas with more interaction between the groups, the consequences
of the restricted experiences of Belfast children make their views extreme
and difficult to change and, I argue, also motivate involvement in the
conflict.

Local and inborn conflict identities

One result of the local life of children in these two working-class areas is
that they understood the group terms Catholics and Protestants as referring
to their own local community, on the one hand, and to the closest community of the opposite religion, on the other hand. This is exemplified by
Nadine, who drew me a map explaining where 'we' and 'the Catholics'
live:

> There's . . . do you know the Strand,[6] that's where all the Catholics live
> and we live past the . . . and that's where we live, just in that area,
> and a few Catholics live up near the town.

(Nadine, 8 years old, Protestant)

This contrasts with adult practice, which understands these terms as
referring to much larger, more abstract and more geographically dispersed
groups. As a result of this understanding, and in contrast to adults who
view the conflict as a historical one of some complexity, the children from
New Lodge and Avoniel evidently understood any talk of the conflict

between Catholics and Protestants as referring to the strife they experience between their local community and one or two neighbouring communities of the other religion.

As the children understood the conflict as a local strife between two local groups, it was of strong personal concern to them. The conflict is one between a group that they know only as evil and violent, and as opposed to their own group, which is the group of immediate significance to them. To the individual child this latter group is *Us*, which includes *me and my loved one*s as well as my neighbours, all being people that I know as friendly, peaceful and not deserving violent attacks from the others. In accordance with this, the children understood their identity as either Catholic or Protestant as a local identity connecting them to the people they knew from the local community in opposition to a perceived hostile neighbouring community. This identity was thus a positive and relevant identity that the children readily accepted. They knew of its religious significance and they could tell me a number of religious differences between the groups, but what they stressed was the local group aspect of the identity, as well as its most important characteristic, namely that it is a *conflict identity*. This requires some explanation.

In everyday life within the purely Catholic or Protestant areas – which, it should not be forgotten, are predominantly peaceful – other identities such as gender and age seem to be more important to the children than being Catholic or Protestant. Psychologists rating Northern Irish children's identifications have seen this as proving that Catholic and Protestant identities are of little importance to young, pre-adolescent children (Trew 1983: 117; Cairns 1987: 104–11, citing the work of Lawless, Cairns and Mercer, Trew and Mullan). I assume that this conclusion results from a lack of recognition of the situationality of identities. An individual's identity is multifaceted, situational and relational, in such a way that the aspect of one's identity that comes to the fore in a specific situation depends on the particular context, such as the activity being engaged in, and the present or merely imagined others involved in this specific situation. It is even more important to keep this in mind when questioning children about their identities, as one cannot expect them to abstract from the current situation and make a general cross-contextual evaluation of their self-understanding. As Barth's work on ethnic groups shows, identity is defined by the boundaries that are marked between oneself and others in the particular situation (Barth 1981 [1969]). In the peaceful everyday life in the local areas where most questionnaires and interviews with Northern Irish children are conducted, it is the boundaries between people within the children's local social group, such as age and gender, that are relevant to the children. Nevertheless, I found that most of the 7–11-year-old children I interviewed were both knowledgeable and proud of their Catholic or Protestant identity – their local group identity – but this was predominantly brought to awareness and thus only of real importance when the boundary between the religious groups was marked. This marking mainly occurs in talking about the conflict, that is, within the conflict discourse, and in the actual and only interaction between the groups that the children experience, which, due to their physical restriction to the local area and the local group, consists overwhelmingly of conflict situations. As such, the identity mostly has relevance in relation to the conflict, and consequently the children mainly understood their Catholic or Protestant identity as a *conflict identity – that is, what signifies being Catholic or Protestant is being participants in a conflict* – and if you are one of them you are naturally involved.

This understanding is evident from the way the children explained being Catholic and Protestant. Although they rarely explained these formally religious identities in religious terms, what was mentioned every time was Catholics or Protestants being in conflict with each other:

> What does it mean to be Catholic?
> The Catholics fight with the Protestants.
>> (Meriad, 9 years old, Catholic)

> What is an Orangie?
> They shoot Catholics.
>> (James, 8 years old, Catholic)

> What does it mean to be a Protestant?
> It means to be good or . . . doesn't it? We're Protestants, and Catholics don't like Protestants. Protestants don't like Catholics, Catholics don't like Protestants.
>> (Thomas, 11 years old, Protestant)

As adults treat both Catholic and Protestant identities as inherited and inborn, this understanding of the identities as conflict identities has serious consequences for the children's involvement in the conflict. Being in a subordinate position regarding knowledge of this kind, the children accept the identity ascribed to them by their parents and other adults. Here Tracey shows her acceptance of her parents' authority on this matter and thus her acceptance of her ascribed identity:

> You told me before that you thought you were a Catholic when you were small?
> Yes, I didn't know what I was. If someone asked me at school: 'I'm a Catholic', you know, 'No, I'm a Protestant', no just: 'I don't know, I think I'm a Catholic' . . . 'cos I didn't know what I was!
> Yeah. . . . Do you remember when you found out what you were?

Yes, it was . . . . Someone turned around to me and said: 'What are you, Protestant or Catholic?' And my Mummy heard it and she said: 'No, you're Protestant, remember that you're a Protestant'. I just found out that I was a Protestant.

(Tracey, 10 years old, Protestant)

Thus the children's understanding of the two religious identities as conflict identities signifying positions in the conflict and being inherited from their parents means that what the parents actually pass on when they teach their children about their religious identity is that they have been born into a conflict identity, which makes them natural participants in the conflict and gives them natural groups of allies and enemies. And, as the conflict discourses of both groups present this identity positively and ascribe its holders the moral high ground of the conflict, the children rarely have reason to refuse it.

It is important to stress here that the children's understandings are not wrong or misunderstood. Toren points out that children's understandings make sense in relation to their experiences and often show us those parts of the adults' understandings that are not expressed and often unconscious, but are embodied in and conveyed to children through actions and non-verbal communication (Toren 1993: 466, 473). I argue that adult Northern Irish have also come to understand the two religious identities as inborn identities and to use them as synonyms of ethnic identities. This is not peculiar, as historically they have correlated with the ethnonyms Irish and English/Scottish. Also, although many Northern Irish would deny it, the understanding of Catholic and Protestant identities as conflict identities does not seem basically different from adults' expressed perceptions of these identities. Apparently, centuries of conflict have facilitated these understandings of what are nominally religious identities.

The combination of restricted experience with the others and an understanding of the conflict as being a local conflict between the local Us and Them – both factors connected with the practice of restricting the children to their local area – makes the conflict of great importance and emotional relevance to these children. Through their inborn identity as Catholics or Protestants, they are solidly placed in the conflict, in its inward spiral of identification, participation, competence and emotional involvement. Borrowing the term from Lave and Wenger these Belfast children have the role of 'peripheral legitimate participants' in the conflict, and they have the motivation to stay there and work their way inward to full involvement and competence in the conflict (Lave and Wenger 1991). Here it could be argued that children's agency in conflict situations, and probably also in general, is profoundly influenced by this kind of motivation, which is derived from being 'legitimate participants' in specific 'communities of practice' (ibid.).

Cross-community interaction, anti-sectarianism and the avoidance of conflict

In spite of all these factors ensuring the children's involvement in conflict, there are practices as well as social forces within Northern Irish society that presumably work against this process. Sadly, though, these only rarely seem to make any real difference to the children. As mentioned before, most Belfast children inevitably meet members of the other group in peaceful situations. In spite of the existence of pure sectarian areas, members of the other group actually pass through their local areas from time to time. Also, Catholics and Protestants meet in the city centre, in the big shopping malls or on the bus and in the taxi, as taxi drivers and passengers are frequently of different religions. In both the play centres where I worked, one or two of the play workers were actually of the other religion, thanks to the council's fair employment policy. But nevertheless, many of the children I interviewed in the play centres claimed that they had only seen people from the other group in the violent clashes, or even that they had never met one.[7]

From my conversations and interviews with and observations of these children, it became clear to me that they automatically regarded peaceful members of the other group as members of their own group, just as they regarded all normal-looking people situated in their local area as one of their own. As such they categorised people as Protestants or Catholics according to their behaviour and according to their location in the physical and social landscape. Due to the similarity of Catholics and Protestants in physical appearance and dress, and the children's image of the others as unfriendly and violent, which is upheld by their restriction to the local area, they never realise that they actually meet members of the other group that do not match this image and might challenge their stereotype of them. They automatically expect such people to be members of their own group. In the same way, they never questioned my identity as one of them. Andrea, an 8-year-old Protestant girl, explained me why quite neatly:

> What about me, what am I?
> Protestant.
> Yeah? Why?
> Because I know you don't go around starting troubles and things like that, so you don't, and you can tell that by the way you're dressed and all, by the way you comb your hair properly, because, like, if you were Catholic you would keep your hair messy and go out and start trouble and never worry about your hair, you would say like: 'Oh I have to go out early and start getting ready for the troubles'.
> (Andrea, 8 years old, Protestant)

Like Andrea, many children expected that the others would actually look different. This is very much due to a practice of conflict avoidance in all mixed areas and situations, which are not conflictual either by accident or tradition.[8] In mixed situations, people of different religions interact with caution and avoid mentioning the conflict and politics, and especially identifying others using the terms Catholic and Protestant. Likewise, all Northern Irish, even people not actively or emotionally involved in the conflict, use what Burton has called a system of *telling* to identify strangers' religious identity for the sake of avoiding conflictual subjects and episodes in otherwise peaceful situations (Burton 1978). Because of the sectarian division of most physical and social spheres, simple questions of people's surnames, what school they went to, where they live, as well as looking out for identity markers such as particular expressions, the pronunciation of certain letters,[9] sport interests, which bus they take and what newspaper they read, can tell any insider whether they are facing a person of the same or the other group.

The avoidance of conflict in mixed areas and situations is also marked through a code and ideal of anti-sectarianism, and an anti-sectarian discourse is dominant here. Sectarianism – that is, defining and evaluating people according to their belonging to different religious groups – is, like racism in other countries, politically incorrect in these mixed areas and situations, but people also avoid making sectarian remarks in order to prevent violent or stressful situations, simply because they want a peaceful everyday life. These practices of *telling*, taboo and conflict avoidance, which seem to have helped uphold the peace that actually dominates everyday life in Northern Ireland, have the grave side effect that children either never realise that they have met members of the other group who challenge the negative stereotype, or else conclude that the interaction with the others is restrained because it is dangerous. This is the main reason why the cross-community projects that a third of my group of informants (all 9-year-olds or above) had attended in many cases only served to support the bad image the children had of one another.

Neutral places: cross-community projects

In Northern Ireland cross-community projects in schools are part of an official programme for the improvement of relations and understandings between the two conflicting communities. Through interviews with the organisers of these projects, I learned that these are directed towards children because children are 'the adults of tomorrow' and regarded as more capable of changing than their parents. But the very same image of children is what makes them vulnerable in the eyes of their parents. Parents have the right to decide what their children should be exposed to, and if they feel that the children are being 'indoctrinated' into a different understanding of the conflict, or to take a critical stance to their parents' opinions and actions, they often react by forbidding or threatening to forbid their children to participate in the projects. The adults involved in these projects – the teachers and organisers – are keenly aware of the parents' authority over their children, and, as they told me, are careful not to challenge their authority and world view. Thus the efforts of the adults who are actually most likely to challenge the views of the children are limited because of the vulnerable image and subordinate position of children in the generational order of Northern Irish society.

What we can see in these projects is that the adult organisers use place actively to try to influence the children, at the same time as they use it in operating in a politically sensitive arena. The first meetings of a cross-community project normally take place on neutral ground, somewhere that is neither Protestant nor Catholic. Moving the children out of their local places has important symbolic value, as it is presumably meant to demonstrate the neutrality of the projects to the parents and the public. The project's aim is to introduce the children to other experiences and discourses and thus influence their negative understanding of 'the others'. For this goal they move the children in space, away from their doxa experiences, so to speak, and put them into an ambiguous and 'heterodoxic' place (cf. Bourdieu 1977), where it is thought that they can throw away old stereotypes and be susceptible to influences through other experiences and discourses. Moreover, moving the children from a local to a neutral place also challenges the parents, as it is opposed to their desire to keep their children in the safe physical and discursive place of their own group.

In accordance with the anti-sectarian discourse and practice of avoidance in mixed situations, the children involved in the projects are only told that they are supposed to meet a class from another school and are supposed to make friends with them. Any naming of the others as Protestant or Catholic is prohibited as sectarian, and any direct confrontation or verbalisation of the sectarian divide and conflictual relationship between the groups is avoided so as not to awaken any harsh feelings between the children and provoke their parents to forbid them to take part. Thus the children are told that they are not allowed to speak of Catholics and Protestants and are forbidden to wear the highly fashionable football outfits, as this shows their membership of the religious group and signifies opposition to the other group.[10]

At the projects I attended, the children behaved according to the rules, except for some minor events, and some returned with good experiences of individual children from the other group. But due to the strength of their stereotypes, most often they apparently understood these children as individual deviations from the group, rather than as challenges to their view of the other religious community, as the adult organisers intended. It was striking that the children were very aware of the ties that were

imposed on them and felt that this proved the potential danger of interaction between Catholics and Protestants. Many told me how the two
groups of children had started abusing each other as soon as they left the
neutral premises such as the bus, as Angela tells me here:

> . . . and then when everybody goes home, when they get off the bus,
> they give us the finger and all.
>
> (Angela, 9 years old, Catholic)

To the children, these events proved that the peace at the projects was only
a fragile one that was imposed by the teachers and adult organisers. These
cross-community projects therefore do not seem to have the desired results.
In line with this, researchers evaluating different cross-community projects
also conclude that the interaction between the groups do not change the
children's and youngsters' general opinions of one another (reviewed by
Cairns 1987: 160–1, and Hughes 1992: 196).

New discourses and discursive phrases

Instead of the intended understanding that the others were friendly and
normal children like themselves, what I found to be the primary lesson of
these projects for the children was learning the main rules of conflict
avoidance, that is, the practice of not talking about the conflict, not using
the terms Protestant and Catholic, not wearing sectarian symbols in
neutral places, as well as the discursive phrases of the anti-sectarian
discourse. The children who used discursive phrases such as 'We are all the
same', 'There's no difference to me', 'I don't mind Protestants/Catholics',
'It's not like they're green and we're orange' or the like, were always
children who had attended these cross-community projects, where they are
acquainted with the anti-sectarian discourse. By discursive phrases I mean
sentences with specific wording or just a specific content that is taken from
a specific discourse and has an air of truthful triviality. Members of a
community have common knowledge of these phrases, ascribe them almost
the same meaning, and regard them as culturally legitimate in accordance
with the shared discourse they are taken from. As such they are condensed
entities of a discourse that are uttered over and over again and can be used
to awaken and refer to the discourse as a whole (see also Gilliam 1998). I
would like to stress that the cross-community projects are not useless, as
some of the children I interviewed, mainly the oldest girls, seemed to be
honestly convinced of the truth in these discursive phrases. However, many
of the children seemed to use them only as phrases that they knew were
politically correct, as at other times they conveyed their bitter disgust of
'the others' to me. Thus what the children generally learned on the projects
was the anti-sectarian discourse and the conflict avoidance practice – both

important social skills in Northern Irish society. As such, to many children the projects mainly served as an eye-opener to heterodoxy, 'the universe of the discussed' (Bourdieu 1977: 168–9), here the existence of different views on the conflict and the two different religious groups.

These examples of the factors that ought to break down the practice of restricting Belfast children to a local area, a single social community and a specific conflict discourse show that the understandings the children have constructed from their experiences within this area, community and discourse have so much force, and correspond so well with one another, that the children do not recognise experiences that do not match these understandings, nor are they challenged by a few experiences of a different sort. Thus while children who experienced that 'the others' could be quite friendly show that the projects are not entirely without effect, the latter also show us that nice words of anti-sectarianism and sporadic changes of place and experience are not enough to change children's understandings.

Conclusion

One possible way to weaken the motivation of these children to become emotionally and actively involved in the Northern Irish conflict – and thus a possible way out of the circle of conflict, restricted experiences in childhood and identification with a conflict identity – is for children to have continuing neutral and positive experiences of the others and for them to experience the others as part of the same community. When children are restricted to a local area that is also a homogeneous social and discursive place, when they are kept away from the other group, and when membership of all the important social groups, such as school, local community and family, never cross the boundaries of the religious groups and always divide them, then the children are restricted to contra-identification as well as negative and violent experiences of the others. In Northern Ireland the prolonged restriction to a physical, social and discursive place is one of the main reasons why children become involved in the conflict with heart and soul, even before they know the political reasons why they should continue fighting the battles of their forefathers.

As such, the tendency of these children and those older than them is to reproduce their parents' conflict involvement and understandings. This fact has often brought observers as well as the Northern Irish themselves to marvel about the consistency of the patterns of conflict and the non-progressiveness of new generations. Seen from one point of view, therefore, Northern Irish children show us how restriction to place in certain social arenas puts a firm limitation on children's agency. Restricted to what Bourdieu called 'the universe of the un-discussed', the children have the kind of doxic experiences where experiences and presentations fit so perfectly that other possibilities are not considered (Bourdieu 1977:

164). At the same time, their restriction to the physical, social and discursive place of the local area limit their experiences of their own and the other group and of the conflict, resulting in an understanding of their own role in the conflict as participants that motivates them towards reproduction rather than innovation. One could also argue that, given the strong cultural forces that serve the continuation of the conflict, conflict involvement is strategically wise for the children in that it assures them positive identities and positions within their local community, which are of the utmost importance to them as long as they are restricted to the local physical, social and discursive place. But even if we see this as a positive choice, it is merely a limited agency within a restricted space. Thus the case of children in Belfast also questions the extent of children's agency, which has received great emphasis in new social studies of childhood (Prout and James 1990: 8, 24). In extreme cases such as the present one, children's agency can be severely limited, or at least heavily influenced, by their restriction to place, as this restriction has important consequences for children's experiences and understandings, and thus for the choices and kinds of behaviour that form the basis of this agency. In these cases, therefore, concerned adults tend to control and regulate children's bodies as well as their minds.

Notes

1 All names are pseudonyms.
2 In this way, as well as showing us something about growing up in a conflict society, the understanding of the experiences of Belfast children can demonstrate some of the factors that serve the continuation of the Northern Irish conflict and conflicts like it.
3 The colour green is a symbol of Catholics and Ireland, as green is the colour of Ireland's national saint, St Patrick. The colour orange as a symbol of Protestants is a reference to King William of Orange, the Dutch Protestant king who defeated the Catholic James II at the Battle of the Boyne in 1690 and thereby ended Catholic rule in the British Isles.
4 Fenian is a derogatory term for a Catholic.
5 Orangie is a derogatory term for a Protestant.
6 The Strand is a Catholic area in East Belfast
7 I did not question the children about the play workers of the opposite religion in their play centre, as the play workers preferred that this should not be discussed with the children and their parents. Religion is not a secret, but it is preferably not discussed in mixed situations.
8 For a description and discussions of conflict avoidance in Northern Ireland, see Harris 1972, Leyton 1974, McFarlane 1986.
9 When saying the alphabet, Catholics often pronounce the letters A and H in the Irish way.
10 Football games between Catholic and Protestant teams are thought of as a part of the conflict, and therefore any expression of support for a football team expresses conflictual opposition to the other group.

References

Barth, F. (1981) *Process and Form in Social Life.* London: Routledge and Kegan Paul.

Bourdieu, P. (1977) *Outline of a Theory of Practice.* Cambridge: Cambridge University Press.

Burton, F. (1978) *Politics of Legitimacy: Struggles in a Belfast Community,* London: Routledge and Kegan Paul.

Cairns, E. (1987) *Caught in the Crossfire: Children and the Northern Ireland Conflict.* Belfast: Appletree Press.

Gilliam, L. (1998) ' "When Catholics and Protestants fight": En analyse af konfliktforståelser blandt børn i Belfast', unpublished M.Phil. Thesis, University of Copenhagen.

Harris, R. (1972) *Prejudice and Tolerance in Ulster: A Study of Neighbours and 'Strangers' in a Border Community,* Manchester: Manchester University Press.

Hughes, J. E. (1992) 'Formation and management of national identity and inter-group attitudes among school children in two polarised Belfast communities', unpublished Ph.D. Thesis, Queens University of Belfast.

James, A., C. Jenks and A. Prout (1998) *Theorising Childhood.* Cambridge: Polity Press.

Lave, J. and E. Wenger (1991) *Situated Learning: Legitimate Peripheral Participation.* Cambridge, MA: Cambridge University Press.

Leyton, E. (1974) 'Opposition and integration in Ulster', *Man* 9: 185–98.

McFarlane, G. (1986) 'Violence in rural Northern Ireland: Social scientific models, folk explanations and local variation', in R. Riches (ed.) *The Anthropology of Violence.* Oxford: Basil Blackwell.

Prout, A. and A. James (1990) 'A new paradigm for the sociology of childhood? Provenance, promise and problems', in A. James and A. Prout (eds) *Constructing and Reconstructing Childhood: Contemporary Issues in the Sociological Study of Childhood.* New York: Falmer Press.

Toren, C. (1993) 'Making history: The significance of childhood cognition for a comparative anthropology of mind', *Man* 28(3): 461–78.

Trew, K. (1983) 'Group identification in a divided society', in J. Harbison (ed.) *Children of the Troubles: Children in Northern Ireland.* Belfast: Stransmillis College.

Vigh, H. (1998)' "They're trying to destroy our culture": En analyse af konflikt-narrativer blandt paramilitære protestanter i Nordirland', unpublished M.Phil. Thesis, University of Copenhagen.

Whyte, J. (1990) *Interpreting Northern Ireland.* Oxford: Clarendon Press.

Chapter 3

The Smith children go out to school – and come home again

Place-making among Kuku-Yalanji children in Southeast Cape York, Australia

Francine Lorimer

This chapter is an exploration of the place-making activities of Kuku-Yalanji children in Southeast Cape York, Australia. Drawing on my fieldwork among an extended Kuku-Yalanji family in Southeast Cape York, I present a dense description of everyday lives in order to show how the culturally specific shape of the children's social relationships to places gave meaning to their choices of movement, including movements out to school and back home again. I argue that the children's experiences of belonging to a network of paternal and maternal kin as well as engaging with bush, sea and town life constituted the grounds of the social world that the children – each in their own way – drew upon as their movements expanded outwards to embrace more distant places. I discuss the school-attending practices of three children to illustrate how what might to an outsider seem irregular and unpredictable choices on the part of the children were in fact the ways in which each child maximised their particular support network, as they took the big step of leaving home to go to school. I end with some reflections on the experience-near nature of place, and of the experience-distant map that we are left with of the children's movements to and from school.

The Farm

The children in this chapter were all members of one extended Kuku-Yalanji family that I will call the Smith family, with whom I lived during my fieldwork in 1993–4, and visited during return trips in 1996 and 1998. I had been invited to do fieldwork in this area by a Kuku-Yalanji woman in her late fifties, Denise, whom I had met at the Laura Dance Festival earlier that year. Throughout the year, the issue of Native Title had been in every newspaper[1] and Denise and I shared an interest in the prospects of future land claims. Kuku-Yalanji have a history of owning almost no land.[2] Earlier that year, Denise had already managed to gain back a small plot on her land, which I call 'the Farm', by applying for an ATSIC grant.[3] But this represented a tiny portion of what she spoke of as her traditional country.

The life of Denise's extended family became the focus of my research. Almost all of the children that I discuss spent months at the Farm at one time or another. Although they were never all there at the same time, the Farm was rarely without the sounds of their voices, and the adults preferred to have children around, complaining that the place was lonely without them. These children all had some kind of right to be there, either because they had a parent (e.g. Denise) who belonged to the Smith family by birth, or they had a close relative who had married into the Smith family. [4]

The children that my account describes (there were others) are: Karen (14),[5] John (13), Janina (2), Jack (7), Janet (14), Daniel (2), Flora (15), Trenton (7), Phyllis and her sisters and cousins (ranging between 3 and 17), Katrina (7) and Jason (9). The children that had one parent from the Smith family had a strong claim to the Smith land at Lowrel. In addition, they each had a particular relationship to the land of their other parent, each who described themselves as belonging to a different land area (see Map): **Karen**'s father, Martin, hailed from Port Stewart. Karen had relatives through her father at Coen, Laura, Cooktown, Wujal Wujal and Mossman. **John**'s father, who was separated from Margaret, grew up at Woorabinda. John had relatives through his father at Woorabinda and Brisbane. Helen, the mother of **Janet** and **Jack**, came from Hope Vale.[6] Most of Janet's mother's family lived at Hope Vale, but some lived at Wujal Wujal. **Flora**'s father was a traditional owner of land close to Mossman; Flora lived at Mossman Gorge but visited the Farm. **Trenton**, **Phyllis** and her sisters and cousins, as well as **Katrina** and **Jason** did not have a parent in the Smith family, but they lived for extended periods of time at the Farm through other relationships.[7]

My interest in these children's movements on the land was initially aroused when I became intrigued and concerned by the amount of time they spent away from school. I was intrigued because it was clear from

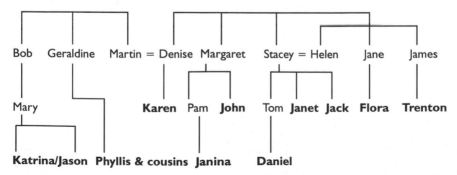

Figure 3.1 A selected representation of the Smith family (names in bold are the children discussed in this text).

comments that the children's parents made that the parents valued school highly. The first thing that I became aware of, then, was that it was ultimately up to the children to decide whether they went to school or not. I also noticed that, even when they had dropped out of school the year before, they generally chose to return to school the following year. But they all returned to different schools.

How could I make sense of this pattern, especially given that, despite coming from the same extended family, each child's school-attending pattern was unique?

I decided to begin analytically within the nexus of relationships that was relevant to each child, and look at how the children lived in places in terms of these initial relationships. I then followed the children out, in the style of an extended case analysis (van Velsen 1967), exploring where they went, and how this pattern of movement was socially meaningful in terms of the personal placement of each child. In this way, I attempted to grasp the social growth of these children as a process that encompassed the range of the different places they lived in, for the children themselves lived all their various placements in a fully engaged way.

Figure 3.2 Map of Southeast Cape York.

In my case studies, I will indicate how patterns could be found in each child's movements that resonated with movements in earlier generations, which were meaningful to Kuku-Yalanji in terms of clan connection to certain areas of country. But first I will sketch some impressions of how the children interacted socially, physically and imaginatively with their environments.

Home as a lived place

During the time of my fieldwork, the children that I have described above could often be found at the place to which they all had some claim – the Farm at Lowrel[8] – and it is around this place that the activities I describe are clustered. Constituting the children's place-making activities around life at the Farm allows me to illustrate that these children's activities brought into play a myriad of factors that cut through a classical anthropological divide of 'traditional' Aboriginal life and 'urban' Aboriginal life. Spearing a snake, going fishing, collecting berries or visiting one's other relatives' country were just as important for these children as watching videos, listening to reggae, watching a fight or going shopping at Cooktown. All of these activities slipped in and out of focus in the children's talk with me or with each other, as the children accompanied me on car rides or as the older children played with and scolded the younger children in the front yard of the Farm.

The children let their attentions be grabbed by one or another detail as they moved across a landscape that was at once socially and ecologically meaningful. I noticed that they often became engrossed in a very specific activity, and it was in terms of these activities that the children related to me. It was thus through children that I learnt much about the social and physical environment: when I went to the beach, Karen gave me a stick and took me out to the reef, showing me how to probe for a certain kind of shell; Phyllis showed me how to dig for clams, and later, despite her own lack of food, gave some of the clams that she had collected to my 2-year-old son; Jack pointed out marks that showed that a pig had passed by, then showed me a red crab claw, which he said was poisonous. On these occasions, their actions drew on a store of knowledge that had been built up over many such events, and constituted a kind of body of 'how to' knowledge.

When we looked for the various kinds of food that the land offered, the children's talk often included past events on the same place, or of the same nature. I reflected how children brought these past events into their present activities, and concluded that, apart from this 'how to' knowledge, they also drew on a store of memories in which they personally had experientially grasped aspects of the environment through their own bodies and thoughts. In the following case, for example, a routine dig for *jarruka* eggs[9] was an occasion for Jack to evoke, more than his knowledge of the habits of bush fauna, the thrilling danger and intimacy of previous bush trips. As we dug, Jack pointed to an area of the ground:

> Look there, that's where a pig was sitting. We go pig hunting with our best uncle. And I'll tell you something funny. When we was hunting up at – there was a vine, this thick – look! – And it went around and around, round, round, round [Jack twisted his hands in a spiral motion upwards]. And John was hanging on it and he was saying: 'Help!' He was scared of the pig!
>
> After a short silence, Jack said:
> Hear that?
> I heard a very faint sound.
> There again! That's the bush hen looking for somewhere to lay her eggs. One time, when we were digging one came right here – look! And laid her eggs. Well, we hid and then we chased her away and took the egg! Well, she chased us too a bit!

The children's measure of the world embraced all things that moved around them, whether they were tourists, planes, boats, the tide, the wind or animals. Jack pointed to a boat on the horizon and observed, 'that one goes up to Cooktown, then down to Cairns'. On the morning after a storm, Jack described its course:

> That lightning came this way [his hand swept towards the west], then this way [towards the east].
> Jack paused.
> Then: bugbugbugbugbugbugggggggg [thunder]. Then it went to the beach.

This 'tracking' was also implicit in the way that the children described relationships between people, whether in real life or on television. Thompson (1983) has described how children in an isolated community in the Northern Territory would claim 'ownership' of a heroic character in a Kung Fu movie by calling out 'starring, starring'. At Lowrel, children localised the characters on television by remarking 'eeeh, like Jack!' or 'like Karen!', or as they worked out together how the characters in the movie were related to each other and what the intrigue was ('that woman had that man's baby'). In the same way, children would work out with me how I was related to my immediate family and the *Bama*[10] who invited me there and how, by extension, they should relate to me. It seemed to me that part of the children's willingness to talk with me and with other people, especially in their pre-pubescent years, seemed to be connected to an insatiable desire to engage with (and know where they stood in relation to) all the people, animals and other elements they came across. And with this same energy, the children explored how to relate to the foreigners that came into their familiar worlds; this took place even while they were still on their home ground, as when they drew the characters from the television screen into their local worlds. Most visitors to isolated Aboriginal communities will have the experience of being swamped by children, who befriend them and 'get their measure' within the first three days.

In this way, the children engaged with different aspects of their home ground, and home had the quality of that which had been personally experienced. Casey (1996) has argued that place is lived before it is conceptualised in an abstract way. I have shown how the children lived in the place of the Farm in an immediately sensual way while they also were in the process of absorbing ideas about place. And yet this sensual living did not entail a straightforward ontological merging of each child with the surrounding environment. Elements in the landscape – the storm, the bush turkey, television characters – were also separate from the children, and in their talk and play the children *acted* to make these objects their own. Thus, this everyday living was very much about grasping. It was vital for children to grasp the terms of the world they were born into, just as they were taught to express their wants and to fight for what was theirs.[11]

This important activity that the children were caught up in of making places their own must be understood in relation to Kuku-Yalanji practices of affiliation to land through birth and marriage. In an Aboriginal environment, the terms of connection to land have the same social importance for a person's identity as gender (Merlan 1988). People are born with a land-identity.[12] Kuku-Yalanji are born with rights to their father's land, and to some extent, to their mother's and their in-laws' land. In the course of their upbringing, they realise these rights as they grow, and to some degree, will be able to extend them when they marry. In general for Kuku-Yalanji, the activities of growing up and moving away from home draw on rights to land based on what are considered social connections (to people or ancestors), primarily through conception, birth, long-term residence, marriage and patrilineal or matrilineal descent.[13]

Growing away

All children, then, were born with a unique place in the kinship-country matrix. This matrix, while given meaningful expression in cultural ideology and partly determined by the place of the child's conception and birth, was constituted through the social and physical movements of the previous generation. In a direct way, then, the movements and marriages of the Smith children's parents gave shape to the places and kin that the Smith children were structurally a part of. Thus, when children moved on to foreign land, this land was not *altogether* foreign: it was 'aunty Flo's' land, or 'cousin Jimmy's' land, and, to the extent that each child was connected with these people, they had a right to spend time on this land, too. The children then played an active part in making these extended places and kin really and truly their own by *being* there – at least for a few weeks.

Indeed, Smith (von Sturmer 1980) has written that for Kugu-Nganychara in Western Cape York, it was important for children to spend time in the places of their maternal relatives. In this way, the children became part of their relatives' social group, and this gave them strength as they grew into adulthood. For Kuku-Yalanji, too, it was regarded as a child's right and responsibility to live for some time on the country of close relatives. Sometimes these extended relatives would live nearby, and sometimes they lived a few hundred miles away.

I observed this principle at work at every level of relatedness. At the age of 2, a child might spend the morning fishing with her grandmother, and then, on the way home, get passed over to an aunt who was in a different car driving in the direction of where her primary caregiver was. These movements took place frequently and with little ritual.

As they got older, children's range of movements grew less frequent but larger, incorporating more distant kin: Karen and Janet often lived at Wujal Wujal with Janet's older sister; Jack often lived at Hope Vale with his mother's family; Trenton often lived at the Farm. But from a very early age, it was the children themselves who decided where to stay and when to leave. And their choices were almost always respected by their parents or other caretakers, who often went far out of their way to drive the children to where they wanted to go.

It is clear from this description that, just as relationship to place was a vital part of young Kuku-Yalanji children's lives, so, too, was movement. Children were born as part of a place, but they were related to kin *across* places (consider the tension between consanguinal and affinal relations) and they activated these relationships with their presence. The choices that these children made when going to school in some way drew on these family links. Thus, like all children, these children moved away from their home place as they matured. But they did this at every step through social relationships that were relevant to them in terms of their personal placement in the socio-environmental field. I will now show how three of the children that I knew best moved between home and a range of schools during the time of my fieldwork; and I will describe how these movements were built in relevant ways on to those of their fathers and mothers a generation earlier.

Moving between school and home

John

John had attended the Aboriginal boarding school in Brisbane the year before I arrived. This was the furthest away that any of the children went to school. And yet, the placement follows the patterns of the movements of John's mother and father. John's father was from Woorabinda, and although he had lived for several years at Lowrel and had been an active member of the community, he had now returned south. He and John's mother were divorced. However, Margaret's children were at an age where she could begin to get out and meet people, and she was keen to extend her social contacts beyond the range that most Kuku-Yalanji live within. Perhaps this is due to having spent fifteen years – her entire childhood – forced to live within the missionary school system that was set up by the Lutheran Church. In this environment, Margaret's freedom was severely restricted.[14] She once observed bitterly, 'I was not even allowed to go to my own father's funeral'. On the other hand, she got an education of sorts at the Lutheran mission, and the choice of Brisbane as a school suited Margaret's preference for a Lutheran school as well as her desire to travel and meet people. Nevertheless, Margaret lived with relatives even when she was in Brisbane. She also accompanied John home when it was holiday time – and remained home when John chose to not return to Brisbane.

I came to Lowrel after John had already 'bailed out' of the Brisbane school. At this time, he lived at his family's newly acquired Farm. He spent much of the day in the yard, minding his sister's child, 2-year-old Janina, while his mother did things in the house. John's sister lived for the time being with a new man in a different community, and Janina had become Margaret's charge, with John doing much of the active caring-work.

He did sometimes though go pig hunting with his uncles, or out on the reef to spear *ngawiya*, sea turtles. John's school photo from Brisbane arrived in the mail after he had 'bailed out'. His mother hung it on the wall. When his aunt, Jane, popped in to get some clothes, she looked at me and then indicated the photo with her chin, 'Smart eh?' I agreed. John himself said nothing. A few days later, as he was gathering some clothes to take to Wujal Wujal, his mother complained, 'I don't know what you kids see there. You might as well *live* there!' John replied as a kind of threat, 'I might as well go back to *school*!' At which, Margaret shouted back, 'Yeah, you might *learn* something!'

John did return to school, but not in Brisbane. The next year, a new Lutheran school was set up in Cairns. The Lutheran pastor left his ten-year station at Wujal Wujal in order to run the Cairns school. The building of a Lutheran school enabled the Lutheran Church to maintain some influence over the Aboriginal population following the Church's enforced marginal-isation from the administration of Hope Vale and Wujal Wujal since the 1980s (Anderson 1984). Margaret travelled to Cairns to buy clothes and school things for John. When I asked her why she wanted John to go to the Lutheran school, she commented: 'They look after them there. Not like those other [government] schools, where they let the kids go wild'. Despite her hatred of the treatment that she had received from the Lutherans as a child, Margaret's early experience may be responsible for her belief that a Lutheran institution was better for her children's education than a government school. And Margaret cared about her children's education. As Margaret prepared to bring John down to Cairns, she remarked to me that, since her daughter had already dropped out of school for good, John was her 'last hope'. I later asked Margaret how John had adjusted to his new school. She remarked: 'John wandered around until he found a piano. He sat there playing it then.' John stayed in school until the first holidays, when he came home and did not return.

During my first year of fieldwork, there seemed to be a lot of turmoil going on in John. He often gave vent to bursts of anger. This anger was generally vented at people who were younger than him, and he himself seemed to feel weak and powerless within the wider society. This some-times came out when the subject of whites came up. As we passed Karen and Janet walking on the road one day, he muttered, 'They better watch out, *Wybala* gonna rape them'. And when some tourists on motorbikes stopped at a fishing spot close to where John stood, I saw him race down to join his family.

When I went back in 1999, John hung around with his mother's brothers. He had changed. He was one of the men now. He no longer expressed the same kind of frustration, but took care to look after other people's interests. I have described elsewhere how the 'hanging around' of one of John's uncles, Steve, had intrigued me because it was not at all associated by Kuku-Yalanji people with laziness, but rather with 'taking care' of the land, or looking after the land (Povinelli 1993), including often looking after the children. During my return visit in 1999, I had the impression that this role of custodian also suited John.

Karen

The year before I arrived, Karen had attended the high school at Cooktown, where she lived with her father's family. But Karen left after getting into some trouble at school. 'She didn't like it there', commented her father. As Margaret was preparing to send John back to school, I asked Denise whether Karen would be returning to school as well. Denise responded, 'I don't know. Well, we *want* her to go to school. We asked her, "You goin' back to school?" And she said, "If you're so keen about school, why don't *you* go? They got classes for adults, you know!"' That was the end of the matter, until about a week before the new school year, when Denise remarked to me: 'Karen wants to go to school, down at Mossman. She'll be with Flora then. They can keep each other company.'

Denise and Martin packed their jeep with Karen's mattress, clothes and stereo and drove her to Mossman Gorge, where the whole family moved into Jane's two-bedroom house, so that Denise and Martin could be near

Karen while she settled into school. Later on, I asked Denise how Karen's first day was. Denise replied that Karen had cried at first because there was no one she knew in her class. But then a councillor at the school found another Aboriginal girl from Hope Vale and asked Karen, 'Do you know this girl?'

'Yeah, she's my cousin', Karen had replied, and from that moment, things ran smoothly.

After a month, Denise and Martin drove back to Lowrel, with Karen happily set up in her Mossman Gorge family. However, rumours soon got back to Karen's parents that Karen was skipping school and getting into trouble. Soon, Denise and Martin had to drive down to Mossman to pick her up because she had gotten into a fight with some *Bama* girls. It was rumoured that the fight had been about a boy. After this, Karen bailed out of school. I asked Denise why Karen had left the school. She replied, 'The white girls were "teasing" the *bama* girls'.[15]

In 1999, Karen and her mother and father were all in Cairns: Karen had a newborn baby, and Denise and Martin were in Cairns keeping her company while she lived near the clinic during her baby's early weeks. When I had known Karen in 1993–4, she had been very quiet around me, and I had had to rely on Denise to talk to me on her behalf. Four and a half years later – and a new mother – Karen was very vocal and had a good grasp of the politics of interfamily life, and of her own plans. She told me that she was planning to go back to school as an adult, and enrol in a TAFE[16] computer course.

Jack

Because Jack was only 7, he could go to the local primary school. This may account for the fact that Jack was the only one who kept up a sporadic attendance at school throughout the year. It was up to Jack, however, whether he chose to go to school on any given day, or do something else. I remember sitting with his mother one morning as she stared down the driveway. I asked her, 'What are you looking at?' Her mother replied, 'I'm watching to see if Jack goes to school.' When he didn't, he often hung out with Trenton, his cousin from Hope Vale. I remember on one of these days hearing Jack and Trenton's thoughts about school and community. I had asked Trenton why he didn't go to school very often. He hadn't responded, but Jack helped him out, 'The other boys beat up on him', to which he added, 'Anyone touch *me* and I'd *bash them up!*' Trenton's response was: 'When I grow up, I'm going to be a policeman. I'm gonna arrest people and put them away.' Jack added: 'When I get older, I'm gonna fix up this road. Get rid of all the potholes. I'm gonna get a Mercedes and round up all the cattle. I'm gonna give lots of meat to my Mum and Dad and Aunty and Uncle.'

When Trenton went back to Hope Vale, Jack went with him and started going to school up there. I had earlier asked Jack why he often didn't show up in class at the Lowrel primary school. His response was: 'The school bus doesn't stop at the Farm.' Her mother's response was different: 'Jack has sores. You can't go to school with sores.' But both of these answers seemed to me to be less convincing than the reason they gave me for why Jack was now going to school at Hope Vale. Jack and Trenton both told me that, even though they didn't always go to school at Hope Vale, it was better than the one at Lowrel because it was actually in the Aboriginal community. The important thing that both the children stressed about a school being in the community was freedom of movement. As Jack's mother said: 'At Hope Vale, you can just walk down the road [to school].' During one trip to Hope Vale in 1993–4, when I was visiting Trenton's mother with some other people, I happened to ask her where Trenton was. She said, 'When I woke up this morning, Trenton wasn't around. Then I found out he'd already got up and went to school!'

In 1996, during my trip back to Lowrel, I was told that Jack was now living at Hope Vale with Helen's mother. When I asked Helen if she was missing him, she responded: 'But he's going to school. I'm happy about that.' By the time I visited again, in 1999, Jack's father had died. His mother had remarried and was now living back in Hope Vale. But Jack was in Cairns, going to the same Lutheran High School that John had spent time at. A community leader told me: 'Jack's doing real well in school. We're all proud of him.'

The relevance of the 'place' of school

Each of these three children had their own field of movement, the parameters of which were partly set by their own particular family history. John's range extended further south than that of his cousins, and this is not unconnected to the living-place of his father and the travels of his mother; Karen's movements to Cooktown were made possible by the living-place of her father's family, and her movements the next year to Mossman relied on the care of her aunt and the company of her cousin, Flora. Jack's decision to go to school at Hope Vale involved a choice to be both freer (to be able to just 'walk down the road to school') and to be contained: living with his mother's family. In other words, the children's movement between places followed the tracks that had been made in an earlier generation and linked up with the settling down of family members that had occurred at particular spots in the course of these movements. Each individual's lifepath has its own antecedents, just as in Kuku-Yalanji mythology: each formation in the environment comes about because of a mythological figure moving from one place to another, before.

This pattern of moving in the tracks of kin may be evoked as mythological, but it is a history, or rather a collection of personal histories. And these histories are about following the marriage options and resources that have presented themselves over the past hundred years, each time along a course that does not diverge too much from the course that the previous generation took. The Lutheran Church has had a marked influence on these patterns of movements, first confining a generation of children to dormitories, and more recently setting up a Lutheran school in Cairns for a new generation.

Jack's very family structure was intertwined with Lutheran activity in Southeast Cape York. The Lutherans had set up a mission at Wujal Wujal only after having established themselves at Hope Vale. There was almost no contact between Guugu Yimidhirr at Hope Vale and Kuku-Yalanji further south until the Lutheran pastor, as Helen put it, 'drove up a truckful of Wujal boys to meet the Hope Vale girls'. Stacey was one of the first Wujal Wujal-based boys to marry a Hope Vale girl, added Helen: 'He set the ball rolling.' When Jack was of age, he benefitted from the new Lutheran High School in Cairns, and the environment obviously gave Jack enough support for him to return to school after the first holidays.

Karen's parents moved literally along the pathways of Karen's mother's family, which in the 1920s and 1930s travelled up and down the Daintree coast with the seasonal changes, dividing their time between working for an early white settler at Daintree and living near Wujal Wujal during the rainy season. Denise's father also took Denise to a mission school at Daintree, until he got tired of being there and took them out again ('spoiling us for school', as Denise put it). Denise then lived with her aunt, Hilda, who had moved to Mossman because she had the chance to work for a white shopkeeper there and escape an unhappy relationship at Lowrel. In the holidays, remarked a Mossman woman, Hilda's relatives would come down in a canoe to take her for a visit home: 'We'd know they were coming, because we'd see a light in the distance.'

This sketch of the movements of the Smith family over the areas of Wujal Wujal, Woorabindah, Hope Vale, Cairns and Mossman allows us to appreciate the density of contact over time that these children have had with the places that their schools sit on. Theirs is a history of engagement with particular colonial activities in Southeast Cape York. And yet, at every point in time, when people moved of their own accord, like Karen's family did, they followed paths that had been laid for them by earlier family members. Even when people were forcibly moved, such as when Stacey was trucked up to Hope Vale to meet some Hope Vale girls, these men were following an established pattern in which young men journeyed out beyond other people's average ranges, often found work in less familar areas, got married and settled down there for a time, only to create a new link between their new place and their old place. And each time a new path was created, it became the grounds for new personal histories of connectedness. Children were conceived and born in these places, and new claims to land were forged.

If we think about the Smith children's school-attending practices in terms of 'movement' and '(family/land) placement', which is consistent with Kuku-Yananji practices, the shifts and decisions that the children made in this area of their lives begin to look quite consistent with the rest of their lives. On the one hand, the places that they moved to were consistent with the places that they knew and already had some kind of claims to, and the children made their own choices to expand on these choices (returning home from time to time) in ways that worked for them. On the other hand, the places of the schools were not wholly foreign to them. It is worth reflecting on how often in the literature there is a categorical distinction between an 'Aboriginal' environment and a 'White' environment. Aboriginal people made this distinction to some extent, as well. But it is important to remember that these 'classroom spaces' were situated on 'places' that had specific and distinctive meaning for the children, and generally contained other children to whom the Smith children were related. Thus, in *this* sense, school had meaning for the Smith children in terms of their own personal histories, and the movements they made to and from schools confirms this.

Looking at these children's school-attending practices from the perspective of place has allowed me to represent these practices as at once historically constituted and experientially open-ended. In a Kuku-Yalanji environment, children are always welcomed – for one reason, because the presence of children promises a society future strength in numbers (von Sturmer 1980). I have tried to show that, as children grew older, they were keen to widen this world by travelling further away from the place(s) of their early childhood, still along family/familiar links. And where they did not have already established connections, they acted as much as possible to create them, such as, for example when Karen found a Hope Vale cousin that she could link up with and even in a way when John, who had cousins at the Cairns Lutheran school, found a piano to play on.

In my view, we can appreciate both the structures and the fluidity of the Smith children's experiential worlds because we can understand how their thoughts arise out of and are built upon their relationship to place. Such a perspective is consistent with Casey's suggestion that we *put culture back into place* (Casey 1996: 33, italics in original).

Building 'culture' up from 'place'

The thought of school usually evokes thoughts of the state, and it has often been pointed out that Aboriginal Australians have been marginalised by state institutions. Despite the tragic fact that the Australian school system has generally sidelined and reified Aboriginal history and society, I have argued that there were ways in which the children brought the classroom environment into line with their already known worlds. In my view, such a perspective allows the reader to grasp the tangible but complex nature of how Kuku-Yalanji children live in place – and move between places – and to appreciate that the school-attending patterns that I witnessed among the Smith family have meaning in terms of these children's lifeworlds, and are not the undisciplined actions of children who have missed out on responsible parenting.[17] But I was only able to come to this understanding by focusing specifically on how children lived in place, both at home and away from home, and how they experienced their movements between different places.

Such an approach required that I employ an experience-near concept of 'culture', grounding 'the cultural' in the range of personal ways that the Smith children lived in place. In particular, I had to disregard the substantive model of culture that I had brought with me to the field, namely, the idea that there was 'a Kuku-Yalanji culture' or even 'an Aboriginal culture'. Neither was I happy with the alternative approach, namely that Kuku-Yalanji participated in a 'culture of opposition', the definition of which could only be a kind of reverse-reflection of main-stream society (Trigger 1997). These notions had some relevance, of course, and this comes through in some of the comments of the children. As elsewhere in Australia (Cowlishaw 2001), ideological models and oppositional activities are part of the grounds on which people in South-east Cape York interact with one another.[18] But I felt that such approaches overlooked the formative value of the family support structures and ecology that these children were so fully immersed in during their growing years, and the specifically Kuku-Yalanji meaning that these elemental presences had for the children.

In my view then, it was necessary to understand children's engagement in the world in an emotional, physical, sensual and mental sense in order to grasp how Kuku-Yalanji children lived in and moved between places. Focusing on the children's experiences and movements on a daily basis meant that I worked with a notion of culture that began with the grounds on which the children acted and spoke – both physically and imaginatively. By looking at the places that these children lived and moved in, and by combining all their movements, I could have some grasp of the broader historical and social field in terms of which they exercised their choices.

Such an approach required that I thought of culture primarily in terms of personal horizons of experience, and less in terms of macro-construc-tions, such as notions of race or class (even though these macro-construc-tions continue to have their place, and influence people's thoughts and choices). This way of prioritising agency over comprehensive social or cogni-tive constructions is inspired by ethnography as diverse as the Manchester

School's methodology of extended case analysis and Bourdieu's (1977) theory of habitus.

On an ethnographic level, my findings are consistent with Schwab's (2001) and Carter's (1991) observations in other parts of Australia that Aboriginal children's experiences of school were connected with their particular histories and relationships to place (see also Gray and Saggers 1990). But such an approach is also a development of the more analytical problematics that anthropologists today are grappling with as they attempt to fashion new ways of grasping experience that can go beyond reified notions of culture without disregarding the specificity of different ways in which experiences are meaningful. The suggestion on the part of some contemporary anthropologists that we ground culture in experience of place (Ingold 1993) or in the activity of talking (Duranti and Goodwin 1997; Ochs and Capps 2001), or in the specificity of different bodily and social experiences (Hutchins 1994; Tamisari 2000) or particular histories (Donham 1990) or the politics of specific relationships at hand (Fabian 1983; Bhabha 1994) are all expressions of the tendency today to break down the notion of culture into a more experience-near world. Such an approach has been essential for me in my efforts to grasp the threads of meaning that informed each Kuku-Yalanji child as he or she engaged with particular places, and expanded out into others. For it allowed me to complement both the experience-near engagement and the structural positioning of these children in a way that cut across and embraced both immediate and extended family, and both urban and rural contexts – as the children themselves did.

Let me end on a pragmatic note concerning the topic that drew me in the beginning to focus on Kuku-Yalanji children's movements, namely the place of school in these children's lives. I have argued that the Kuku-Yalanji children I lived with incorporated a range of places into their lives, and that the classroom was one of these places. This may allow us to rethink the place of the classroom in terms of how these children experienced it, rather than as simply an alien space that these children occupied, like fish out of water. The children were the ones who chose where and when to go to school, and when to come home. If we focus on the meaning of school for Kuku-Yalanji children as though it were one aspect of a web of relatedness that extended across place and time, it seems to me that we might better appreciate the reasons why these children made the choices they did.

And yet, there are ways in which the children obviously *did* feel like fish out of water. These are reflected in the excuses that the children and their parents gave for why they came home again. In my view, it was to some extent due to critical moments of loneliness felt by the children when they were away from home, that they decided to remain at home rather than return to school after the initial holidays; after all, the most reliable and important support came from their home place. Only after being at home again for a time did they venture out into a new place, to try out a different school environment through either a different branch of their extended family or the Lutheran School system.

How do we assess the localised nature of these children's support structures against the demands of the mainstream Australian classroom that the children actually *be there* all year long? No matter how much connection and nourishment the Smith children received when they chose to remain home rather than return to school, they did miss out on the kind of education that might allow them to make significant changes to their inferior socio-economic situation in Australia. It is arguable, since they periodically felt the need to return to their own home-places, that despite the strength and agency that these children demonstrated, and despite the kinship networks that they drew upon, it was ultimately very difficult for them to adapt to the demands of the various schools that they participated in. It is worthwhile reflecting, for example, on whether there was too wide a gulf between John's momentary thought of returning to the Brisbane school, after receiving his school photo – and actually going back; or to what extent Karen's life in Mossman would have been different if the fighting in school could have been resolved with some support from the school staff.

The obvious solution seems be to reverse the system, and make the schools spatially central to the children's experiential lives instead of marginal. Even the primary school available to Wujal Wujal children was a twenty-minute drive away from the Aboriginal community, located in the local mainly white town of Ayton. And, despite the support structures that the older children drew on to sustain them during school time, the fact remains that they had to travel far from their homes to be able to attend high school. If the system was reversed, the children's 'living at home' time and their 'going to school' time would be synchronised, and the important activity of visiting other places and relatives that figured in their family network could be reserved for holiday time.

I began this article by focusing on the Smith children's experiences of living and moving, and how these practices drew on and built on established social networks. I then made sense of the children's irregular school-attending practices in terms of these social networks, thereby indicating that these children drew school into their field of meaning, and practised school-attendance in terms of this. The Smith children were not impoverished, they had a rich history of connection to draw on, and they chose their personal movements – of which school was one aspect – in terms of this history. The irony is that if one simply looks at where school is plotted on these maps, we end up – once again – with a map of marginality: the schools are situated miles away from home in every case; in other words, children had to go *out of their way* to perform the compulsory activity of going to school. I might have told quite a different story if – instead of the Smith children *going out* to school – school had come to them. One solution to the educational problems raised by this account, then, might be as simple as building more high schools that are 'just down the road'.

Notes

1 The Native Title Act was passed on 21 December 1993.
2 See Anderson and Coates (1989) for a history of Kuku-Yalanji failed and successful land acquisitions up until 1989.
3 ATSIC stands for Aboriginal and Torres Strait Islander Commission.
4 Two-year-old Janina was cared for by her grandmother, Margaret, since her mother lived in Hope Vale at the time. Two-year-old Daniel spent some time with his grandparents, Helen and Stacey at the Farm.
5 The numbers in brackets represent the children's approximate ages in 1993–4.
6 Helen and Stacey had other children, but they are not described in this paper.
7 Trenton was Jack's age-mate and cousin, who lived at Hope Vale, and was the child of Helen's brother, James. Phyllis was cared for together with her eight sisters and cousins by her grandmother, Geraldine, who came to stay with her brother, Martin, after her husband died in a shooting accident. Katrina and Jason visited the area with their mother, Mary, who was the daughter of Bob, Martin's brother.
8 'Lowrel' is a fictitious name for an area near Wujal Wujal.
9 *Jarruka* is the Kuku-Yalanji word for a kind of bush turkey that buries its eggs in a large mound of dirt and foliage.
10 Aboriginal people in Southeast Cape York refer to themselves as '*Bama*', as opposed to '*Wybala*' (Whitefella).
11 Schieffelin's (1990) description of how Kaluli children are trained to demand food for themselves also applies to socialisation in Cape York. See also Peterson's (1993) description of demand-sharing.
12 Among other studies in Cape York, Smith (von Sturmer 1980: 283) states that, for Kugu-Nganychara, patrilineal claim was 'immutable', but that people could argue for claim to matrilineal land if they had spent their 'small time' there. Von Sturmer (1978: 72) writes that the ideology of patrilineal descent is only one of a number in social life. Sutton (1978) also emphasises the flexibility of individual choice among the people of Cape Keerweer. He suggests that the earlier ethnography by Sharp (cf. Sharp 1934) paved the way for this more fluid understanding of Cape York society. Thus an ego-focused approach to social interaction can make apparent the flexibility that operates for any individual's choice of action at any one moment (Sutton 1978: 32). Nevertheless, Sutton points out that 'even for the very ego-centric individuals of Cape Keerweer,' society is heavily segmented in corporate and non-corporate ways. 'The set of available or potential alliances, plus their realisations, do form a rough pattern which may be regionally defined' (ibid.: 32). For a discussion of contemporary Aboriginal connections to country, see Sutton 1996 and 1997.
13 Among Kuku-Yalanji, claims to land based on patrilineal connection are particularly strong and claims based on marriage are weak.
14 Contemporary Kuku-Yalanji have all had some experience of missionisation, and many Kuku-Yalanji living conditions have changed following colonisation (Anderson and Coates 1989). Nevertheless, Kuku-Yalanji continue to

experience affiliation to country in totemically relevant ways and these affiliations are consistent with clan-based kinship affiliations (Anderson 1984; Wood 1997; Lorimer 2001).
15 'Teasing' has more serious connotations in Aboriginal English than in mainstream Australian English.
16 TAFE, which stands for Technical and Further Education, provides technical training courses.
17 The notion that Aboriginal children's behaviour is the product of undisciplined parenting was the subject of a debate surrounding Yolngu child-rearing patterns, fought principally by Hippler (1978), Hamilton (1979) and Reser (1982).
18 Due to lack of space, I am not able to describe the importance of oppositional practices, or of fighting and conflict for children's social development (cf. Lorimer 2001: 132–64).

References

Anderson, C. (1984) 'The political and economic basis of Kuku-Yalanji social history', unpublished M.Phil. Thesis, University of Queensland.
Anderson, C. and S. Coates (1989) 'Like a crane standing on one leg on a little island', unpublished report to the National and Islander Legal Services Secretariat.
Bhabha, H. K. (1994) *The Location of Culture*. London and New York: Routledge.
Bourdieu, P. (1977) *Outline of a Theory of Practice*. Cambridge: Cambridge University Press.
Carter, J. (1991 [1988]) 'Am I too black to go with you?' in I. Keen (ed.) *Being Black*. Canberra: AIAS, pp. 65–76.
Casey, E. S. (1996) 'How to get from space to place in a fairly short stretch of time: Phenomenological prolegomena', in S. Feld and K. Basso (eds) *Senses of Place*. Santa Fe, NM: School of American Research Press, pp. 13–52.
Cowlishaw, G. (2001) 'Performing Aboriginality: The politics and poetics of citizenship in everyday life', *UTS Review* 7(1): 153–69.
Donham, D. L. (1990) *History, Power, Ideology: Central Issues in Marxism and Anthropology*. Cambridge: Cambridge University Press.
Duranti, A. and C. Goodwin (1997 [1992]) *Rethinking Context. Language as an Interactive Phenomenon*. Studies in the Social and Cultural Foundations of Language 11. Cambridge: Cambridge University Press.
Fabian, J. (1983) *Time and the Other. How Anthropology Makes its Object*. New York: Columbia University Press.
Gray, D. and S. Saggers (1990) 'Autonomy in Aboriginal education: A quest at Carnarvon', in R. Tonkinson and M. Howard (eds) *Going it Alone? Prospects for Aboriginal Autonomy*. Canberra: Aboriginal Studies Press, pp. 185–200.
Hamilton, A. (1979) 'A comment on Arthur Hippler's paper', *Mankind* 12(2): 164–9.
Hippler, A. E. (1978) 'Culture and personality perspective of the Yolngu of Northeastern Arnhem Land: Part 1 – early socialization', *Journal of Psychological Anthropology* 1(2): 221–44.
Hutchins, E. (1994) *Cognition in the Wild*. Cambridge: Cambridge University Press.
Ingold, T. (1993) 'The art of translation in a continuous world', in G. Palsson (ed.) *Beyond Boundaries: Understanding, Translation and Anthropological Discourse*. Oxford: Berg, pp. 210–30.

Lorimer, F. (2001) '*Ngayku bubul* "My bit of dirt". Themes of belonging, difference and separation among Kuku-Yalanji of the Bloomfield Valley in Southeast Cape York, Australia', unpublished M.Phil. Thesis, University of Sydney.

Merlan, F. (1988) 'Gender in Aboriginal social life: A review', in R. M. Berndt and T. Tonkinson (eds) *Social Anthropology and Australian Aboriginal Studies: A Contemporary Review*. Canberra: Aboriginal Studies Press.

Ochs, E. and L. Capps (2001) *Living Narrative. Creating Lives in Everyday Story-telling*. Cambridge, MA: Harvard University Press.

Peterson, N. (1993) 'Demand sharing: Reciprocity and the pressure for generosity among foragers', *American Anthropologist* 95(4): 860–74.

Povinelli, E. (1993) *Labor's Lot: The Power, History and Culture of Aboriginal Action*. Chicago and London: University of Chicago Press.

Reser, J. (1982) 'Cultural relativity or cultural bias: A response to Hippler', *American Anthropologist* 84(2): 399–404.

Schieffelin, B. B. (1990) *The Give and Take of Everyday Life: Language Socialization of Kaluli children*. Cambridge: Cambridge University Press.

Schwab, R. G. (2001) '"That school gotta recognize *our* policy!": The appropriation of educational policy in an Australian Aboriginal community', in M. Sutton and B. A. Levinson (eds) *Policy as Practice: Toward a Comparative Sociocultural Analysis of Educational Policy*. Westport: Ablex Publishing.

Sharp, L. R. (1934) 'The social organization of the Yir-Yoront Tribe, Cape York Peninsula', *Oceania* 4: 404–31.

Sutton, P. (1978) 'Wik: Aboriginal society, territory and language at Cape Keerweer, Cape York Peninsula, Australia', unpublished M.Phil. Thesis, University of Queensland.

—— (1996) 'The robustness of Aboriginal land tenure systems: Underlying and proximate customary titles', *Oceania* 67: 7–29.

—— (1997) 'Families of polity: Post-classical Aboriginal society and native title', National Native Title Tribunal Discussion Paper 1. Perth.

Tamisari, F. (2000) 'The meaning of the steps in between: Dancing and the curse of compliments', *Australian Journal of Anthropology* 11(3): 274–86.

Thompson, D. (1983) 'Claims of stardom', *Education News* 18(3): 10–13.

Trigger, D. (1997) 'Land rights and the reproduction of Aboriginal culture in Australia's Gulf Country', *Social Analysis* 41(3): 84–106.

van Velsen, J. (1967) 'The extended-case method and situational analysis', in A. L. Epstein (ed.) *The Craft of Social Anthropology*. London: Tavistock, pp. 129–49.

von Sturmer, D. E. (Smith) (1980) 'Rights in nurturing. The social relations of child-bearing and rearing amongst the Kugu-Nganychara, Western Cape York Peninsula, Australia', unpublished M.A. Thesis, Australian National University.

von Sturmer, J. R. (1978) 'The Wik Region: Economy, territoriality and totemism in Western Cape York Peninsula, North Queensland', unpublished M.Phil. Thesis, University of Queensland.

Wood, R. (1997) 'The contemporary land holding system of the Eastern Kuku-Yalanji', unpublished report to the Cape York Land Council, Cairns.

Chapter 4

How will the children come home?

Emplacement and the creation of the social body in an Ethiopian returnee settlement

Laura Hammond

I.

Intay leyao iye?	What do I need?
Sudan aytemeleso	I don't need to return back to Sudan.
Ye'akileni iyu aboy ze haresu.	What my father harvests is enough for me.

II.

Atta wedi aytekeydar hika	You, boy, don't go far from here.
ab Ada Bai wetsiu fabrica.	Ada Bai has new industry.

(Children's songs in Ada Bai returnee settlement, 1994)

The experience of repatriation has often been considered in monolithic terms. There is little acknowledgement of the different ways that refugees' or returnees' experiences may vary according to the gender or age of the individual. The generational aspects of the repatriation/return experience are often overlooked. In particular, there is insufficient understanding of the meanings that children associate with such a shift in their lives. In my experience over the past decade in the Horn of Africa, this neglect of children's viewpoints seems peculiar, particularly since Ethiopian, Somali and Eritrean adult returnees have all told me that the desire for their children to have a better life is a key reason for repatriating.

Despite such well-intentioned motivations on the part of parents, children often experience the greatest upheaval upon return, especially if their families have lived in exile for several years. In protracted refugee cases, such as that of Ethiopians living in Sudan from 1984–3 (upon which this chapter is based), a new generation was born and raised in refugee camps. For a significant percentage of those returning then, the refugee camp was the only home they knew. Others, who entered the camps as children, repatriated as young adults, often with young children of their own. For those who were born or came of age in exile, the notion of 'returning' to their country of origin held vastly different meaning than it did for those who fled their country as adults.

I argue in this chapter that return involves an experience of *emplacement*, both individually and collectively.[1] Emplacement is the process by which *space* (a geographic area that initially holds no special significance for the protagonists, and is a 'vessel' or 'receptacle' for the generation of meaning [Casey 1997: 41]) becomes transformed into *place* (a geographical entity imbued with personalised and affective meaning).[2] Place is made meaningful through the interaction of 'self, space, and time' rather than being a 'secondary grid overlaid on the presumed primacy of space' (Feld and Basso 1996: 9, referring to Casey's contribution in the same volume, pp. 13–52). Place is the arena for the generation of social meaning, and forms the basis for social action and identity formation in the new geographic setting. Emplacement is thus essential to the construction and evolution of identity, and as such can be seen as the *opposite of displacement*; that is, as the act of forging a relationship between person (individual or collective) and geographic and social space.[3]

Space becomes meaningful through daily interaction with the physical and social environment to generate associations, relationships, attitudes and beliefs that serve to bind individuals and groups to the new place. These interactions constantly alter relationships between the individual, the group and place. Bender notes that landscapes (arrangements of spatial significance) 'serve as palimpsests of past activity, incorporate political action, encompass change – both past and present – , are half imagined or something held in the memory, are about identity, or lack of identity, roots or lack of roots' (Bender 1993: 9). In Hirsch's terms, landscape represents the interplay between foregrounded actuality and backgrounded potentiality, place and space, internality and externality, and image and representation (1995: 4). Representations, or conscious reflections on or about place, are born from the relationship that individuals and groups forge between themselves and their environment through these practices, and are complementary to the immediate experiences of inhabiting place through social practice. Emplacement thus involves the integration of the material and moral aspects of practice (Migdal 1988: 27). Practice and representation work in a dialectic to mould 'senses of place' (Feld and Basso 1996) that are at once utilitarian, reflective and creative.

When former refugees or displaced persons return to their area of origin, emplacement can involve an adjustment or reconciliation of past and present associations between individual and community on one hand, with space on the other, towards the creation of a new place infused with personalised meaning. This process can be exhilarating but also disturbing for returnees. Returnees sometimes discover that in their absence relatives and friends have died or moved away. They may be given a cool welcome by those who remained behind: jealousy between stayees and returnees is often great, as each side may perceive themselves as having sacrificed more by leaving or staying. They are often in direct competition for scarce resources, including humanitarian and development assistance. In many cases returnees find that infrastructure and their own physical property has been destroyed, damaged or taken over by another person. As a result they are unable to enjoy the same living conditions or social status that they had prior to migrating. Returnees often find that the environment does not conform to their memories or expectations. The 'imagined homeland' is, it seems, never the same as the actual one, as several authors writing about the return of people who were born 'displaced' or away from their ethnic areas of origin have recently reminded us (Rogge 1994: 32–4; Akol 1994; Clifford 1997; Pilkington and Flynn 1999).

The process of emplacement in Ada Bai was enacted through the innumerable practices that made up everyday life: house-building, farming, cooking, tea-drinking, trading, attending the church or mosque, celebrating public holidays, etc. Such use served to define public and private spaces, roughly divided along gender lines.[4] Movement from exile to country of origin was the impetus which 'offered [strategies] that lock[ed] horns with prevalent norms and modes of social control, proposing new forms of social life' (Migdal 1988: 27). Tradition and innovation were combined to varying degrees to create new webs of meaning in the area of 'return'.

In this chapter, I describe the complex and sometimes seemingly contradictory experience of emplacement that Tigrayan children encountered when they returned with their families to Ethiopia following an 8-year period of exile in Eastern Sudan. The people I lived with in the Ada Bai returnee settlement in northwest Ethiopia were returning to their country of origin but not to the villages that they had originally emigrated from. In this case, people experienced emplacement in the short to medium term as their attempt to create safety and stability in a dramatic and threatening environment. Without familiar landmarks to guide them, returnees faced the task of creating a meaningful 'home' (a term which, we will see, may have multiple connotations) from a space with which they previously had no association at all.

The social practices that adults used to protect their children and guide them towards total membership in the community formed part of adults' own emplacement process, even as they also served to partially define children's emplacement experiences. Parents sought to manipulate the environment so as to minimise risk to their children. At the same time, children functioned as independent and purposive actors in their own emplacement, much of which lay outside the grasp of their parents. This tension between children being passive recipients of emplacement-generated meaning, and being active and creative architects of their own emplacement, created a complex and ever-changing relationship between children and their lived environment.

This dual role of children as actors in their own emplacement and vehicles through which adults sought to create meaning in the new, unfamiliar space is a major theme that has emerged from my research over the past 10 years in the Ada Bai returnee settlement. While the bulk of my research was carried out between 1993 and 1995, I have returned to the village nearly every year since then and have closely followed approximately twenty families from their early return experiences to the present.[5] In each family, I have watched children grow and mature, in some cases to marry and start their own families. I have researched the ways in which young people conceive of their physical surroundings, the relationships between physical place and personal identity, and the role of emplacement in the construction of a sense of 'home'.

This chapter describes several moments of emplacement in the lives of children, and to a lesser extent their parents: first, as it was enacted in the Sudan; second, as it was pursued in the first months following repatriation to Ethiopia; and finally as it was pursued in relationship to the creation or maintenance of a sense of home in the returnee settlement. In each of these moments, parents' and children's notions of space as being safe or dangerous, the nature of its gendered division, and its relation to home, is distinct. As Ada Bai residents further emplaced themselves, and as people came to feel comfortable in this, their new home, ideas about the relative degree of security in their lives also changed.

Emplacement through displacement – life in the refugee camps

In 1984, global media attention rested for a moment on a scenario of desperation, as thousands of starving and exhausted people stumbled across the border from Ethiopia to Sudan to escape civil war and famine.[6] The refugees had walked by night for up to six weeks under escort from the guerilla movement known as the Tigrayan People's Liberation Front (TPLF) and its humanitarian branch, the Relief Society of Tigray (REST), to reach the relative safety of the Sudan. Children were carried strapped to their mothers' backs, tied to donkeys, or if they were able to walk were given a bundle of household goods to help carry with the rest of the family.

In 1986, the United Nations High Commissioner for Refugees (UNHCR) estimated that there were 677,000 Ethiopian and Eritrean refugees living in the Sudan (Mebtouche 1987). One of the largest crossing points from Ethiopia into Sudan was Wad Kowli camp, which in February 1985 – the height of the crisis – hosted 100,000 Tigrayan refugees (MSF 1985). Most of the people that I lived with in Ada Bai had spent their first months in Sudan living at Wad Kowli.

Conditions in the camp were extremely poor, as neither the Sudanese Government nor the UNHCR had been prepared for the sudden arrival of so many severely weakened people. Mortality rates skyrocketed out of control in the camps in Eastern Sudan. During the first quarter of 1985, monthly crude mortality rates in the camps were reportedly nearly twice the rate of famine-affected sedentary populations within Ethiopia and eight times the baseline mortality rate (CDC 1992). Children were the most vulnerable in the camps. High rates of morbidity and mortality continued throughout the first year after the refugees arrived. Malnutrition and overcrowding contributed to the spread of measles, cholera, meningitis and tuberculosis (CDC 1992).

Such high incidence of sickness and death contributed to refugees' conviction that the camp was an unsafe space. They believed that overcrowding caused illness to spread, but rather than considering the vector of disease to be viral or bacterial, they saw it as spiritual. In the first weeks and months after their arrival in the camp, families were directed by the authorities to share tents with strangers from other parts of Tigray. Losing the ability to choose one's neighbours, a basic element of control over their own lives, they recalled, created a dangerous situation in which they were vulnerable to the attacks of evil spirits, particularly *buda*, also known as Evil Eye.

Belief in the Evil Eye is common throughout East Africa (Young 1970; Bishaw 1988; Boddy 1994 and 1989). While there are many local variations, spirits (known as *tebib*) carrying the Evil Eye are generally believed to be capable of possessing a person through biting, pinching, hitting, or establishing direct eye contact with him or her. Once resident inside a human host, the *tebib* is said to make the victim ill and eventually cause his or her death. People believe that if detected early enough, the spirit may be exorcised by traditional healers using herbal remedies, incense (potash, bits of bone, or rubber tyre burned over a bed of charcoal) and prayer to coax the spirit from the victim. In the course of the treatment, the exorcist may also try to compel the victim to reveal the name of the person who passed the spirit to him or her; the victim is said to speak in the voice of the *tebib* when revealing him/herself.[7]

Because it is impossible to tell by looking at a person whether he or she is a *tebib*, strangers are immediately suspect. Only by knowing a person's character, their family history and the history of the village he/she has come from can one be sure that that person does not carry the spirit and thus poses no threat. In the refugee camps and later in Ada Bai, pregnant women and children were considered particularly vulnerable to the attack of the Evil Eye, and the presence of so many strangers increased the risk. Children were said to be susceptible for two reasons: first, they were weak and innocent, and therefore were often unsuspecting of the advances of the *tebib*; second, children too young to be able to speak could not reveal the name of the person who had transferred the spirit to them and thus could not easily be exorcised.

People responded to the perceived threat of strangers in the refugee camps by moving their tents or straw huts so that they could live with others who were from the same part of Tigray. In so doing, they were surrounding themselves with people who were known to them, either personally or through the reputation of their families. Nearly every *woreda* (similar to a county) in Tigray was represented by a small neighbourhood in the camp. In creating this 'Little Tigray', people said that the danger of being targeted for spirit possession by a stranger was minimised. In taking control over their own living arrangements, they felt better able to ward off evil spirits.

This point was explained to me by Gebre Selassie, a 70-year-old man who described to me how one of his daughters had died in Wad Kowli:

> In 1978 [1985 G.C.] my girl who was 12 years old died from diarrhoea. But I do not believe that was the reason – she was sick only for three days, from Friday to Sunday. She was killed by the *tebib*. I could not find a *habesha medehanit* [the generic term for traditional medicine from Ethiopia]. [People from] my [area] were not there. [He refers here to the difficulty of losing his social network through displacement.] They were all at Jirba [another refugee camp nearby]. I was living with Keyih Tekeli people [i.e. those who had come from Keyih Tekeli, a place said to have many *tebibs*]. [Another child] my boy [also] died from diarrhoea like the others [as a result of being attacked by the Evil Eye]. It is the worst thing to live with unknown people.

People's inability to locate *habesha medehanit*, either because they could not find traditional healers from Ethiopia or because much of the medicine was extracted from plants that grew only in the Tigrayan highlands, contributed to a sense of insecurity and endangerment. They thought that rearranging the residential space helped to reduce the threat, particularly for children.

In this example of emplacement, the dangerous potential of the environment was made manifest through the human body. The threat posed by the unknown (strangers, spirits and camp authorities who assume control over the refugees) served as an imperative to the refugees to reclaim control over at least some aspect of their lives by reorganising their living arrangements such that they were protected by a zone of safe space. The consideration of the body as a vehicle through which place is given meaning runs throughout Casey's phenomenological history of place (1997, particularly pp. 202–42) and is a theme to which I will return.

Life in the camps after the cameras have gone

Although the media's attention had moved on to the next global disaster a few months after the refugees had entered Sudan, most of the refugees remained in the camps for eight more years.[8] UNHCR supported the establishment of schools in the camps, and children worked to help support their families by selling water and fuel, taking care of their siblings, and engaging in petty trade. Many children learned to speak basic Arabic, though they were raised according to Tigrayan, Orthodox Christian customs.[9] There was a remarkable degree of cultural continuity between life in the camps and that in the Tigrayan highlands, bolstered by the strong role that religion played in the refugees' lives as well as their close association with TPLF political ideology, which blended Marxist Leninism with a strong Ethiopian/Tigrayan identity. The oral poetry and songs that emerged in the camp, often sung by children, recalled the famous battles and many places in Tigray where the attacks of the then Ethiopian government, known as the Derg, had been repelled.[10]

Despite their adaptations to life in the camps, the refugees remained highly politicised. The TPLF encouraged them to keep thinking about and planning for return. Unlike those who integrated into the Sudanese cities of Gedaref, Kassala and Khartoum, camp residents remained poised to return to Ethiopia as soon as conditions would permit.

The emplacement that occurred in the camps shows the flip side of displacement. Whenever people move from one place to another, they become involved in creating meaning out of a new environment. This, I argue, is a necessary survival strategy, for it renders the new environment usable. Even when movement is conceived of as temporary, emplacement always accompanies displacement.

Emplacing an empty space

In May 1991, Derg was overthrown by a rebel coalition, known as the Ethiopian People's Revolutionary Democratic Front (EPRDF), which was dominated by the TPLF. Many refugees considered their years in exile to have been their contribution to 'The Struggle', as the war came to be called by Tigrayans. With the 'rebel army' now in the seat of power in the Ethiopian capital, Addis Ababa, most felt that the conditions were right for a return to their country of origin. Actual finalisation of plans and funds for assisted repatriation did not begin until June 1993.

Before their return, refugees were told by Ethiopian political leaders in Sudan that their farmland in the highlands of Tigray, and in many cases their houses, were occupied by others. Population density and demand for farmland had necessitated redistribution, so the local councils had re-allocated the land to those who remained behind. Even then, landholdings were smaller than a hectare (2.5 acres) for each household, and in many places were as small as 0.25 hectare. The officials advised them that instead of returning to their villages of origin, they should resettle to the flat, hot, but much more fertile lowland plains in Western Tigray, where they would be given land. It was assumed that they could also work on the nearby commercial sesame and sorghum plantations.

The first group of returnees came from two camps in Sudan and were settled by the government in three settlements near the town of Humera. Some 7,500 of these returnees were brought to Ada Bai, which means 'Big Land' in Tigrinya. The name was fitting, for Ada Bai was literally a huge empty field before the returnees arrived. It was a space, rather than a place, which held no personalised meaning for its new inhabitants. None of the new arrivals had lived there before, and the environment's potential was largely unknown. To make return viable, they had to learn to grow new crops (sorghum and sesame, rather than the crops commonly grown in the highlands – barley, wheat and teff). Some sought off-farm income, including daily wages for work on commercial farms, although there was not sufficient work for everyone. Traders built a business district in the new village, but many had spent all their money on the move and could not afford to buy stock to sell, so they too tried their hand at farming (Hammond 1996).

Residents' organisation of space in Ada Bai reflected their desire to develop a community that borrowed features from both pre-flight highland Tigray and the refugee camps, but also included new innovations that rendered the environment productive and gave it meaning (for some) as a home. As they had in Sudan, they organised themselves into neighbourhoods made up of people who had originated from the same area in Tigray. They assisted each other in building houses and fences, gathering firewood and caring for children. Social networks were renegotiated so that neighbours and distant kin came to be thought of as close kin.

Men and women encoded space differently, largely into domestic and public spheres. Areas where a person felt most comfortable were considered 'safe'; this included areas where work was done, as well as social spaces to which the individual had a recognised right of access and areas that were shared by these residential and kin groupings. Unfamiliar spaces were often those to which access was prohibited or which their daily activities did not normally bring them into contact with; these spaces were considered dangerous and threatening.

Women's safe places included the home, parts of the market-place, the public water taps and the clinic. Houses of other women who lived in the same residential cluster were considered safe spaces for women as well. Agricultural fields, the forest, bars in the market-place, and the neighbouring town were all considered dangerous to women; the first two places were referred to as *berekha*, or wilderness, to be avoided by women unless accompanied by a man. Men's safe and known places included parts of the market-place that 'respectable' women would not venture into (including bars and some tea-houses), the agricultural fields and areas of the forest that they knew well. The geographic area that they felt most comfortable in was wider than it was for women, but was still not unbounded. In 2002, the most significant unsafe place for men was considered the Tekezze River bank, which forms the border between Ethiopia and Eritrea and which was vulnerable to attacks and raids from Eritrean militia.[11]

Children's safe and known places spanned both male and female domains. Very young children (younger than age 4) tended to stay with their mothers in the residential compound and house or at the houses of neighbours. Boys 5 years of age or older were tasked with tending the household's sheep, goats and cattle in fields close to the village where water was available. Some enterprising families offered their sons' shepherding services to other households that did not have a child to work for them: the child's family was paid 3 *birr* per month (approximately 60 US cents) for each animal the boy tended. Thus, at an early age, boys' safe space was enlarged from the house to the field. Boys brought their animals to central grazing and watering areas, keeping one eye on their animals while playing football, hunting for wild fruits and greens, or swimming in the river with the other shepherd boys. The river-bed (*jirba*) became a place for social interaction with boys of a similar age from all over the village, who might not otherwise have seen one another if they had remained in their homes.

The eldest son was often tasked with fetching water using two 20 litre jerrycans, or saddlebags made from old tyres, loaded on to a donkey. The boy brought water to his mother's house first, then refilled his donkey's load with water to deliver for sale to other houses. This helped ease the work burden of the boy's mother, who otherwise had to carry the jerrycans unaided on her back from the water point to the house, a distance of up to 1 km.

The mobility enjoyed by young boys stood in contrast to that of mothers and daughters. The mother tended to remain close to the house; she was responsible for childcare, cooking, cleaning and tending suckling or ill livestock that could not graze with the rest of the herd. The mother's social network usually consisted of her immediate neighbours who were real or fictive kin (extended family who came to be thought of as closer relatives). Young girls tended to stay close to their homes as well, helping their mothers with chores and playing with other children nearby. Girls were less likely to herd animals, but when they did, tended only those animals that stayed close to the house such as goats and sheep. However, girls often went uninvited to other houses in the immediate area, and in general were more mobile than their mothers.

As part of its initial assistance to the village, UNHCR had built an elementary school in Ada Bai for grades 1–5. (Subsequently, the school added classes for grades 6–8, and now provides scholarships for the strongest students to attend high school in Humera town, 20 km away.) During the first few years, enrolment in first grade was exceptionally high, as most children had not attended school in the refugee camps. With large classes, and with demands from parents who needed them to work at home, absenteeism and drop-out rates were high. During these early days most boys expected to be farmers for the rest of their lives. Over the years, school attendance rates improved, as more parents came to see education as an important key to upward mobility. They began to encourage their children, particularly boys, to imagine a future that did not involve farming. Parents often said that they wanted their sons to become teachers. In 2002, I asked several boys what they wanted to be when they grew up: one wanted to be a pilot and another wanted to be a policeman.

Just as residence was based on area of origin, so too was marriage based on attempting to keep bonds between families intact despite displacement. Marriage of a man and woman from the same area was actively encouraged, on the grounds that 'you can trust a person if you know he is from the same place as you. You know his family, or at least you know what kind of person he is.'

The space in which children felt at ease as part of their personal landscape tended to narrow as they matured and became more tightly bound to the social rules of the adult world. Several of my young informants had to relinquish elements of their childhood landscape when they married. They made the adjustment with some awkwardness, and girls in particular were often embarrassed to talk about their married lives. Girls became more tied to the home once they married, and were less able to visit their friends, linger in the market-place or chat at the water source. Young married men had less free time to loiter in the tea-shops; their associations with other men became more rooted in kinship as well as in the likely benefit to be derived from sharing resources or labour on a particular project for the benefit of their household.

Children as independent agents

Children in Ada Bai were given a great deal of independence which affected their emplacement within the community. Where parents were divorced, children were often allowed to choose which parent they wanted to stay with: some alternated between staying with one parent one night and the other the next. One girl of about 6 years of age, whose mother had remarried after her father left to join the military, chose to stay with her maternal grandmother. She would spend the days with her mother, but would usually return to her grandmother's house in the evening. When the girl's father eventually appeared, having taken up a job as a truck driver and also remarried after the war ended, he took her regularly to his home in the Tigrayan highlands to stay with his new wife and his mother. The girl's mother told me, 'I didn't want her to be worried, [but] to be free to be with both parents. If she wants she can come here or she can stay with her grandparents. I leave her free to do what she wants.'

Although always on hand to supervise young children, adults tended to consider them able to decide whether to go to school or not, whose house to sleep in at night, and how best to carry out household chores. Discipline for inappropriate or ill-advised action was swift, however, so children did not act with impunity. Children frequently acted so as to attract their parents' approval and thus to avoid being disciplined.

Despite the independence they gave them, parents played an important role in managing their children's longer-term emplacement. They attempted to guide a child's entry into the social world of the community, and to ensure that he/she would be able to avoid spirit attacks and other hazards that could result in death. Such emplacement was largely carried out through the medium of the body: bodies were literally used to forge a connection between the individual, community and place. Place was encoded into rituals and everyday practice so as to inscribe the landscape into the fabric of socialised meaning that gave the person both individual and group identity.

Christening: entry into the Christian community of Ada Bai

The Christena, or Baptism, was the most important ritual involving a new-born child in Ada Bai, as it is throughout Christian communities in Ethiopia. Tigrayans considered a child to have a soul as soon as it is baptised (40–80 days after birth) and to be fully capable of individually purposive action from a young age. Although the form of the ritual is similar throughout Tigray and other Orthodox Christian areas of Ethiopia, its significance in forging a permanent link between the child and its birthplace gave it local significance in the context of emplacement. The Christening ceremony itself involved a manipulation of space and a rite of passage that served to inscribe the physical landscape on the social and spiritual identity of the child. The Christena marked the child's entry into the Church (both as a member of a particular parish and in the wider Christian world), and acceptance into the Christian community.

A baptised child could enter the church, attend the church school, and ultimately could be buried in the cemetery with other baptised souls. Thus the number and types of places that became meaningful and part of the individual's personal landscape increased through this ritual. Space to which access was previously forbidden was made accessible and was incorporated into the social life of the individual.

Ada Bai parents said that one of the most important benefits to a baptised child was that when the child died (either as a child or adult), he or she could be buried in a sanctified church cemetery together with others who had been baptised, rather than in a separate grave for unbaptised newborns and infidels (i.e. those without souls). Those who were buried outside the Christian cemetery brought shame to their families. Priests disagreed about whether an unbaptised baby could be expected to go to Heaven. Some said that at such a young age a child was innocent and thus its place in Heaven was assured. Others said they did not see how anyone who had not been baptised as a Christian could ascend to Heaven. In cases in which the child was seriously ill and was expected to die before the Christena, a priest told me, he was obliged to advise the family to christen the child early, so that it could be buried as a Christian. Failure to advise the family in this way, he said, could bring God's punishment to both the family and the priest.

Herein lies another example of the intrinsic role of the body in imbuing space with meaning. Even in death, the location and status of the interred body continued to generate meaning for relatives who remained, and also served to ensure that the individual's membership in the community was perpetuated into the afterlife.

Mapping the body into the community through healing

In addition to the emplacement of the child on the physical landscape through the opening of spaces for meaningful interaction throughout and beyond his or her life, the process also worked in reverse, whereby the place was literally inscribed on the body of the child.

Several illnesses were believed to exist only in the lowlands around Ada Bai. These illnesses were believed to be caused by malevolent spirits who caused the blood to 'turn bad'. The only way of curing an afflicted person was thought to be through making incisions to allow the poisoned blood to drain out of the body.[12] Again, children were considered particularly vulnerable to such maladies. One of these illnesses, known as *waz* (leishmaniasis), was treated with a series of 44 incisions made on the patient's body, in groups of two or three, with a cross cut into the head.[13] Another illness, known as *shofer* (probably a form of hepatitis) was treated with 16 burns, administered with a needle or piece of metal heated in a fire, to the wrists, forearms, elbows, upper arms, and top of the head (in the shape of a cross).

The reasoning behind cauterisation and incision was explained to me in the following terms: when a person is burned, he or she inhales and exhales sharply, forcing the spirit that has taken up residence within the body to be expelled. When the person is cut, the 'bad blood' is able to leave the body, taking the disease with it. Both adults and children were treated in this way. This explanation struck me as interesting, but only after I had witnessed the treatment being applied to infants and very young children did I find it personally disturbing. Two of my closest friends, Tibbletz and Ambachew, had a son, Kiros, who received several cuts and burns during his first year of life. When he was four months old, his parents brought him to a traditional healer to have the skin under his tongue (*anker*) removed. I was told that removal of the *anker* was necessary to prevent the child from becoming unable to swallow the mother's breastmilk. On the same day, Kiros had had the cross in his forehead re-cut, to protect him from the Evil Eye. Tibbletz told me that she had been concerned that he was not eating well, and wanted to make sure that he had not been attacked by a *tebib*. A few days later, the child had a high fever and was vomiting. I brought him to the clinic and he began a course of daily injections of procaine penicillin. That evening, Ambachew, his father, came to my house looking extremely distraught and asked me to come and see the boy. The following is an excerpt from my notes of that day:

> I got there and found a house full of people – Berhan was making coffee; Lettemariam [the boy's paternal aunt] was holding Kiros, who had finally fallen asleep. Aboy Gebreselassie [an older man who, though distantly related had come to be thought of as the boy's grandfather] was there – whether he knew that Kiros was sick or not I don't know. Medhin was also there with her tiny baby – so tiny I can't believe she's alive, and now marked with burns all over her body from attempts to treat her with *habesha medehanit*. Medhin herself still has her TB cough and it is likely that her baby has it too . . .
>
> Tibbletz was sitting there listlessly, exhausted by the day. Kiros . . . wasn't feverish, so I suspected that the worst had passed. Whatever it was that his body had wanted to expel from his stomach seemed to have gone.
>
> Meanwhile attention turned to Aboy Gebreselassie, who had found Tibbletz' old umbrella, ripped and broken, hanging under the [straw shade outside the house]. He started examining it closely: I thought he was under the impression that it was the umbrella he had [recently] given to Tibbletz. Then Tibbletz got up to go to the field [which was used as an open-air latrine]. I thought she wanted to get away on her own. Aboy Gebreselassie put one of the rods of the umbrella into the fire. I was still under the impression that he was trying to fix the umbrella. Then the scene suddenly all became horribly clear to me when Lettemariam pulled up Kiros' shirt and Aboy Gebreselassie stuck the burning rod into his stomach in two places. I started screaming at them to stop, as did Kiros. The others laughed uncomfortably and Ambachew tried to explain to me that this was 'medehanit nay buda' [medicine for Evil Eye]. I retorted that I thought his sickness was only of the stomach, not from *buda*, but I realised that they thought I was crazy or just plain wrong. I also realised that that was why Tibbletz had left – so she wouldn't have to watch her baby being tortured, even if it was meant for his own good. [After the procedure was finished, she returned to the house, looking disturbed.]
>
> Kiros stopped crying relatively quickly, and drank a lot of breast-milk, which seemed to stay down. But then Tibbletz [tied] him [on to] her back and walked around with him, his stomach rubbing against

her back and no doubt hurting him. [He started crying again and could not be consoled.]

In this example of the use of traditional medicine, the body is seen as the battleground between evil spirits who seek to gain control over the body, and the child's social network, which seeks to displace the spirit. Although I attributed Kiros' recovery to the procaine penicillin injections he had received, his family considered that the burns had successfully exorcised the spirit. His father, knowing that I had been disturbed by the painful impact of the traditional medicine, tried to explain why they administered the burns. 'We are doing this because we are scared', he said. 'We are scared of losing him.'

Those treated with incisions or burns for *waz*, *shofer*, or other forms of spirit possession would carry the scars for the rest of their lives that would mark them as having lived in the western lowlands of Tigray. This made them distinct from highland Tigrayans (who may have a different set of scars), and was a permanent indication of the person's having been 'marked' by the place.

Parents made a direct link between the relative danger of the new place and their lack of familiarity with it. A father of several young children explained the fragility of the environment: 'We do not know this place; that is why we and our children are dying.' As people came to 'know' the place better, and learned to avoid dangerous spaces or to protect themselves against harmful agents and spirits in their environment (through amulets, traditional medicine and avoidance of places such as rivers where spirits were thought to lurk) morbidity decreased.[14] As a way of counteracting the threat posed by dangerous spaces, cutting and branding of children served to mark the place on the body, and was likely more important as a means of literally inscribing social membership and identity on the body than it would have been had the community felt 'safe' in its new place. However, it should be noted that emplacement never entails full rendering of the physical landscape as safe, and therefore cutting and branding practices have continued as a response to changing perceptions of threat and risk in the environment.

Emplacement's role in the creation of a sense of home

In 1993–5, during my longest period of fieldwork in Ada Bai, I would often ask people how long they thought it would take them to feel that they were 'home'. The variety of responses I received shows that age played a decisive role in determining the nature of emplacement and the conception of home.

Most elderly people considered their birthplace to be their home, as that was where their families had come from and where, they said, 'people knew me best'. Home was tied to birthplace and family lineage and was not influenced by conditions in their lives in Ada Bai. The elderly commonly said that they wanted to be buried in the village in which they had been born, where they could be appropriately mourned and remembered by those who had known them when they were young.

Younger adults, many of whom had entered the refugee camps in Sudan as children, had a more utilitarian, pragmatic view of home. They reported that they felt that home could be created from a new place. They said that they had started their lives over so many times that the concept of 'going back' to a life they had once known was so unpractical as to be unthinkable. One man told me: 'We see our life as two lives. The life before [1984] and the life after. The life before was better because we were in our homes. But this is a new life and we must try to make it as complete as possible.' Another said that he considered that he had lived three lives: one in the highlands, one in the Sudan, and one in Ada Bai. He said that he had no desire to go back to the highlands. Since leaving he had had numerous occupations, married a second time, had several more children, and made a complete break with his family in the highlands. These men were typical of the middle-aged group that had chosen to begin a new life in Ada Bai without apparent regret or longing for their birthplace.

Such pragmatism was also found among parents of small children. They expected their children to eventually develop an identity as Ada Bai people. A woman from a town in the central highlands said that her children 'know that they are from Abi Adi [a large town in central Tigray] by story [i.e. they have heard me talk about the place], but they do not know it so [instead] they can say "Ada Bai is our home"'. Another man said 'We are teaching our children now to be Ada Bai people. They should say they are from Ada Bai when someone asks them.' Over time, songs and oral poetry emerged within the village that reinforced the idea that Ada Bai was home. The songs quoted at the beginning of this chapter were composed by children and sung at home, school, or while children were attending to their herding, water fetching, or other responsibilities. The verses were sung repeatedly, with variations in intonation or melody with each repetition. Often girls would sing these songs to their younger siblings as they played with them in the family house.

While the idea that Ada Bai was the best or most practical home for their children played an important role in parents' sense of home, their children did not always adapt in the ways that their parents envisioned they would. On a visit to Ada Bai in June 2002, I asked several children, who had either been born in Sudan or in Ada Bai, which place they considered to be 'home'. Questions about home were complicated by the fact that Tigrayans have several words to refer to places that in English would all be referred to as home. *Addi*, the place to which one's family belongs, is distinct from *hager*, meaning one's country (Ethiopia), and distinct from *bota* meaning a highly localised place which may or may not hold meaning for the speaker (in the context of this discussion, space may be known as *bota*). *Geza*, meaning house, is never considered a locus for notions of home, in the way that Western cultures might use house and home interchangeably. A 14-year-old girl, who had been born in the Sudan, said to me 'our home [*addi*] is Axum' [the district in the central highlands from which her parents had come] – then she looked to her mother and asked, 'What is it called?' 'Adiet [meaning the name of the village]', she was told. Although she had never been to Adiet before, she considered it to be her 'home' because of her family's connection to the place. Other children agreed that their *addi* was not Ada Bai. A few children who had paid a visit to the family home in the highlands since repatriating to Ada Bai said that they preferred Ada Bai, either because the school was closer to their houses, the water was closer, or, in the words of one 7-year-old girl, because the highlands are 'full of stones . . . [and] you have to walk so far [to get from the village to the house]'. Despite their preference for living in Ada Bai, they still felt some identification with the place that the family had migrated from in the highlands. The responses of these children indicated a sort of bilateral construction of home, with Ada Bai occupying the role of 'everyday home' and the highlands that of 'family home'.

In an earlier essay (Hammond 1999) I surmised that children would form associations of emplacement with Ada Bai such that they would eventually come to think of it, rather than the highland point of origin, as their home. This would happen as the process of emplacement served to forge stronger associations between these children and their physical and social community. On visits to the community in 2001 and 2002, I observed that emplacement is occurring as I predicted it would, but that the process is more gradual than I originally anticipated it would be. I now see that for those children growing up in families with active memories of life in the highlands, home may always be a double-sided vision. On one hand, the place that they know best and where they expect to continue to live for the rest of their lives is Ada Bai. On the other, there is a sense in which the highlands will remain an absent, and somewhat vaguely defined, home. Home for these young children may not be entirely dependent upon emplacement.

In revising my conclusions about the relationship between place and home for children and young adults in Ada Bai, I see that I should have listened more closely to the parents I interviewed during the mid-1990s. When I asked parents and grandparents then how long it would take before their children thought of Ada Bai as home, some told me that it would take three generations. At the point when a person could say that their father and paternal grandfather were both born in Ada Bai, they told me, they would be a true Ada Bai person. Others saw the process as being even more prolonged. Incest prohibitions stipulate that a man and woman cannot marry if they have had any common paternal ancestors within the past seven generations. Children are taught to be able to name their paternal ancestors. Parents said that when all relatives in the seven generation lineage were Ada Bai residents, then the tie to the highland home would truly be broken.

I did not take this statement as seriously as perhaps I should have. I assumed that they were speaking more rhetorically than literally. Perhaps at a subconscious level I discounted their words because I did not think that the funders of my research, who were aid agencies involved in repatriation, would take me seriously if I were to say that the return process would take seven generations to be completed. I also did not realise how important it was for parents to teach their children to remember their lineage. In 2002, I asked several children to name their paternal ancestors; to my surprise, even 6-year-old children could name their grandfathers five or six generations back. Though they did not know the details of these men's lives, they knew that they had lived in the highlands. Thus, they were able to place themselves easily into a historical legacy of emplacement that tied them to other areas outside the village into which they had been born, even if the returnee settlement was the only place they had any direct memory of. Through longitudinal research, I have come to see when people told me the process of redefining home would take seven generations, they were in fact speaking quite literally.

Recently I have been grappling with the question of whether I should continue to consider Ada Bai to be a returnee settlement. Outward appearances suggest that it is a stable village rather than a temporary settlement. The population is no longer dependent upon food aid or other forms of humanitarian assistance, and it is fully integrated into the local political landscape as a village. Thus, I have wondered at times whether it is in fact still a migrant community. However, the responses of the children I have interviewed suggest that the process of homecoming is not yet complete. Although the idea of 'family home' may be a hazy concept for those who have no personal memory of the place, it continues to influence their lives in Ada Bai.[15]

Conclusions

Understanding the emplacement processes of returnee children requires a multi-step process. First, it is necessary to consider the gendered aspects of emplacement, whereby space is made meaningful for adult men and women. Then the observer must consider the ways in which children inhabit each of these spaces, transcending boundaries that their parents cannot or will not, and creating new meaning for themselves in the process. Children follow two paths of emplacement. First, they are conduits for emplacement enacted by adults, whereby parents define their own relation to physical space and social identity through their children. Second, they are active agents in their own right, forming new and independent bonds with their geographic and social environment that serve to define individual and group identity. Emplacement is a never-ending process that changes character throughout the life-cycle of the individual and the community.

Understanding children as fully participant actors in their own emplacement processes widens the scope of anthropological enquiry and enriches the study not only of the return experience of children, but also of their parents and other relatives. In the process of trying to understand the former, the latter comes into sharper focus.

Notes

1 See Hammond 2000 for a full explanation of the notion of emplacement.
2 Casey's seminal examination of space (1997) and place in philosophical history consistently refers to space in these terms, and to the notion of place as being space made particularly meaningful. For Casey, space is not devoid of meaning, but rather the meaning is unactualised, not fully integrated into the person's associational framework so as to influence individual and group identity.
3 It should be noted, however, that every experience of displacement, in which a person leaves a meaningful place, involves emplacement as well. Emplacement occurs in refugee camps and other temporary havens, as well as in return contexts.
4 Bodenhorn (1995 [1993]) discusses the construction of gendered spaces according to public/private frameworks proposed by Engels (1896) and M. Z. Rosaldo (1974) through emplacement.
5 My yearly visits were disrupted by the border war that was fought between Ethiopia and Eritrea from 1998 to 2000.
6 At the time, Eritrea was a region of Ethiopia fighting a war of secession. In 1994, Eritrea was recognised as an independent state.
7 The best description I have found of the behaviour of the Evil Eye spirit in Ethiopia is given in Allan Young's Ph.D. Dissertation (Young 1970). In Ada Bai, I read passages of this text to a traditional healer, who confirmed that the descriptions agreed with his own experience. Bishaw (1988) and Boddy (1994 and 1989) also cite the Evil Eye as being commonly cited by people as a cause of generalised illness.
8 50,000 refugees did return to Ethiopia in 1985, claiming that they needed to tend to their farms even if the war was still ongoing (Hendrie 1996).
9 Approximately 90 per cent of those who repatriated to Ada Bai were Orthodox Christians, and 10 per cent were Muslim. Most of my research was done with Tigrayan Christians.
10 The Derg and its leader, Mengistu Haile Mariam, came to power in 1974 after overthrowing Emperor Haile Selassie. Tigrayan rebels began fighting against the Derg in 1975 and finally defeated the government forces in 1991.
11 From 1998 to 2000 the governments of Ethiopia and Eritrea fought a war along the border. The cause of the fighting stemmed from disputes over the location of the border, but were also influenced by economic and nationalistic factors.

12 The association of blood with illness, either as a cause of disease, the host of disease, or as a vehicle for spirit possession, is common throughout the Horn of Africa. See Young 1970: 73–6; Boddy 1989: 249; Hutchinson 1992: 496; 1998: 171.

13 In 1993–5 while I was in Ada Bai, the local hospital did not have a diagnosis for *waz*; this reinforced local residents' belief that it was attributed to evil spirits. In 1996, Médecins Sans Frontières and the regional Bureau of Health identified the illness as leishmaniasis and began a treatment programme.

14 It should also be noted that river-beds were commonly frequented by mosquitoes, sandflies and poisonous snakes, and thus were dangerous even to those who associated illness with biomedical causes.

15 Gow (1995) discusses the impact of older relatives' personal histories in 'distant landscapes' as being important in tying individuals to their genealogical history.

References

Akol, J. O. (1994) 'A crisis of expectations: Returning to Southern Sudan in the 1970s,' in T. Allen and H. Morsink (eds) *When Refugees Go Home*. Trenton, NJ: Africa World Press, pp. 78–95.

Bender, B. (ed.) (1995 [1993]) *Landscape: Politics and Perspectives*. London: Berg Publishers.

Bishaw, M. (1988). 'Integrating indigenous and cosmopolitan medicine in Ethiopia,' unpublished Ph.D. Dissertation, Carbondale: Southern Illinois University.

Boddy, J. (1989) *Wombs and Alien Spirits: Women, Men, and the Zār Cult in Northern Sudan*. Madison: University of Wisconsin Press.

—— (1994) 'Spirit possession revisited: Beyond instrumentality,' *Annual Review of Anthropology* 23: 407–34.

Bodenhorn, B. (1995 [1993]) 'Gendered spaces, public places: Public and private revisited on the North Slope of Alaska', in B. Bender (ed.) *Landscape: Politics and Perspectives*. London: Berg Publishers, pp. 169–204.

Casey, E. S. (1997) *The Fate of Place: A Philosophical History*. Berkeley: University of California Press.

—— (1996) 'How to get from space to place in a fairly short stretch of time: Phenomenological prolegomena', in S. Feld and K. H. Basso, *Senses of Place*. Sante Fe, NM: School of American Research Advanced Seminar Series, pp. 13–52.

Centers for Disease Control (1992) 'Famine-affected, refugee, and displaced populations: Recommendations for public health issues, *Morbidity and Mortality Weekly Review* 41(No. RR-13).

Clifford, J. (1997) *Routes: Travel and Translation in the Late Twentieth Century*. Cambridge: Harvard University Press.

Engels, F. (1972 [1896]) *Origin of the Family, Private Property and the State*. New York: Pathfinder Press (quoted in B. Bodenhorn (1995 [1993])).

Feld, S. and K. H. Basso (1996) 'Introduction', *Senses of Place*, Sante Fe, NM: School of American Research Advanced Seminar Series, pp. 3–11.

Gow, P. (1995) 'Land, people and paper in Western Amazonia', in E. Hirsch and M. O'Hanlon, *The Anthropology of Landscape*, Oxford Studies in Social and Cultural Anthropology. Oxford: Clarendon Press, pp. 43–62.

Hammond, L. (1996) 'Returnees, local farmers and big business: The politics of land allocation in Humera, Ethiopia', in J. W. Bruce, A. Hoben and D. Rahmato (eds) *After the Derg: An Assessment of Rural Land Tenure Issues in Ethiopia*, proceedings of a workshop held at Addis Ababa University, 5–6 May 1994. Trondheim: Trondheim University Press, pp. 248–63.

—— (1999) 'Examining the discourse of repatriation: Towards a more proactive theory of return migration,' in R. Black and K. Koser (eds) *The End of the Refugee Cycle: Refugee Repatriation and Reconstruction.* Oxford: Berghahn Books, pp. 227–46.

—— (2000) 'This place will become home: Emplacement and community formation in a Tigrayan returnee settlement, Northwest Ethiopia', unpublished Ph.D. Dissertation, University of Wisconsin.

Hendrie, B. (1996) 'Assisting refugees in the context of warfare: Some issues arising from the Tigrayan refugee repatriation: Sudan to Ethiopia 1985–1987', in T. Allen (ed.) *In Search of Cool Ground: War, Flight and Homecoming in Northeast Africa.* Trenson, NJ: Africa World Press, pp. 35–43.

Hirsch, E. (1995) 'Introduction: Landscape: Between place and space' in E. Hirsch and M. O'Hanlon (eds) *The Anthropology of Landscape: Perspectives on Place and Space*, Oxford Studies in Social and Cultural Anthropology. Oxford: Clarendon Press, pp. 1–30.

Hutchinson, S. (1992) ' "Dangerous to eat": Rethinking pollution states among the Nuer of Sudan', *Africa* 62(4): 490–504.

—— (1998) *Nuer Dilemmas: Coping with Money, War and the State.* Berkeley: University of California Press.

Mebtouche, L. (1987) 'Refugees in Eastern Sudan: Aid and development (5–30 Oct. 1987)'. Geneva: UNHCR/TSS Mission Report 87/50.

Médecins Sans Frontières (1985) *Mass Deportations in Ethiopia.* Paris: Médecins Sans Frontières.

Migdal, J. (1988) *Strong Societies and Weak States: State–Society Relations and State Capabilities in the Third World.* Princeton: Princeton University Press.

Pilkington, H. and M. Flynn (1999) 'From "refugee" to "repatriate": Russian repatriation discourse in the making,' in R. Black and K. Koser (eds) *The End of the Refugee Cycle: Refugee Repatriation and Reconstruction.* Oxford: Berghahn Books, pp. 171–97.

Rogge, J. R. (1994) 'Repatriation of refugees,' in T. Allen and H. Morsink (eds) *When Refugees Go Home.* Trenton, NJ: Africa World Press, pp. 14–49.

Rosaldo, M. Z. (1974) 'Theoretical overview' in M. Z. Rosaldo and L. Lamphere (eds), *Women, Culture and Society.* Stanford: Stanford University Press (quoted in Bodenhorn 1995 [1993]), pp. 17–42.

Young, A. L. (1970) 'Medical beliefs and practices of Begemder Amhara'. unpublished Ph.D. Dissertation, Philadelphia: University of Pennsylvania.

Part II

Place as a site in the field of generational relations

Growing up between places of work and non-places of childhood

The uneasy relationship

Olga Nieuwenhuys

Introduction[1]

The way anthropology has conceptualised place is no doubt linked to its main preoccupation with the 'here and now', and the problem of delineating the spatial, temporal and symbolic fieldwork area. The consequence has been that socially important public centres, as well as meeting points and itineraries, have by and large been chosen as markers of place, to the neglect of the unremarkable places where everyday life is carried out. Place has tended to reflect dominant power relations and to obfuscate what happens behind the official façade in what are, for the anthropologist, often fuzzy, inconspicuous or inaccessible private places. This may help explain anthropology's traditional neglect of children's places. However, turning the approach upside down by looking at place from the perspective of children may carry the danger of implicit assumptions about the nature of childhood slipping into research. These assumptions are related to urban middle-class values that inform the anthropologists' gaze and that may, if left unquestioned, distort the perceived world.

According to these values, places of childhood coincide with clearly demarcated physical spaces in which children are both spatially and socially segregated from adults. In the urbanised areas of the Western world, segregation is born out of an ambiguous concern with children's safety and a pressure on space which results in children being seriously hampered in their mobility (Tonucci and Risotto 2001). The overriding concern is that children should at all times be in safe, supervised, controlled spaces. Outside these spaces their safety, and with it their very experience of childhood, is deemed to be at risk. Children who spend much of their time outside the safe spaces of childhood are not only deemed to be out of place, they are also perceived as being outside childhood. The problem with an approach to children and place, then, is that the notion of childhood is both historically and culturally predicated on spatial separation. In other words, when taking the notion of childhood as the frame of reference, children appear: 'sited, insulated and distanced, and their very gradual emergence into wider, adult space is only by accident, by degrees, as an award or privilege or as part of a gradualist rite of passage' (James *et al.* 1998: 37).

Understanding both children's and adults' sense of place requires that the anthropologist be prepared to question personal experiences that are his or her primary reference point when entering the field. Childhood icons such as children's playgrounds, children's rooms and furniture, classrooms, clothing, baby food, toys and books need to be critically recognised as encoding an urban middle-class childhood and separating it from the world of adults. Their absence, rather than signifying a lack of childhood, points to a deeply different understanding of children's place. In the local societies that are the concern of anthropologists, children's social place rarely appears to be as neatly compartmentalised spatially as is increasingly the norm in highly urbanised areas. The lack of a clear spatial positioning entails that children, particularly young ones, are immersed in places thick with meaning that entwine them from their youngest age in the continuous building and sustaining of their local worlds (cf. Sack 1997: 8; 1986).

Instead of being spatially segregated, children live in spatial contiguity with adults. However, spatial contiguity is matched by strong social distancing that articulates complex patterns of authority, dependence and support. Their constant intercourse with adults does not entail in the least, as Ariès believed for pre-modern France, that children are considered to be mini-adults – quite the contrary. Rather, children are perceived as occupying a liminal position at the margin (or *limen*) of society, somewhere between the imprecise outer world of the gods and the situated society of men (cf. also Turner 1970 [1967]: 93ff.). It is only in time, upon growing up, that children find their own ways in society and accede to the position of authority held by adults, becoming in the process as clearly spatially situated as their elders are. In most societies today, however, spatial segregation – and this is the core of my argument – is never totally absent, even in childhood. At the margins of local society, there are arenas controlled by the state or by voluntary organisations, such as schools or NGO sites, that offer children access to what are deemed to be the privileges of modern childhood. In these arenas children are spatially segregated from adults for part of the day and learn to challenge local conceptions of childhood as socially distanced from adulthood, being offered an alternative world view that contests local rules of authority and acquiescence. It is with the tension that arises from the multiple arenas in which children's identity and sense of place is shaped that anthropologists must engage.

The argument is based on a comparison of field material from Poomkara,[2] a village in South India, and data gathered through research on street children in NGO project sites in Addis Ababa[3] (cf. Nieuwenhuys 1994 and 2001). Poomkara's 3,000 or so inhabitants, packed together in a densely populated strip of coast in the central part of the Indian state of Kerala, live mainly from fishing and making coir yarn. The majority are Muslims, but a sizeable minority consists of low-caste Hindus. Birth rates are high among Muslims, children under 15 forming about 40 per cent of the population. The vast majority of children go to one of the government schools, many continuing their schooling till they obtain the Secondary School Leaving Certificate. Schooling is fairly accessible even for the poorest, as the government makes schoolbooks and other necessities such as school uniforms available at cost price and levies no fees. However, living standards are so low and poverty so widespread that children have to work to help their parents make ends meet even while they are at school. Intricate patterns of authority and intra-generational exchange, based on gender, class, kinship, birth rank, generational order and personal inclination, position Poomkara's children both physically and symbolically vis-à-vis meaningful others. These positions are continuously negotiated, making individual children's places spatially, temporally and symbolically multi-dimensional. The evidence from Poomkara emphasises that children's embeddedness in society does not necessarily depend on spatial segregation. With a few exceptions, related to modern institutions such as schools, Poomkara has no spaces of childhood. Yet, children are seldom in the wrong place.

What, then, makes children find themselves in the wrong place? Looking at how the staff of NGO projects for street children construct 'proper places' in Addis Ababa, I suggest that the idea of a 'wrong place' is intimately linked to the notion of childhood. If childhood is indeed, as sociologists claim, 'that status of personhood which is by definition often in the wrong place' (James et al. 1998: 37), then by the same token it is childhood that, by powerfully delimiting proper spaces for children, designates spaces beyond these limits as wrong places. Nevertheless, the case of Addis Ababa's project sites also highlights the fact that spatial segregation does not translate automatically into social place. The spaces of childhood that NGOs offer to street children are, to use Augé's expression, non-places.

Augé (1992: 100) defines anthropological place as a geographical space endowed with the following qualities:

A. *Relationships* among the people who live there.
B. *A sense of history* shared by these same people.
C. A place with which one can *identify,* grounding a shared sense of belonging.

Starting from this definition, Augé distinguishes between anthropological place and non-places, the latter being for him the typical spaces of high modernity. Shopping malls, airport lounges and highways would all be examples of spaces where one can find oneself regularly and even for protracted periods, but that lack the qualities of place. Rather than grounding the shared experiences of a stable community, these spaces distance people from meaningful markers of time and place and reinforce solitary individuality. Their idiom is not addressed to anybody in particular but to the average person, thus suggesting an inter-changeability of temporary roles suspended in time and place. Non-places are in Augé's argument like a huge parenthesis, which presupposes that meaningful social relations are grounded and enacted 'somewhere else' (Augé 1992: 139).

In what follows I shall first use Augé's approach to anthropological place to map out broadly Poomkara children's sense of place (pages 102–6). In the section that follows I contrast one of the important places of work where children are found in numbers – the fish-landing place – with the government schools, the only arena in which children find themselves segregated from the adult world. Following Augé, I contend that schools are, to some extent, non-places. The work place, however, is not a place for children.[4] This brings me to amend Augé's dualistic approach to place by highlighting that, next to anthropological place and non-place, there is at least a third, liminal dimension in which children find themselves immersed (pages 106–8). Next, on pages 108–13, discuss NGO project sites for street children in Addis Ababa, which bring out even more forcefully the fact that spaces of childhood created for the children of the poor are, in the context of the city's slums, non-places. But they also articulate children's structural liminality, thus functioning as zones of passage that enable children to accede to and negotiate assigned place in local society. In the final section (pages 113–17) I argue that the anthropology of children should examine children from the liminal places that articulate them to places that are locally of social, economic and cultural significance. Though lacking in coherence or being largely invisible, these places provide children with the meaningful relationships that govern their gradual incorporation into the world of adulthood. I also take issue with Augé's approach to non-places, suggesting that they should not be merely qualified by a 'lack'. Their roles can be highly dissimilar and can only be understood when seen in the wider context of the places of reference (Augé's 'somewhere else') that ground them.

Anthropological place from the perspective of children

In this section I shall first use Augé's definition of place to investigate the place of children in Poomkara. This will allow me to argue that, in village society, children are typically not insulated in any particular space, their place being everywhere and nowhere, but above all liminal. I start with a short description of the empirical data. I then focus on children's mobility and relate their omnipresence and disregard for boundaries to the strict rules of gender segregation that govern adult intercourse. I finally argue that children's places are liminal because place can only be acquired after a long period of socialisation into the rules governing local society. Children are perceived, in fact, as not yet being completely part of society.

What does place in Poomkara look like from the perspective of children? When I started my fieldwork and looked for children's places, I assumed that such places would have to be spatially demarcated. I soon realised that they were not. Where does then one start research on children when there are no playgrounds or sport grounds, no children's rooms or birthday parties, and no special events or spaces where children congregate except schools? Was I to infer from this that, apart from schools, there were no spaces for children, or was I to question the gaze with which I looked at childhood, and were there things that had escaped my attention? I soon realised that the answer to these questions required my being more agile and mobile than if had I worked on adults. Instead of participant observation, tied as it is to more or less stable places, I combined informal chatting with mobile observation, a method better suited to mapping children's itineraries as they unfolded during the day and varied with the seasons. Endlessly criss-crossing Poomkara in pursuit of children's whereabouts, my eyes often glued to the ground, I gradually became familiar with the intricate pattern of inconspicuous or even fleeting markers of place that articulated most of the villagers' experience of everyday life. I remember nearly stumbling over the tomb, no more than a heap of earth, of a forgotten elder and treading on the sacred ground of a tiny temple, only a few inches high, inhabited by one of the lesser gods of popular Hinduism. I walked over workplaces, bathing and toilet areas, backyards and children's playgrounds, often unaware of boundaries other than an occasional palm-leaf stuck in the ground, a few low shrubs planted in a row, a simple piece of coir yarn tied between two coconut palms or even nothing more than signs drawn on the sandy ground. Children's tiny kitchens of leaves and sand, the little holes into which marbles had to be tossed, or the imaginary roads on which palm-leaf cars were made to ride were largely invisible unless one was bent upon questioning every inch of children's local landscape. The house likewise lacked a clearly defined space for children. Although it was divided into the front, male space and the rear, female space, the location of children's spaces was imprecise: pre-puberty children could be everywhere in the house but could claim none of the spaces as theirs. Children had no rooms of their own in the tiny huts. School books were often simply stuck under the palm roof and children's clothes hung on a rope. Children did their homework sitting on the same mat on which they slept at night. Even this mat was often shared with others.

Importantly, it was difficult to find places where children were absent, even in a society in which male and female domains are often strictly segregated. These domains were primarily work places: for men, the beach where they kept and launched their boats, landed their catches and bargained with itinerant fish vendors, and the only tarred road where, next to the main mosque, shops were located and occasional vendors displayed their wares. Even if children were habitually there in large numbers, the fish-landing place was not a place of or for children. Small children were always present to pick up any fish that escaped the nets during the hauling or the small fry that remained stuck in the meshes after the landed fish had been taken away. Older boys helped with cleaning the boats and carrying the net and other gear to be stored in the house of the boat-owner. But this work did not give any of them a legitimate claim to the place. Significantly, the work was rarely remunerated: to underline the fact that the children were outsiders to the place, they were rather presented with 'gifts' (fish, tea and snacks) in return for their help. Entering this kind of exchange was deemed to be entirely free, and it was only after many years of displaying an interest in their operations and trying their hand at the different parts of the job that fishermen would ask some of the boys to join their crew. Children's presence was legitimised on the ground that they were close to the sea goddess Katalamma, who made a gift of her wealth to the fishermen. Fishermen did not believe that they had an exclusive right to her gifts. They believed that chasing children away could endanger the propitious inclinations of the goddess and entail great dangers, such as storms and loss of life and gear while at sea. In addition, as some of the children were the next generation of fishermen, they also felt that one could never tell in advance who would have the pluck and the stamina. Only years of informal intercourse would tell them so. In sum, connected as it was to local beliefs and charged with underlying potential, even though symbolically invisible (because yet inconspicuous), children's place was real.

For women, the workplace was often indistinct from the domestic domain, their main activity, coir-yarn spinning, being carried on in between domestic chores. The house was an important place of work, whether in the kitchen or in the backyard, where women made coir and where both boys and girls spent long hours working by their side. Most of the children of coir-making households would start helping out while still very young, 3 or 4 years old. But it would take them a long time before they acquired a fixed workplace. Boys never did, for as they got older they refrained from spending long periods in places reserved to the opposite sex. Girls would normally be assigned a fixed workplace only by the age of 14 or 15, when they had fully mastered the skills of yarn-spinning. Before that they had to remain at adult women's beck and call, switching continuously between tasks according to the demands of yarn-spinning, looking after the younger children, and doing the household chores in between.

In other places too, strict male and female segregation was matched by the omnipresence of children of both sexes.[5] The teashops and grocers on the main road were, as said, adult male terrain. Women had to content themselves with buying tea or groceries from the back or the side of the shops, through a small window which had generally been made for the purpose. However, boys and girls who had not yet come of age could enter them without objection. When asked about children's tasks, most people answered that drawing water was an important one. I therefore expected to find enough children near water taps, wells and ponds to consider it a space for children. In reality, however, a survey revealed that, although children were often sent to draw water, these places were frequented by everybody, including men.

There were places for play and recreation though: unremarkable, liminal places such as paths, fallows lands, the beach, the river bank, the wells and public taps. It is there that children played in between work or while they looked after the young ones, collected fruit, cut grass for the goat or fished, or where they just stopped on their way to somewhere else, such as the grocer's or the rice mill. While carrying out their customary foraging tasks, children displayed an impressive degree of spatial mobility. Teenage boys could travel quite far from the village in search of occasions to obtain some fish for vending. However, the further afield they went, the more they faced hostility, even violence, from fishing communities that felt their presence to be illicit and suspected them of going there to steal. Smaller children would remain closer to home, but they displayed a similar contempt for boundaries. It was normal for them to trespass on the precincts of fields, compounds or houses. They considered it their privilege to enter the fields to glean the paddy remaining after the harvest, catch fish, or collect fallen nuts and fronds from the coconut trees. Similarly, they freely entered private compounds to gather firewood, grass, mangoes and other fruit. They would sometimes congregate at the kitchen door of a wealthier neighbour in the hope of being offered some of the food being prepared on the occasion of a feast, not refraining from entering into the rooms if their curiosity drove them there. I seldom saw adults show impatience at these intrusions when the children were relatively young or behaved in a respectful manner. Rather than being blamed on children's uncontrolled behaviour, impatience would have been seen as a display of greediness and loss of decorum on the part of the adult.

In short, children's place in Poomkara is multi-faceted, ambiguous, ever-changing and difficult to pinpoint. Rather than being sited, children enjoy greater mobility than adults and have easy access to spaces that are closed to the latter. The best explanation for this lack of consistency of both place and space is, in my view, that positioning oneself in the shared history of such a society is not a birthright, but something one acquires slowly as relationships unfold and as one passes through the important stages in life that lead to wisdom and respect, which are acquired only in old age. Children are believed to keep links to the outer world of the gods before becoming part of the society of men for quite some time. To a large extent, this explains the tolerance for children's spatial mobility and contempt for boundaries. The situation changes radically for girls when they reach menarche, and for boys when they have ripened both physically and mentally and are thought fit to start taking the responsibilities of adulthood upon their shoulders. However, Poomkara children do have a clearly defined, recognisable space, allotted to them purely on the basis of chronological age, and irrespective of their physical and mental maturity, namely the school. But in the village landscape, as I shall argue in the next section, the school is a non-place.

Places of children and the non-place of childhood in Poomkara

If schools are non-places in the local perception, it is because what goes on there remains largely unconnected to the relationships that lace local place together. For most people, workplaces are at the core of village social life. By contrast, the government schools are associated with non-work. The activities carried out there are not regarded as having an economic purpose or a definite social meaning. These activities are about acquiring skills and internalising the rules and knowledge that are deemed important in supra-local intercourse. Locally, schools are non-places, both physically and socially. Physically, they are spatially separated from the village centre: the government primary school is located on the roadside and is not near other places of public importance, such as the mosques, the main shops or the only temple. Socially, when at school the children lack the opportunity to nurture enduring relationships that inform local place. To highlight what I am hinting at, let me contrast the typical workplace, the stretch of beach where Poomkara fishermen land their catches, with the government school by looking at how they perform as place in Augé's definition (see Table 5.1).

From this comparison it emerges that, compared to the fish-landing places, schools lack the qualities of anthropological place. The place of children outside school being as subordinates and invisible helpers in the world of adults, even when going to school they still have to submit to initiation into the different trades that will lead them, in time, to acquire a place in the local economic cycle. Alternatively, they will, as the spatial and social organisation of the school symbolises, simply have to leave to find a place elsewhere. This elsewhere is preferably a government office or jobs in Indian or Middle Eastern cities.

Schools in Poomkara (or for that matter Kerala) do not represent spaces of childhood aspiring to replace parents, homes or children's roles in local economic activities. Schools do not pretend to play a socialising role beyond forging the qualities thought to be essential in a prospective government official or migrant worker. They are silent, for instance, on issues of gender socialisation, religion, rituals, domestic and family matters, and above all on

Table 5.1 Qualities of place: comparison between place of work (fishing place) and the government school in Poomkara

Qualities of place	Fishing place	Government school
Relations	Hierarchy based on seniority, skills and wealth.	Symbolic equality based on socially neutral chronological age.
	Membership based on long-term mutual obligations.	Clear-cut and immutable division between children and teachers, no passage is possible from one position to the other.
	Central importance of trust in sharing of work and takings.	Central importance of competition and measurement of achievements.
	Assiduity and application lead in the long-term to entry into the job and a durable work relationship.	Assiduity and application translate in expulsion from the place and dissolution of teacher–pupil relation.
History	Common history of conquest of the place from other fishermen.	Symbolic lack of prior history of the pupils.
	To be accepted on a crew entails becoming part of this history.	Formalised history in the form of passage to various classes and passing of examinations.
	Skills, know-how, traditions and myths are transmitted gradually as one gets initiated.	No relationship between teacher's and children's life histories.
Identity	Becoming a fisherman totally engages the individual, his family and his immediate surroundings. Fishermen are always easily recognisable by their tan, their language and their particular habits and beliefs.	Being a schoolchild is by definition a limited and temporary identity assumed for the time one is in school. Uniforms are worn at school and removed back in the village.
	Identity is acquired in face-to-face intercourse.	Temporary identity is assumed by adopting standardised speech and behaviour which demonstrate successful adaptation.
	Success depends on the demonstration of locally valued virtues such as courage, application, compassion, trust and perseverance.	Success depends on the display of virtues such as diligence, neatness, punctuality and order, which are valued in government offices.

children's work obligations. Their social place, even though prominent from an outsider's perspective, is tangential. The link between diplomas, seniority and status is not as evident as one may be inclined to think. At the time of my first fieldwork, this was precisely what many secondary school diploma-holders who lacked the networks that would help them get a government job or extra money and support to get a 'passport' for the Middle East complained of. They had discovered that performing well in school failed to provide them with any clear advantage in the local economy. Young boys dropping out of school to work after the very first years had often been able to obtain a fixed place on a fishing crew, something those who had obtained diplomas failed to achieve. Girls likewise argued that if they had spent the time and money invested in schooling to earn themselves a dowry, they would at least have been able to marry and set up families of their own. Now they were still on the look-out for a government job, which would anyway remain, they feared, out of reach. The risk of staying unmarried amounted to remaining a placeless child forever.

Somewhat paradoxically, therefore, schools are not only non-places that refer children back to real places, but also zones of passage through which anthropological place may be exited. Over the years, Poomkara's schools have produced hundreds of diploma graduates, who have migrated to work in other parts of India or the Middle East. These migrants now supply the local community with much-needed cash to build new houses and marry off daughters. These remittances give young men an entirely new, ambiguous place of absence-cum-presence in the village. They are much-wanted sons-in-law who open up access to modern consumer goods to their kin. As these young migrant workers epitomise, one can then leave one's place but still keep some sort of a place in the locality by regularly sending remittances back home.

The grounding of children's lives in local places, particularly places of work, gives schools the character of non-places that, however, are also zones of transition to other, faraway places, such as jobs in the Middle East or government employment. However, faraway places remain linked to the anthropological places to which migrants remit their savings. Remittances reinforce rather than weaken anthropological place, a process Sahlins has termed the 'indigenization of modernity' (Sahlins 1999: ix). As schools are part of the logic of migrant work, they may therefore not turn out to be non-places equally for all the children who frequent them, particularly those who succeed in reinforcing anthropological place through long-distance migration. But reinforcement, as I shall argue in a moment, works only as long as a certain degree of distrust of non-places is maintained. For children it is crucial that they spend most of their time immersed in local society and that their primordial bonds remain unaffected. When this is no longer the case and children find themselves fully dependent on non-places, as is shown by the NGO project sites in Addis Ababa to which I now turn, non-places can indeed become Augé's alienating no-man's-lands.

Children's projects in Addis Ababa as non-places of childhood

The staff of NGOs dedicated to helping the so-called 'street children' of Addis Ababa have a very different conception of the place of children from that of Poomkara people. They offer a space of childhood to children who are perceived as lacking a proper place in urban society (the 'street' being the antipode of 'home'). Paradoxically, however, their very structure undermines children's local embeddedness. I have described elsewhere the work of these largely foreign-funded and -staffed organisations (Nieuwenhuys 2001). Here I shall only recall that the government closely scrutinises the kind of services that NGOs offer, which are consequently surprisingly unimaginative: the formula is essentially to select poor children whom the local authorities consider to be in danger of becoming 'street children', and providing them with free lunches and other assistance, such as an occasional set of second-hand clothes, medical care and recreational opportunities in open centres, where most of the children do not spend the night. The selection procedure for the children is carried out by local authorities and is based on the largely uniform criteria of age and family situation. The great majority of children come from large, female-headed households. There are also a few projects that cater specifically for orphaned children, children who have come to the city unaccompanied, or girls. They offer places to sleep in addition to the standard kinds of services provided by open centres.

NGO sites may be seen as poles that attract or select children from what is perceived to be an undefined, chaotic urban zone designated as 'the streets', that is, everywhere and nowhere. Although NGO staff recognise that children use this zone for both work and play, the emphasis is on its negative connotations: the street is primarily viewed as a space where crime, prostitution, gambling and drug abuse thrive unhindered, thus exposing children to the loss of their childhood innocence. Project sites symbolise, by contrast, safe havens where children are offered the markers of what the staff considers proper childhood: neat clothes, fees for schooling, school material, free meals and supervised recreation, such as games and watching videos. In the imagination of the staff, in short, the project sites would be places of childhood par excellence.

What are the parameters of such places? They revolve around the disciplining and homogenising of bodies, time and space, the standardisation of what is 'a child', what he or she is supposed to do and when, where it should be at fixed times, where this is supposed to lead to, and an insistence on icons that separate childhood from the outside, adult world. The project site is above all a place where all children are approached as equals on the ground of a supposedly shared, innate commonality. It is a place of proper work for children, where they engage in homework and domestic chores, receive counselling, are engaged in recreational activities, etc. – in short, all that the NGO staff and those who fund and support them associate with non-work. The activities contribute to defining the project site by opposition to the 'bad places', where children risk exploitation and danger (such as the street) and where they would not be loved and cared for properly (as in their home).

The site is therefore also the place where the time and whereabouts of children are regulated: there are fixed times for lunch, homework, recreation, the weekly bath, counselling and the distribution of clothing. Failure to submit to the schedules is interpreted as unwillingness to appreciate the efforts of the staff and is punished, if need be, with expulsion. Submitting to the schedules purifies a child from the filth and vice that breeds unchecked in the disorderly world of urban poverty, turning the child in time into a new person. Time schedules are matched by an organisation of space that underlines ideas of purification, regulation and separation: children have their own personal space in which to keep their belongings, separate places to pursue recreation, do their toilet and sleep, etc. There are clearly demarcated forbidden spaces as well, such as the staff's rooms and offices. NGO rooms and offices are generally more airy, clean and well-furnished and located on a higher floor or in the central building, the children's areas being located in shacks around it. With a few exceptions, this symbolises the fact that the staff are not themselves in any need of redemption. Most sites are also gated, with a gatekeeper controlling entrances and exits. Within the organised space of the site, one finds childhood icons linking the local project with the global childhood programme: children's books, posters, coloured pencils, toys, games, a TV and a video, often donated by distant carers, and all testifying to the quality and ambitions of the project. Indeed, the evaluation of projects hinges on their success in emulating what is held to be a superior model of childhood, rather than on their ability to support local conceptions of 'the good child'.

NGOs alienate the children in their care from their families, not only because they denounce the latter as bad parents, but because they ritually open up spaces leading to a supra-local world that is presented as being more respectful of children's innate nature. Importantly, Augé's definition applied to these sites draws out their lack of the essential qualities of anthropological place (see Table 5.2).

Although NGO staff may claim that they provide a place of childhood to children who have no place in urban society, this space is but weakly linked to the place the children may occupy in future: staying regularly in a project site does not guarantee that children develop meaningful and long-lasting relationships, a sense of history and an identity. Quite the contrary, successful adaptation to life in a project site makes it increasingly difficult for children to comply at the same time with their obligations towards relatives and neighbours. Although to begin with the admission may seem to benefit the entire family, in the long run it creates a chasm between the assisted child and his relatives that will often never be bridged. To obtain admission to the project, a child has to internalise the idea that his or her original identity is that of a (potential) 'street child', which his or her family considers deeply wounding. In the site the child eats according to the schedules: often he or she will eat at the site before returning home,

Table 5.2 Qualities of place: NGO project sites in Addis Ababa

Qualities of place	NGO project sites
Relations	The aim of the projects is to be a passage to a better life; the final aim is to make themselves redundant and to rehabilitate (i.e. expel) the children in their care.
	Neither children nor staff have a clear life path within the project. All are there temporarily.
	The staff depend on donations from the elite or from abroad and are closely scrutinised by the government; the long-term viability of projects is often insecure.
	Children are admitted on the basis of negative qualities (abandonment, abuse, neglect, addiction, prostitution) which the staff are supposed to be able to dispel because of their higher moral qualities; relations are by definition temporary and impersonal.
History	Children are admitted because they have experienced or risk experiencing things that contradict the ideal of childhood innocence.
	Personal history is equated with the history of these experiences or risks and matters in so far as it contrasts with the purified person the child will become after staying in the project.
	Nobody knows or is really interested in knowing where the children come from and who their families actually are.
	Admission and treatment are deemed successful when the parenthesis in the personal history of the child can be closed and s/he can be delivered back to the parental home.
Identity	On admission children must accept a negative identity ('street child'; 'child prostitute') based on an assumed 'lack of childhood'. The passage through the project implies gradually shedding this identity and emerging, purified, as an 'ordinary' or 'normal' child.
	The staff perceives its work as a personal sacrifice and an initiation into middle-class values of public service. In that sense, the project site is also a zone of passage for most of the staff.

displaying in the eyes of parents and elder kin a penchant for egoism and ingratitude. Since the child leaves home in order to avail him-/herself of the services provided by NGO projects, family members left behind may feel particularly acutely that they are dealing with an unsupportive child who is shunning effort and self-sacrifice.

The example of the beds that were distributed to children in some projects thanks to the generosity of Dutch churchgoers was telling. As some children came home with a bed, a quarrel arose as to who should lie on it: the father, whom a 'good' child ought to respect and obey, or the child who had received the gift? If a child were to lie on the bed, this would involve displaying such a lack of respect that he could be expected to be turned out of doors in minutes. If he did not, he would certainly bear a grudge against a father who denied him or her enjoyment of the space of childhood that distant well-wishers had so generously offered to supply. Children were faced with the dilemma of either accepting a rupture that with time becomes inevitable, or of living double lives by deceiving the NGO staff about their behaviour and whereabouts during long periods of the day in order to maintain reciprocity with their kith and kin.

Children attracted by NGO tales of a childhood liberated from the cruel fetters of parental discipline and work demands probably failed to anticipate that in time the project would expel them because of their age, and that some of them would then find themselves placeless. However, long mysterious absences and sudden disappearances from the sites suggest that many of them were aware of the necessity of maintaining relationships outside the project, and that they sometimes preferred trading the comfortable but ambiguous security it offered for the hardships of sharing the lives of their kith and kin. Indeed, although training the children in skills that would enable them to get a proper job in the city stood high on the agenda, it is precisely this that is the least successful aspect of NGO work. Even with a diploma, it was difficult if not impossible for most youngsters to find a job, particularly in the sectors of the economy that catered for the demands of the local poor. Expatriates or other NGO projects, where many found work as peons, cooks, drivers or gatekeepers, were their most likely employers.

To sum up, then, the anthropological approach to (and indeed, pre-occupation with) place poses a dual challenge to the anthropology of childhood. First, there is the problem of the liminality of children's places that makes it confusing for the anthropologist to deal with the issue of children's place. This is the more problematic in that a preoccupation with children's place is, as already mentioned, linked to assumptions about childhood as spatial and social segregation. While occupying indistinct places, children may be oppressed by hierarchical orderings based on gender and seniority, but they are not segregated or disempowered. The process of negotiation and adaptation starting in childhood leads to a gradual incorporation into the relationships, shared history and sense of belonging that form the texture of local society.

The second problem arises when children's places are, as is the case with Poomkara government schools and NGO project sites in Addis Ababa, clearly demarcated spatially. These places paradoxically underline the fact that children's real place is elsewhere and later. Although not liminal when seen from the perspective of the state or, for that matter, the global market, they lack the anthropological qualities of place. They are all the more difficult to negotiate for the children who are disciplined in them, as the Addis Ababa NGO sites demonstrate, in that they actively seek to sever children's primordial bondings. When they grow up, children in these sites may very well discover that the comfortable homes that held out the promise of a better life turn them into strangers to their own kith and kin. In that sense they are even more on the margins of local society than the liminal places assigned to children before adulthood, which make them eligible for a place in local society.

An anthropology of childhood that limited itself to observing children 'in place' would give a partial and distorted view, not only of children's use of space, but also, and *a fortiori*, of how liminality articulates a sense of place. Such an anthropology may fail to appreciate the importance of places in which children's relationships are shaped and give exaggerated weight to the non-places that children also use but cannot translate into a sense of place because of the nature of the relationships that are enacted there. The true role of non-places, however, cannot be fully understood unless, as I argue in the next section, one seeks to uncover how anthropological places can be challenged through the zones of passage that non-places also are.

Negotiating place and the anthropology of children

What is the impact upon children's perspective of place of having to submit to long periods of socialisation in which one is treated more or less as an outsider, or at least as a subordinate constantly at adults' beck and call, before being admitted fully into places that really matter? Does it explain why, notwithstanding adults' misgivings, Poomkara children seek identification with a childhood in school or why children in Addis Ababa espouse the identity of the despicable 'street child' in order to be rescued by foreign philanthropists? If children seek identification with these non-places of childhood, it is, I contend here, to abscond from an adult world that has little else to offer than the perpetuation of a life of hardship. Their passage into zones that hold out the promise of being better places offers children a ground to renegotiate assigned place from those who hold, locally, positions of authority. This positive aspect leads me to refine Augé's notion of non-place. Liminal local places and spatially segregated non-places should not be seen as mutually exclusive, but rather as a complex matrix that informs a process of renegotiation.

Some Poomkara children have been able to renegotiate their place at work in local society. Claiming that they had to incur costs to attend secondary school, they demanded and obtained payment for the assistance they offered to the fishermen. This translated, though never without a struggle, into a more clearly defined task and place at work. In a society in which children are just supposed to be working all the time, wherever they find themselves, while common opinion denies that what they do is in fact 'work', being paid makes work visible. Occupying a non-place in school thus helped define place in local society. However, the reason why these children were paid for their work was precisely because going to secondary school forestalled any future claim to membership of a fishing crew. The boys who received wages were typically assigned work which 'true' fishermen, however young, looked down on. They were not allowed on the sea-going canoes, and had to work the shore seines instead, fishing gear with highly seasonal and uncertain catches. In fishermen's eyes non-school-going children, by contrast, demonstrated by the same token real devotion to the fishing occupation, since they remained submissive and accepted for a longer time being treated as undefined helpers. It was they who were gradually introduced into the intricacies of the fishing craft and taken, in due course, on to a sea-going crew. In sum, an immediate, visible place was demanded at the expense of a future but lasting one.

To a lesser degree, the same holds true for the children in the NGO projects sites in Addis Ababa. Many children had come to the sites looking for places that would enable them to escape excessive parental discipline and heavy work demands. Many felt that devotion to the family put their ability to remain in school and improve their future prospects at risk. Upon admission, most still lived with their families. But the sum of tensions and conflicts arising from the demands of the NGO staff soon translated into a growing estrangement between children and their families. At first children may have smuggled free lunches and other items out of the project to share at home, supplying the ground for renegotiating their place in the family. But the immense distance between the foreign conception of a good childhood and local practices was difficult to bridge in the long term. Children to whom foreign well-wishers had given a bed could not, for instance, resign themselves to offering it without grumbling to their fathers, as custom demanded. By using the donated bed to create a segregated space of childhood within the parental home, NGOs legitimised the affirm-ation of individuality against local conceptions of deference to the older generation. These and similar conflicts might make children decide to leave their families for good. But the opposite was more often the case. For instance, it was unusual for children to remain for the full four years required within a Dutch-funded NGO that offered foster care: they normally disappeared without trace before this period had elapsed.

The ambivalent relationship of children with schools and project sites highlights the fact that non-places may be viewed as zones of passages providing spaces to challenge and renegotiate seniority. As already noted, seniority assigns each child a subordinate position *because* s/he is a junior. In spite of the tensions that junior status may generate in a child, it allows room for manoeuvre in the use of space that adults generally lack. This applies not only to children's mobility within village society, but also to the distances that teenagers may travel outside it. In Poomkara it was far easier for an unmarried young person, even a girl, to leave his or her village to study or earn money than for married people. Marriage took place around a girl's fifteenth birthday and signalled the end of a period of relative freedom of movement. Boys took on family responsibilities at the age of about 18 and thereafter were not supposed to stay away from home for long periods of time. Unmarried girls could go to colleges in nearby towns, or seek employment to earn themselves a dowry as domestics or even as migrant prawn-peelers in North Indian fishing harbours thousands of kilometres away. These absences were never unproblematic, however, and fathers only accepted them with great reluctance, and only if they were too old or too ill and there were no elder sons who could take upon themselves the task of earning dowries for their sisters. Boys travelled even farther afield, as they migrated to the Middle East and were thus able to support a village economy in which fishing had become an increasingly insecure venture. In all cases, those departing were looking for an opportunity to find a place in a local society in which obtaining a livelihood was increasingly difficult. While stable, organised workplaces often did not provide children with more than a marginal place where they had to await the insecure possibility of becoming the next generation of workers, the passage through the non-places of childhood could give them leverage to contest this fate. Reinsertion into the local economy after a passage through these non-places is a powerful motor of the type of indigenous modernisation that we find in so many of today's developing areas.

When applied to children, Augé's notion of non-place, however illuminating, dichotomises the notion of place unduly between an unproblematic anthropological place and alienating non-places. Anthropological places are also the sites of power relations that control access to resources and authority. Being immersed in places dense with meaning entails not only being unquestioningly part of the social landscape, but also remaining 'invisible' and acquiescing in the authority of seniors and village power-holders. For many, the passage from childhood to adulthood is hardly an attractive option, as this entails a life of hard work and privation. In Poomkara, for example, many married women described their adult lives as 'a vale of tears' and remembered with melancholy the short childhood period in which, unaware of the difficulties of life, they freely roamed the village. One must therefore question the idea of anthropological place as the nostalgic place of primal innocence (cf. also Lasch 1991: 87ff.).

Augé's notion of non-places is also problematic. Segregated places of childhood in Western welfare states or in the emerging landscapes of defence of new urban middle-class neighbourhoods (Aitken 2000) provide, ideally at least, access to middle-class lifestyles in adulthood. These places are indeed segmented, thin, often even 'empty' to the extent that they are made to appear non-places. But, as Sack pointedly remarks, they are part of a complex, routinised pattern of life that requires intense interaction and 'the most exquisitely detailed set of rules, regulations and customary practices' (1997: 9). When seen in their interconnectedness, urban middle-class places of childhood are real places, precisely because they are even more segregated and fragmented than the places of adulthood. Being able to deal with the rules and practices of spatial fragmentation is what socialisation is all about, and it is in preparation for this complex way of life that children are locked in places of childhood.

The role of the non-places of the poor, such as village schools and homes for street children, is more ambiguous. Although modelled on the places of middle-class urban childhood, the underlying social and spatial relationships are very dissimilar. The word 'home', for example, suggests that the middle-class urban home and the street children's homes are similar in nature, hiding the fact that the home of street children is a place of rescue where the children are turned into mere victims, bare life that must be saved (Edkins 2000: 10ff.). While urban middle-class schools prepare children to inherit their parents' social capital, village schools do not offer such opportunities. The homes of the middle classes segregate children in order to insert them into their way of life. The 'street children's' homes fail to reinsert them into their local society. The non-places of poor children, in short, may rather be seen as spaces that produce complex patterns of both exclusion and inclusion. They may facilitate the indigenisation of modernity and be instrumental in children challenging seniority, but not without risks of alienation. Their problematic grounding in society turns them into liminal places or 'zones of indistinction' that are both the place for the organisation of state power, in the forms of discipline and objectification described by Foucault, and the place for emancipation from authority (ibid.: 7). But clearly, challenging authority cannot take place in a vacuum. It is therefore crucial to include in the analysis the anthropological places that remain the main point of reference of the children who find themselves in these zones. There are then at least two types of non-places in childhood: on the one hand those that facilitate socialisation and adaptation into the urban way of life; and on the other hand those that, though alienating children from their local society, also offer them opportunities to contest authority (Skelton and Valentine 1998) and are part of a wider dynamic of transformation of intra-generational relations (cf. also Fog Olwig and Gulløv, in the introduction to this volume).

Summing up, it is too simplistic to claim, as development experts have at times done, that when children have no clearly identifiable space of their own, they have no childhood or are outside childhood. Nor is the opposite approach, which takes the absence of special places of childhood as proof of children's autonomy as social actors, of much help. An anthropology of children should go beyond either condemning or legitimising otherness. It should critically engage with the complex patterns that result from the tension between non-places of childhood and the anthropological places where children's place is liminal. Both juxtapositions and discontinuities of place and space give children leeway to develop meaningful social relations. A focus on this tension would help predicate the anthropology of children upon a cultural critique of how childhood situates children. When transposed to radically different contexts, segregated spaces filled with childhood icons – which are normally associated with children's place in urban middle-class areas – may distance children from the places that are of social, economic and cultural significance for their role as future members of society. That they also provide arenas to challenge relations of authority is something that becomes visible if the scope of inquiry is broadened to include both children and adults as they negotiate rules of seniority based in anthropological place.

Notes

1 I am indebted to Maaike de Bruin for the discussions we had about place and space while supervising her thesis on girls' use of space in Mongolia. I am also grateful to the editors for their excellent and inspiring comments on earlier drafts. Thanks go as well to Jan Mansvelt Beck, Lia Karsten, Virginie Mamadouh and Jan Markusse, my colleagues in the Department of Social Geography and Planning in the University of Amsterdam, for their help and suggestions.
2 Data were collected during five successive fieldwork periods undertaken between 1978 and 1996. The fieldwork was funded by the Netherlands Foundation for the Advancement of Tropical Research, the Directorate General of Development Cooperation of the Dutch Ministry of Foreign Affairs and the University of Amsterdam.
3 Data were collected while I coordinated the two-year research programme 'Child Welfare for the Urban Poor' in 1997 and 1998. The programme was funded by the Directorate General of Development Cooperation of the Ministry of Foreign Affairs of the Netherlands and the University of Amsterdam.
4 I focus on places of work not only because my data were gathered in order to analyse children's economic roles, but also because the poverty that confronts most Poomkara people's daily life makes work an important signifier of social relationships.
5 See Schildkrout (1980) for a pioneering study linking children's spatial mobility with gender segregation in Kano.

References

Aitken, S. C. (2000) 'Fear, loathing and space for children', in John R. Gold and George Revill, *Landscapes of Defence*. Harlow: Pearson Education, pp. 48–67.
Augé, M. (1992) *Non-lieux: Introduction à une anthropologie de la surmodernité*. Paris: Seuil.
Edkins, J. (2000) 'Sovereign power, zones of indistinction, and the camp', in *Alternatives, Social Transformation and Human Governance* 25(1): 3–25.
James, A., C. Jenks and A. Prout (1998) *Theorising Childhood*. Cambridge: Polity Press.
Lasch, Christopher (1991) *The True and Only Heaven: Progress and its Critics*. New York, London: Norton.

Nieuwenhuys, O. (1994) *Children's Lifeworlds: Labour, Welfare and Gender in the Developing World*, London: Routledge.
—— (2001) 'By the sweat of their brow? NGOs, street children and children's rights in Addis Ababa', *Africa* 71(4): 539–57.
Sack, R. D. (1986) *Human Territoriality: Its Theory and History*. Cambridge: Cambridge University Press.
—— (1997) *Homo geographicus: A framework for Action, Awareness, and Moral Concern*. Baltimore: Johns Hopkins University Press.
Sahlins, M. (1999) 'What is anthropological enlightenment? Some lessons of the twentieth century', *Review of Anthropology* 28: i-xxiii.
Schildkrout, E. (1980) 'Children's work reconsidered', *International Social Sciences Journal* 32(3): 479–90.
Skelton T. and G. Valentine (eds) (1998) *Coolplaces: Geographies of Youth Cultures*. London and New York: Routledge.
Tonucci, F. and A. Rissotto (2001) 'Why do we need children's participation? The importance of children's participation in changing the city', *Journal of Community and Applied Social Psychology* 11: 401–19.
Turner, V. (1970 [1967]) *The Forest of Symbols: Aspects of Ndembu Ritual*, Ithaca and London: Cornell University Press.

Chapter 6

Common neighbourhoods – diversified lives

Growing up in urban Norway

Hilde Lidén

Introduction

One warm summer afternoon, while doing my turn as a volunteer at the local Children's Farm in the inner city of Oslo, I was watching a newly born calf together with Thomas, a 9-year-old boy. The calf was shaky on his long legs, and Thomas had promised to help me move it from the field into the barn. He asked:

> How old is he?
> About three months, I think.
> Did you see the delivery?
> No, he was born on a farm in the countryside. Have *you* attended the birth of a calf?
> No, never a calf of a cow. However, I did see the birth of a camel.
> A camel? Where?
> On a holiday with my mum, somewhere in the south.
> That must have been exciting! But never a cow calf?
> No, never.

The conversation caused me to reflect upon the diverse frames of reference of the children in this neighbourhood. Established understanding of inter-action in local communities is challenged because the meaning of practices frequently differs in new and unexpected ways. Distinct knowledge is not restricted to television, films and books about other people's lives. The children themselves travel to different places within the city, in the country-side and abroad, as tourists or to visit grandparents and other relatives. They thus approach the same areas in different ways. Schoolmates will often have different frames of reference for learning at school and for playing in the neighbourhood.

The incident at the Children's Farm brought me to reflect upon my immediate response to the children's experiences. From my point of view, seeing the birth of a cow's calf was a more appropriate experience than the birth of a camel's calf. My distinct knowledge of standard farming in

Norway guided my questions. If Thomas had not elaborated on his response to my question, I would never have grasped the range of his experiences. The incident made me aware of generation-specific understandings of events as well as places. This is significant to the way in which we approach how children are connected to place.

Children's attachment to place is frequently associated with peer relations. Children explore their neighbourhoods together with friends. However, inter-generational relations also define some of the conditions for peer relations. School, spare-time activities and family life will influence children's use of the neighbourhoods they grow up in. Large-scale contexts such as migration and modern mass media also have significant implications for peer relations and how the neighbourhood is experienced as a place. The changing contexts of children's everyday lives raise some important questions as to how children are connected to places. The present chapter will discuss how neighbourhoods are converted into places through activities and relations, making experiences of place differ among children and between generations, and according to social class, ethnic background and gender. Changing contexts of childhood influence how children's everyday lives are organised in time and space. Does attachment to a place become less stable when children's activities and relations expand beyond the local? Does the production of culturally specific frames of reference, in peer relations and in inter-generational relations, affect their connections to the neighbourhood as a place?

After presenting an overview of the research on children and their attachment to place in Norway, I shall suggest an alternative approach. I shall discuss how family relations and the rhythms of everyday life shape children's use of the neighbourhood and their feeling of belonging to certain places. I shall do this by discussing four children: Maria, Oliver, Tieko and Nadja. Through domestic life and, for some of the children, extensive use of the neighbourhood, the children develop certain actions and understandings. These processes are mediated through inter-generational relations. I will then discuss how relationships with close and distant places influence the way children position themselves and are positioned when they meet at school and other shared places. Following this I discuss the gendered and ethnic aspects of children's participation in certain places. Finally, I describe children's attachment to a range of places, from the intimate home and neighbourhood to global connections through travelling and television. Both the close and the geographically distant are used in the children's management of their everyday lives.

Children's neighbourhoods

The creation of a place is a cultural activity and can be grasped only in relation to ideas and practices (Bourdieu 1977; Ardener 1993; Gupta and

Ferguson 1997). These ideas and practices may vary both within and
between particular social groups.[1] Children who share the same neighbourhood do not necessarily have the same attachment to the area (Katz
1994; Lidén 2000). This modifies the understanding of childhoods as
locally oriented and connected to specific places that prevails in research
on children in Norway (Tiller 1983; Gulbrandsen 1996).

Research on children and childhood in Norway has stressed above all
the importance of self-governed social involvement in mixed gender and
age groups. To a large extent, both urban and rural districts in Norway
have been considered good surroundings where children can roam about
on their own.[2] Childhood has been associated with playing outdoors
(Hollos 1974; Berentzen 1987), and research has emphasised the role of
play and physical experiences in defining shared places. Children's interactions in certain places have served to reinforce peer relations and a
shared peer culture.[3] Consequently, children's independent and exploring
approach to their local environment is believed to result in a shared
attachment to the local community (Gullestad 1997a, 1997b).

In recent decades, children in Norway have spent increasingly less time
on their own in the immediate neighbourhood. This is because of extended
schooldays and a growing number of organised leisure activities. Also, the
numbers of young children in kindergarten and after-school activities have
increased as a consequence of women's paid work.[4] This influences the
way children use and experience the neighbourhood.

Childhood and local communities are closely interlinked in autobiographical writings, to the extent that a specific place becomes the key
metaphor for a childhood, and childhood itself central to the definition of
self (Gullestad 1996). The place you grew up is where you invested yourself. However, the creation of place involves multiple acts of remembrance
and imagination that inform one another in complex ways. Place is a
particular universe of objects and events in which aspects of the past are
made relevant to the present. In this way, the landscape of childhood is
connected to retrospective world-building and place-making, which in turn
is a tool of identity construction.[5]

This understanding of how people in Norway reconstruct childhood
places is being challenged by changing contexts of peer relations in socially
and ethnically integrated neighbourhoods, which are generating new
understandings of place and belonging. The local community can be
analysed as a place defined by specific social relations (Foucault 1984;
Harvey 1990; Massey 1994). The concept refers to the materiality of the
place and the qualities of social relationships. The subjective experience of
space turns space into place. Merleau-Ponty (1945) connects time and
space to bodily experiences, for, in order to comprehend space, it must be
realised through the body. Space is converted into place through physical
activities, including sensing, emotional involvement and interpretation. As

space is socially defined, interpreted and positionally experienced, it is transformed into place. Consequently, the understanding of place is connected to what happens there. Although children explore and create place by themselves, they are also socialised into places through inter-generational relations when they take part in place specific social traditions.

East Hill in Oslo

I shall use East Hill as a case study in exploring the changing contexts of children's everyday lives. The analysis is based on one year's fieldwork among 6 to 12-year-old children in multicultural schools near Oslo city centre. East Hill is a traditional working-class area. In the past two decades this area, like other inner-city districts, has undergone significant changes because of urban renewal, the construction of new apartment blocks and the gentrification of existing buildings. This has led to a mixed population with immigrants in the rental apartment blocks, young urban families in the new residential areas, and academics and artists where old wooden houses have been restored.

In the late 1960s immigrants from Third World countries started arriving in Norway, today a nation state of about 4.5 million inhabitants. In 1979, 6 per cent of the immigrant population came from Asia, Africa and Latin America; in 1998 the figure was 49.5 per cent. Some 41 per cent of non-Western immigrants live in Oslo, a capital with approximately 500,000 inhabitants.[6] In the city their presence is visible, particularly in certain inner-city neighbourhoods, such as East Hill.

Approximately fifteen nationalities were represented in the groups of children I followed at an East Hill school. Methodologically I have used participant observation of children's practices within the school, in after-school institutions and in neighbourhoods, interviews with children and video recordings of their activities. During fieldwork, I was particularly interested in how the children handle complex relations and interpreted their experiences in and between different settings (Lidén 2000).

Family life connected to space

Children's use of neighbourhoods is linked with how the home becomes a place of childhood. Often family life is seen as a household linked to one place, namely the home (Brannon and O'Brian 1996). However, household members may be spread over quite a large area, either permanently or temporarily (Simpson 1998). Family life is therefore not necessarily restricted to influence by those present, but may also be part of relationships and processes extended in space. Family life ensures that children acquire specific experiences and understandings. At home, culturally specific values and codes are transmitted through daily life routines that inscribe the children within the specific meaning systems of former generations. In socially and culturally mixed neighbourhoods such as East Hill, children's lives are woven into different religious, ethnically specific and gendered knowledge traditions and systems of meaning. This makes them complex persons, or as Fredrik Barth expresses it: 'each person is "positioned" by virtue of the particular pattern of coming-together in her of parts of several cultural streams, as well as particular experiences' (Barth 1989: 140).

Maria

The everyday life of Maria, 8 years old, in many ways represents an urban experience of growing up in Norway. Maria lives together with her mother and father and a younger brother. Her grandparents live in a rural area on the west coast of Norway. Her parents both have full-time jobs. Her little brother attends kindergarten and she herself attends organised after-school activities after finishing normal school at about one o'clock. After she gets home at half-past four, she mostly stays in the home, finishing her homework and playing with her little brother. All the family members eat dinner together, and then she watches the children's programme that starts at six o'clock. Sometimes she is allowed to watch videos afterwards. If father is home in the evening, he reads to her before she goes to sleep. During weekends the family visits friends in other parts of the city, and they also frequently go on hikes in the forest, where they make fires and play. During the holidays Maria visits her grandparents on the west coast, or the family travels abroad.

Oliver

Oliver is 9 years old and alternates between his father's and his mother's house every second week. His only brother, who is 5 years old, lives permanently with their mother. The father of his brother has recently moved out. Oliver's father does not have any girlfriend, and when Oliver stays with his father, it is just the two of them. This shifting settlement

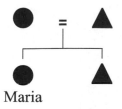

Figure 6.1 Maria's household.

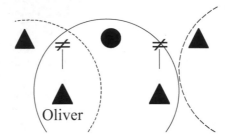

Figure 6.2 Oliver's households.

determines whom Oliver plays with and what his days are like. His mother lives 20 minutes' walk from the school, outside the school district. Most children in Norway used to go to school on foot, but this practice is now changing because parents bring them by car. This is the case with Oliver, and because Oliver has no one to join him on his way back home from school, his mother picks him up in the car in the afternoon. In the evening Oliver and his brother sometimes play in the garden. However, he prefers to play computer games in his room. When he stays with his mother he has regular chores, washing the dishes and looking after his younger brother. He does not know anyone of his own age in his mother's neighbourhood.

Oliver's father lives in a big apartment near the school. Oliver has two friends in the same block, who frequently visit him and play in his room. Some of his best friends at school also play in the same soccer team and live near by. When he stays with his father, Oliver eagerly practises his violin lessons and very much enjoys playing the violin together with his father. He also loves to watch films, soccer games and the news. Often he and his father will do this together in the evenings, his father explaining to him what they are watching. Sometimes his father's friends also visit them in the evenings.

Tieko

Eight-year-old Tieko lives with his parents and a younger sister. He was born in Norway of parents who had both come from West Africa two years earlier. His father moved from West Africa to Norway for educational reasons. His mother also started university education when she moved to Norway, though she now does cleaning work to support the family. Tieko attends school and the organised after-school activities when his parents are working. His sister is in a kindergarten.

Tieko has lots of friends at school, many of whom he knows from when he was in kindergarten. He has two passions, soccer and break dancing. Last year he played in the local soccer team with some of his classmates.

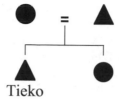

Figure 6.3 Tieko's household.

Now he joins them when they are playing football informally on the sports ground. In the late afternoon he frequently joins friends from school playing football on the sports ground or basketball in the school playground. After dinner at about six o'clock, he watches TV at home. He routinely checks many TV channels, and, like his father and mother, loves to watch American films and music programmes.

Nadja

Nadja is 8 years old. She has two younger sisters and two older brothers. In many ways her parents' work and religious orientation define the rhythm of their everyday family life. Nadja has lived all her life in the same neighbourhood, except for one year she spent with her relatives in the Pakistan countryside. Last year she visited them again for one month. At home they often receive visits from Pakistani relatives living in Pakistan or in other parts of Oslo. Her father's sister and family live in an apartment block in the same street. Nadja visits them almost every day. Her grandmother lives with them almost all the time, and frequently her remaining grandparents come from Pakistan to live with them for a while. When this happens, they receive many daily visitors from other parts of Oslo.

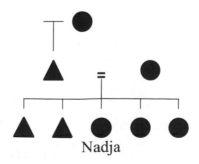

Figure 6.4 Nadja's household.

When school ends at around one o'clock, Nadja returns home. She does not participate in after-school activities. After a light meal with her mother and younger sisters, she does her homework. At about half past two she goes to the Koran school, making the 20-minute walk with her cousin. The Koran school ends at four o'clock. Afterwards she spends the rest of her day at home with her family. After finishing her household chores, helping her mother with the dishes and taking care of her younger sisters, she sometimes plays outside with her older cousins. She only watches the six o'clock children's programme on television if her father or older brother are not at home. If they are at home, they watch the news and films from her parents' home country.

In the winter, Nadja sometimes joins one of her elder brothers and his friends tobogganing or skiing in a nearby park. In the summer evenings she plays with her younger siblings on the nearby playgrounds accompanied by her mother and aunts. Her duties in helping her mother and aunts take care of her younger siblings define how much time she has for outdoor play. In many ways, Nadia takes part in an extended family life, in events and social networks, all of which are interconnected in fields of practices extended in space (Grønhaug 1974).

Discussion of the four examples

Maria's parents give her little responsibility for household chores. She is mainly a recipient of their care, but she is also being brought up to be independent. She is free to do what she likes, but in an expected and acceptable way. The family rhythm frames her free activities. On weekdays her family life is usually restricted to indoor activities, where her parents can supervise her and make sure that she is doing her homework. They worry about letting her play outdoors on her own because they are anxious about older children and 'strange' people living in the blocks next to them. They do not find the green areas and playgrounds in the neighbourhood appealing for family outings. Besides, Maria's parents are too busy on weekdays to play outdoors with her and her brother.

Nadja, on the other hand, is both a caregiver and the receiver of care. She is assigned household chores, and other family members therefore depend on her. Her extended social network offers her the opportunity to explore different places in the neighbourhood. There is always someone around whom she knows well and whom she can join. She also travels long distances by herself, or together with her cousin, to the mosque and to school.

Neither Tieko nor Oliver, when staying with his father, have any obligations at home, and their evening rituals are not as strict as Maria's. Tieko is free to visit a wide range of places and friends. Oliver spends more of his time indoors. When he stays with his mother, he has specific duties. The atmosphere in his mother's house is more tense, with less time for small talk compared with the atmosphere in his father's home. He has a close relationship with his father, enabling him to acquire cultural skills and comprehension through shared interests and activities, and through regular discussions of the media.

In Scandinavian countries, schools and teachers expect parents to be involved in their children's homework, school activities and school meetings (Ericsson and Larsen 2000). These expectations also extend into the family's timetable in that parents are expected to help children with homework, read to them and get them to bed early. Many parents accommodate themselves to these expectations, as is clearly the case with Maria's parents. Maria's and Oliver's parents also emphasise that their children acquire skills such as intellectual curiosity, politeness and playing an instrument. They also acknowledge, although are not always pleased about it, negotiations and independence, skills that are greatly appreciated in middle-class families, as well as at school.

The different ways their everyday lives are organised in time and space affect their relationships with other children. Tieko, Maria and Oliver all attend after-school activities at the end of the school day, playing with classmates until about four o'clock. After this Maria spends the rest of the day with her own family. This divides her day into a noisy, peer-related period at school and quieter, more relaxed hours at home. For Tieko, there is more continuity in relationships throughout the day, and the main difference for Oliver is whether he stays with his father or his mother.

For Nadja, who attends the same class at school as Maria and Tieko, the day is organised in an altogether different manner. When returning from school she hardly meets any classmates, although both Tieko and Maria live near by. Her playmates consist of peers from her family's social network. Her afternoons are also interwoven with events involving both relatives and friends in the mosque, coffee shops, or when visiting certain shops in the part of the city where she lives. In East Hill there are several mosques, which serve as important meeting places for members of different Muslim minorities living within or outside the area. Despite the fact that many minority families share the same mother tongue, original nationality and religion, they are members of different groups and mosques. Members of these communities are connected in multiplex relationships, both economically and politically, and to special shops and restaurants in the area. This results in a strong local attachment. Simultaneously, these networks are also oriented towards relations and events beyond the city and the nation. Consequently, Nadja's experiences of the area differ from Maria's experiences. Maria and Nadja seldom meet and never play together in the late afternoons.

Nadja and Tieko are the most extensive users of the neighbourhood outside the home. Maria is not so familiar with the social and physical surroundings. She stays at home, mainly because her parents feel the area is unsafe. Maria's parents are more familiar with other parts of the city and prefer experiences in nature areas to extending their social life in the neighbourhood. Oliver and his friends do not play outside very often. This is not because of safety fears, but because they prefer to play indoors or to attend organised leisure programmes in the afternoon. At weekends Oliver and his father make use of cultural activities in the city centre on a regular basis. Because of these experiences he recognises places and people he knows from television. In this way, watching TV at home is associated with events in his own life.

A striking change in children's attachment to neighbourhoods, compared with what has been documented in earlier research on Norwegian children, is the absence of work done by children. Children's paid work in the fish industry in northern Norway (Solberg 1994) and as 'baby walkers' (Gullestad 1992) was significant, not at least as a force for integration creating complex relationships between children and adult neighbours. In East Hill, children's paid work caring for younger children or doing errands for elderly people is not part of their outdoor relationships or activities.

Nadja navigates the streets outside the neighbourhood on the way to the mosque, which makes her familiar with a wide range of streets and shops in the area. Oliver, on the other hand, only does this together with his father or mother, as do Maria and Tieko. Most often they will leave the neighbourhood for family outings. Familiarity with places in other parts of the city depends upon parents' or schoolteachers' initiatives and interests. Cultural institutions and hiking in the forests or exploring the seaside become common frames of reference for some children but not for others. This contributes to the strengthening of social ties among these children, whose parents have matching orientations and life-styles, while widening their social distance from other children.

Moving temporarily between parents' homes as Oliver does, as well as moving permanently, not only has consequences for the children involved, but also for their friends. Many of them explain that they are never sure whether their friends are at home. This affects their interest in exploring the neighbourhood. Maria told me that she missed her playmates and added: 'The boys who lived next door moved. And when I ask my friend if I can visit her, she usually answers: "No, not today; I have no time, because today I will stay with my father."' Another girl in the same school class told me:

> It is quite gloomy outside when it is dark and it's raining and hailing. It's gloomy. I try to decide what to do. Not many friends live near by. My classmate near by is never at home or she is at home with some friends or she has no time or she is away. And I never know when she

is at home, because her parents are divorced and she sometimes stays with her mother and sometimes with her father. Her mother is living here, and I am never sure when she is at home.

(Girl, 9 years old)

There may be many children around, but not necessarily the ones she really knows and whom she is used to playing with at school.

So far I have discussed how organising time and space has consequences for children's relationships with their peers. For the children, both those in minorities and others, peer relations alone do not define the neighbourhood experience. I have emphasised the way in which parental life makes decisions that become frameworks for children's everyday lives. Seen together, this leads to many parallel networks between the parents as well as between the children. Borders are shaped by social and cultural distinctions, and codes are learned in family life. To a certain degree this also affects the choice of peers who are considered suitable playmates. Social networks also differ according to where the children spend their free time. Many children prefer indoor life, at home or visiting friends, frequently playing computer games, as Oliver does. In contrast, minority children do not always have computers or a room of their own. Tieko seldom has friends visiting him. Mostly he looks up his friends outdoors in shared places, although he also visits some of his schoolmates in their homes. Nadja, on the other hand, never visits her schoolmates and prefers playing outdoors with her relatives. In this inner-city area, the children of immigrant parents seem to be the most extensive users of the neighbourhood as physical surroundings. Parallel networks thus introduce a paradox: despite several children living next door, the experience of many children, such as Maria, may be one of nearly 'empty' places.

Places and situated knowledge

Situated knowledge is connected both to peer relations in different arenas and to inter-generational relations extended in space. As already illustrated, the family unit is not a natural entity, as the ideology often suggests (Brannon and O'Brian 1996; Simpson 1998). Home is not necessarily defined by just one place. Quite a few children in the two neighbourhoods, ethnic Norwegian children as well as immigrant children, have parents living in other cities or countries, either temporarily or permanently. Children also alternate between living in two homes, and some have sisters or brothers belonging to other households. Both minority children and majority children have strong ties to their parents' and grandparents' home town and home country, and experience contrasts in life styles when visiting their relatives. In this way, family life varies a great deal according to relationships in different places. Consequently, an understanding of what family and domestic life represents is not something the children themselves will necessarily take for granted.

As we have seen, Oliver is one of the children who alternates between his mother's and his father's house. Oliver's parents decide when and with whom he is to stay, adjusting this to their weekly rhythms and routines. Oliver experiences the distinct life style of his father as a contrast to that of his mother. He is aware of the shifting attitudes and behaviours that are consistent with these different contexts. Oliver told me: 'Mamma is always in a hurry; I hate that.' There is something in the atmosphere of his mother's house that makes him feel sad. When he stays with his father, he enjoys the calm afternoons and their shared interest in playing the violin and watching football matches on TV, though he also misses his younger brother.

Domestic life creates certain forms of conduct and routines. The home itself expresses a certain life style, values and social position (Gullestad 2002). When children are attached to more than one house, the life style within these places, and the relational expectations and encouragement involved, are not necessarily consistent. For Oliver domestic life was contextually defined, a condition frequently subject to comparison in alternating between the two homes. When staying in distinct houses, children not only compare their own experiences with those of their friends, they themselves are also acting subjects, experiencing the distinctiveness 'in their body'. They interpret and acquire knowledge in specific emotive relationships and settings, learn to interpret the differences in their parents' behaviour and judgments, and, as a consequence, acquire competence in shifting codes in different relationships and contexts. Through children's interactions at school and in meeting places in the neighbourhood, such as parks and sports grounds, nuances in behaviour and orientations, in values and competencies, are expressed and interpreted bodily as well as linguistically, as what they know something about, their skills and interests. I would therefore like to emphasise *knowledge* and *frames of reference* as central terms in the analysis of how space is converted into place.

Gendered neighbourhoods

Ties to the neighbourhood have to do not only with the parents' life situation, their social networks and interests: they are also gendered. The parents' life styles and the leisure activities of different family members lead them into informal and gendered networks. As we have seen, Nadja's extended family network made her part of relationships and events involving exclusively young children and women. The local soccer team, on the other hand, is associated with local traditions of masculinity. This is where fathers and sons engage in shared interests and physical activity within the neighbourhood. This gendering of places within a neighbourhood is an outcome of children's gendered exploration of places, as well as of locally shared history. The former, however, is guided by a variety of norms and restrictions in their everyday lives. One such constraint is the strict timetable in the lives of families with young children.

In East Hill, Tieko, as well as other children, alone or with friends, venture to specific places to see whether they can meet others. For example, they will go to the school playground or the sports ground to play ball games. Now and then they play in the park, perhaps in the small paddling pool in the summer or on the ice rink in the winter. These are all sites where boys and girls both play. Sometimes the exciting atmosphere when playing in groups of mixed gender is an important reason for visiting these places.

Many of the boys are particularly attached to the main sports ground in East Hill. For many generations the sports ground has been an important symbol of the neighbourhood, associated with the success of numerous local athletes, as well as the local soccer and ice hockey teams. Many of the children's fathers or neighbours have been active in the club and are still enthusiastic supporters. Patriotism is alive, expressing values of masculinity and strength, combined with a working-class identity. In this way young boys playing on the sports ground is likened to the practice of previous generations, reinforcing the uniqueness of the neighbourhood. On the sports ground, the improvised soccer games often consist of groups of mixed age and ethnic background. Everyone is accepted as long as they are skilled and eager. Tieko is often among them. He joins his schoolmates, who always play football in school breaks, at the sports ground in the afternoon, and as regular players in the local soccer team. When playing football at the sports ground, Tieko is included in the gang who define themselves as the 'real' boys. He supports the local football team, although he does not play in it any more. He knows a lot about international teams and football stars from television. In this way the sports ground links affection for football to local identity, as well as to big events in international sport arenas.

Girls do not have the same relationship to the sports ground as do the boys. It is more likely that the girls watch the boys when the latter are playing, although they do attend football games during school breaks, and some also play in the local football team. The girls complain of the gloominess of the remote area of the sports ground when it is dark, and they have heard scary stories about the place. One 10-year-old girl tells me:

> Usually we do not walk in that part of the park. I don't always think it's frightening, however, only when it is dark. Once a shady man followed Eva, a friend of mine. She ran into a shop, and a woman followed her home. Some weeks later we suddenly saw a man down the hill where we were sliding. Eva called to me, 'There is the man!'

Then we ran another way home. It was quite scary. Sometimes I remember this incident, particularly when it's dark.

The girls who seek out the sports ground frequently associate the area with masculinity, insecurity and a somewhat uneasy feeling. However, many also have good memories of playing with close friends or teasing the boys. The place is associated with physical experiences, the testing of skills and independence. They connect such places with gendered images of themselves and with events associated with gendered bodies. In this way, boys and girls reassert places as gendered when they become involved in them. Space becomes place when it is invested with significant persons and events. This continual process is at the same time individual and collective. It is individual in the sense that children involve themselves and make their own narratives. Interpretations are filtered by previous experiences. These, however, are made understandable by using collective systems of meaning. Skills and meaning are extended when taking part in shared practices organised in space, as the gendered experience on the sports ground illustrates. Events are interpreted and transformed as continual mediation, both individually and collectively.

Distant and near places

I have discussed how neighbourhoods are converted into places through activities and relations, and how making place is influenced to a certain degree by social class, ethnicity and gender. In this last section I shall discuss children's attachment to a range of places and the consequence this has for them in defining common frames of reference.

As has been seen, the closest range of places is home together with certain parts of the neighbourhood, such as the school, park, playgrounds and sport fields. Places are made familiar through play and certain experiences. I have emphasised that exploring the neighbourhood is not simply a collective action, however specific in distinct social networks. The children's range of local places is not necessarily an integrated arena, as is often described in research on childhood in Norway (Gullestad 1997b). The children's attachment to local places will also reflect their family's dual orientation to space, simultaneously maintaining strong relationships beyond the neighbourhood, as well as with certain chosen neighbours.

The next range of places that are important in children's lives is more closely connected to inter-generational relations. When they take part in leisure activities or family outings during weekends and holidays, the children are exposed to other areas. Those children who have two homes often commute between two different neighbourhoods on a more regular basis. Most frequently, however, the children may pay regular visits to relatives and friends living in other parts of the city. Some also explore the cultural institutions in the city centre and the green areas and forests in the surrounding area. Only rarely do the children explore such places on their own. Most often they go there on family excursions or with the school.

The next range of places concerns sites that the children know quite well but visit less frequently. This may be a summer cottage, the parent's home town or the place they lived before they moved into Oslo inner city . They may have spent time on their own in these places and acquired important experiences there. Through strong relationships with people and places, they become emotionally involved and gain a sense of belonging. In this way such places assert their identity. They acquire frames of reference from activities and relationships developed over time, although they are grounded in sites that are more distant than their own neighbourhood.

Finally, there is also place attachment connected with contemporary processes of globalisation, represented not least by the mass media and new technology. Television brings images from all over the world into the home. This also affects the way childhood is connected to space. Electronic media make the life of other people and places present within the family, simultaneously influencing the range of knowledge that children are exposed to within their home. This has consequences for inter-generational relations as well as for peer relations. Electronic media introduce new cultural influences into the home beyond the control of parents. This is intensified by the fact that interpreting the input from electronic media is mostly done by peers, not parents. Watching television and videos, listening to music and playing computer games are significant experiences for children in their participation in peer relations. Some films, TV commercials and computer games become a standard repertoire that most of the children are familiar with. For children in East Hill, the media have become a common frame of reference when interacting at school and in after-school pro-grammes. The children develop certain conventions in transforming input from the media to particular games and play scenarios. Those who do not take part in this daily interaction are not as familiar with these skills and conventions as those who do. In this way information about distant places becomes ordinary in specific ways. This also happens when travelling to distant places, as the episode with Thomas and the camel calf demonstrated. What the children know about and what defines their interests and orientations is not necessarily connected with the neighbourhood and local range of places.

Electronic media at home are important for many children's forms of play and peer relations in other settings. Interaction at school becomes an important setting in transforming this visual impact and stream of inform-ation, giving it meaning through play and chatting. In his presentation of self, Tieko, for example, includes fragments of his African background in a way that other children recognise and admire. Referring to Afro-American films, idols and music that the other children are familiar with and enjoy, his black identity is accepted and appreciated. They look upon him as 'cool'. When he moves about he is always dancing or rapping, and his pencil continually taps a beat. In this way expressions of pride and playfulness connect him to 'black' film idols and music, attributes often associated with being black, tough and cool. At the same time, his humour and self-ironic detachment make him less vulnerable to racist remarks. His position among the boys depends upon his ability to grasp and control changing expectations in different relationships. In this way he joins some of the girls in play, since he is quite familiar with their preferences. He succeeds very well in switching between contextually defined codes of interaction. Media and new information technology thus constitute a common repertoire and resources for forming narratives. By means of experimentation and negotiation, he and his friends acquire and explore codes of interaction, creating an understanding of themselves and others. Nadja, on the other hand, who is not a fan of the same films, television programmes and computer games, does not take part in this kind of play. For this reason peer relations at school and in leisure programmes do not offer her the same opportunity as the other children.

With this in mind, Thomas's experience with camels giving birth rather than cows is not necessarily so peculiar. In his school class, he is not alone with this frame of reference. A classmate reveals that his grandfather owns a huge herd of camels, and that he himself is already the owner of three. When sharing such information at school, not only Thomas, but also other classmates, participate with detailed questions. Their knowledge, however, is based on a familiarity with camels from television documentaries. Consequently, when distant places are made familiar through electronic media, family relations and travels, they in turn become potentially shared frames of reference.

The way in which indoor life and media consumption at home have increased in Norway breaks with previous understandings of the sites of childhood. Up till now, the notions of children playing outdoors, roaming about on their own, and exploring neighbourhoods and the nearby wilderness together with their peers have been considered key factors in a good childhood. Until recently, this kind of outdoor interaction was seen as the main source of being informed and included within peer groups. Today, at least in the case of inner-city children, indoor activities such as playing computer games and watching television form a basis for inclusion and peer relations in public settings such as school and after-school programmes.

As already discussed, not all the children develop the same references and skills at home. In East Hill, different commercial and nation-specific media are accessible, and children take part in different networks of information and orientation. As in the case of Nadja, many Turkish and Pakistani families watch the news and films from their parents' motherland. Many of these children also attend Koran school in the afternoon.

Consequently, children in the same neighbourhood take part in different patterns of learning at home, acquiring different information, codes and skills of adaptation and negotiation. This affects the integration process of minority children. As we have seen, however, connections to relations and activities in distant sites are not necessarily central to this process. More significant is how children can transform their experiences in both distant and nearby places into common frames of reference, making their knowledge and competence relevant. However, children are not all in an equal position to define what is relevant.

As I have emphasised previously, interaction at home and in family-related social networks causes the forms of conduct and the values of former generations to be passed on as dispositions, embodied competence and understandings. However, despite the fact that children and adults share family life and the media as participants in a global flow of information, essential interpretations of input and experiences take place in generation-specific settings in or connected to work, school and leisure activities. In this way the interpretations are also to some degree made generation-specific.

Notes

1 In the past decade important texts on gendered use and gendered interpretations of space have been published, for example Ardener 1993; Irigaray 1993; Massey 1994; Moore 1994; Rose 1997. Different understandings of the same surroundings by different ethnic groups have long been documented in anthropological studies, not at least in studies of Indian groups in USA (Basso 1996). In my own work on gypsies in Norway it became obvious how they experienced the main city places occupied by *gajo* as 'empty' in contrast to detailed knowledge of their main travelling routes (Lidén 1990).

2 Comparative research on parents' interpretations of safe outdoor play indicates different culturally specific understandings between different countries and for girls and boys (Hillman 1997; Kyttä 1997; Lidén 1999).

3 Traditionally in Norway, as well as in international research texts (see, for example, Opie and Opie 1969), peer culture is associated with specific outdoor places such as playgrounds, greens and forests; see Kjørholt, this volume.

4 In Norway in 2002, 78 per cent of women aged 25–9 years old and 84 per cent of women aged 30–54 were in paid work.

5 See Basso 1996, who describes place-making as a tool of identity contruction among the Western Apache Indians.

6 The source for the figures in this paragraph is Bjertnæs 2000.

References

Ardener, S. (1993) 'Ground rules and social maps for women: An introduction', in S. Ardener (ed.) *Women and Space*. Oxford: Berg, pp. 1–30.

Barth, F. (1989) 'The analysis of culture in complex societies', *Ethnos* 3(14): 120–42.

Basso, K. (1996) *Wisdom Sits in Places: Landscape and Language among the Western Apache.* Albuquerque: University of New Mexico Press.

Berentzen, S. (1987) '"Eg og ska" bestemme.' Et samhandlingsperspektiv på sammenhengen mellom barns ute og hjemmemiljø, in S. Berentzen and B. Berggren (eds) *Barns sosiale verden. Perspektiver på kontroll og oppvekst.* Oslo: Gyldendal, pp. 126–74.

Bjertnæs, M. K. (2000) 'Innvandring og innvandrere 2000', *Statistical Analysis* 33, Oslo: Statistic of Norway, p. 69.

Bourdieu, P. (1977) *Outline of a Theory of Practice.* Cambridge: Cambridge University Press.

Brannon, J. and M. O'Brian (1996) *Children in Families: Research and Policy.* London: Falmer Press.

Ericsson, K. and G. Larsen (2000) *Skolebarn og skoleforeldre.* Oslo: Pax.

Foucault, M. and P. Rabinow (1984) *The Foucault Reader.* New York: Penguin Books.

Grønhaug, R. (1974) *Micro-macro Relations: Social Organization in Antalya, Southern Turkey.* Bergen: University of Bergen.

Gulbrandsen, L. M. (1996) *Kulturens barn: en utviklingspsykologisk studie av åtteåringers sosiale landskap.* Oslo: University of Oslo.

Gullestad, M. (1992) *The Art of Social Relations: Essays on Culture, Social Action and Everyday Life in Modern Norway.* Oslo: Universitetsforlaget.

—— (ed.) (1996) *Imagined Childhoods: Self and Society in Autobiographical Accounts.* Oslo: Scandinavian University Press.

—— (1997a) 'A passion for boundaries: Reflections on connections between the everyday lives of children and discourses on the nation in Norway', *Childhood.* 4(1): 19–42.

—— (1997b) 'Home, local community and nation: Connections between every day life practices and constructions of national identity', *Focaal* 30/31: 39–60.

—— (2002 [1985]) *Kitchen Table Society.* Oslo: Universitetsforlaget.

Gupta, A. and J. Ferguson (1997) 'Discipline and practice: The field as site, method, and location in anthropology', in A. Gupta and J. Ferguson (eds) *Anthropological Locations: Boundaries and Grounds of a Field Science.* Berkeley: University of California Press, pp. 1–46.

Harvey, D. (1990) *The Condition of Postmodernity: An Enquiry into the Origins of Cultural Change.* Cambridge, MA: Blackwell.

Hillman, M. (1997) 'Children, transport and the quality of urban life', in R. Camstra (ed.) *Growing Up in a Changing Urban Landscape.* Amsterdam: van Gorcum & Co., pp. 11–23.

Hollos. M. (1974) *Growing Up in Flathill: Social Environment and Cognitive Development.* Oslo: Universitetsforlaget.

Irigaray, L. (1993) *An Ethics of Sexual Difference.* London: Athlone Press.

Katz, C. (1994) 'Textures of global change: Eroding ecologies of childhood in New York and Sudan', *Childhood* 2: 103–10.

Kyttä, M. (1997) 'Children's independent mobility in urban, small town and rural environment', in R. Camstra (ed.) *Growing Up in a Changing Urban Landscape.* Amsterdam: van Gorcum & Co., pp. 41–52.

Lidén, H. (1990) 'Vokse opp som sigøyner i Norge. Sosialisering i en etnisk minoritetsgruppe', Magistergradsoppgave, Institutt og museum for antropologi, Universitetet i Oslo.

—— (1999) 'Endringer i barns uteliv. En litteraturstudie og en undersøkelse fra Oslo', *Barn* 1, Trondheim: The Norwegian Center for Child Research, pp. 46–69.

—— (2000) 'Barn – tid – rom: skiftende posisjoner. Kulturelle læreprosesser i et pluralistisk Norge', Ph.D. Dissertation, SVT fakultetet, Trondheim, NTNU.

Massey, D. (1994) *Space, Place and Gender*. Cambridge: Polity Press.

Merleau-Ponty, M. (1994 [1945]) *Kroppens fenomenologi*. Oslo: Pax.

Moore, H. L. (1994) *A Passion for Difference*. Cambridge: Polity Press.

Opie, I. and P. Opie (1969) *Children's Games in Street and Playground*. Oxford: Oxford University Press.

Rose, G. (1997) *Feminism and Geography: Limits to Geographical Knowledge*. Minneapolis: University of Minnesota Press.

Simpson, B. (1998) *Changing Families: An Ethnographic Approach to Divorce and Separation*. Oxford: Berg.

Solberg, A. (1994) *Negotiating Childhood*. Stockholm: Nordplan.

Tiller, P. O. (1983) *Å vokse opp i Norge*. Oslo: Universitetsforlaget.

Chapter 7

Associationless children
Inner-city sports and local society in Denmark

Sally Anderson

> They come when they feel like it and they come in groups, always the
> same ones together. They show up once, and then they don't come the
> next two times, and then suddenly they show up again; [they] can't seem
> to figure out that they need to come every time so there can be some
> development.
>
> (Project coordinator)

Introduction

In this chapter, I explore understandings and practices of 'open' and 'closed'
sociality played out in a children's sports project in an inner-city neighbourhood in Copenhagen, Denmark. In keeping with government policies
promoting social integration through sports, an Open Gym project was
sponsored by the Copenhagen branch of the Danish Gymnastics and Sport
Associations (DGI) to channel 'associationless' children into local sports
associations and through these into 'local society'. The following discussion grew out of trying to understand why Open Gym was not made a
permanent activity when inner-city children often came, enjoyed themselves and certainly obtained the exercise health experts felt they so badly
needed. I argue that while the relationally open venue of Open Gym did
not pose any unsurmountable problems for children's participation, it did
create relational ambiguity and uncertainty among adults responsible for
its daily running. Exploring the relational dilemmas this open venue posed
for adults, I conclude that the key to understanding the demise of the
successful (seen from a child's perspective) recreational activity lies in
dominant notions of 'closed' public sociality that require a particular set of
exchange relations between domestic and public caretakers. Despite Open
Gym's success as an activity venue for neighbourhood children, it could
not be placed within the dominant system of generational relations thought
to constitute 'local society'.

The chapter opens with a discussion of the concept of 'associationless'
children and the power of this category as a mobilising metaphor. I argue

that public practices of organising activities for children feed on and reproduce categories of children whose presence are discursively useful but
relationally problematic. Next, I move to descriptions of Open Gym's
activity venues and main features of child and adult interaction. The aim of
these descriptions is to show the kinds of relations that an open venue
affords and the specific dilemmas it poses for adult organisers. Descriptions
are followed by an analysis of relational tensions embedded in the open
venue as well as cultural models used to explain these tensions. I conclude
by discussing how dominant moralities of civil relatedness and child
exchange produce a category of 'associationless local children' and relegate
this category of child to facilities reserved for marginalised social groups.

Sports associations and Open Gym

Voluntary associations requiring membership registration, modest fees and
fairly regular attendance are the dominant form of sports organisation in
Denmark. Ideally instructors and coaches work on a volunteer basis and,
ideally, all members pitch in to make the association function. Sports
associations are promoted politically as valuable sites of democratic socialisation. Through participation in association sports, children are expected to
develop social networks and civic skills related to democratic organisation.
The Danish Youth Council promotes associations as sites where immigrant
children may learn 'Danish' social skills of membership and networking
(DUF 2000).

Open Gym, requiring no registration, seasonal fees or regular attendance,
was set up as an alternative venue to 'catch' children and channel (sluse)
them into sports associations and, thus, into 'local' and 'Danish' sites of
civil upbringing. It was part of a larger project connected to the opening of
DGI-City, a sports facility built by a national sports organisation in the
Copenhagen neighbourhood of Vesterbro. Municipally subsidised time
slots in this facility were first and foremost reserved for Vesterbro residents
and their children. The Copenhagen branch of DGI designed 'Project
Vesterbro' to connect the facility with the neighbourhood. The idea was to
bring the people to the building and the building to the people, so to speak.
The facility's legitimacy depended on it accomplishing its self-appointed
task of becoming a part of Vesterbro and building 'local society' through
recreational sports.[1]

In cooperation with Vesterbro Sport Union (VSU), Project Vesterbro
encouraged resident groups, families, public day-care institutions and after-
school clubs[2] to form their own voluntary sports associations in order to
gain access to the new facility. The project supported local sports associations in their attempts to establish the children's sections needed to gain
subsidised access to DGI-City. To further this process, the project established
Open Gym to encourage 'non-active' children to join local association

sports. Open Gym was, thus, envisioned as a feeder site for new and existing sports associations that were seeking children but having trouble drawing them. The long-term plan included involving local adults and parents in children's leisure activities through volunteer work in sports associations.

Open Gym was not designed to become a permanent site. It was expected to make itself expendable. The political thrust was on creating strong local sports associations that, in turn, would provide children's sports on a volunteer basis. National laws and municipal administration policies worked together to privilege this particular organisational form which is a prerequisite for membership in sports leagues and access to public indoor facilities. Associations enjoy strong government support because they are recognised as powerful sites of community-building, social integration, civil enlightenment and democratic socialisation. Project Vesterbro's support of local sports associations' efforts to attract more children was, thus, not just a local phenomenon but part of a nation-wide campaign to integrate urban communities by means of new sport facilities and broader provision of children's sports.

Associationless children

Working in the field of Danish children's sport at the end of the twentieth century, it was impossible to ignore the concept of 'associationless' (foreningsløse) children and efforts to channel this category of child into sports associations. Indeed, many government-sponsored social and cultural projects of this period proposed venues that would attract associationless children.[3] The following is a brief discussion of how this concept was contextualised and used.

Like other population segments targeted by policy, children are categorised and the categories created become significant political instruments. In Denmark, both children and the elderly are classified as 'weak' population segments. Children (as well as the elderly) are subdivided into binary categories of 'resource-weak' and 'resource strong', characteristics usually correlated with family background and socio-economic status. With regard to sport, some children, particularly urban and immigrant children are designated as 'sport-weak' or 'sport-foreign' with reference to their lack of participation in organised sports activities.

In a study of Danish children's sporting participation, Ottesen and Ibsen created a profile of 'sport-inactive' children, categorising them as 'sport-passive' (2000: 48–51). On the whole 'sport-inactive' children came from families with social and economic problems. A public health study of children's exercise habits profiled 'inactive' children as socially 'passive' children who did not join after-school clubs, who met less often with friends, and who did not know what to do on a free afternoon. Many children in this category reported being lonely and not particularly happy with their lives (Holstein 1997: 32). These studies produced data for framing policies and designing projects to activate passive children in a political quest to promote physical and mental health and social involvement in extra-domestic spheres. At the same time, the studies created and sustained a prototypical binary opposition between children who fit and children who do not fit standards of 'active' participation in organised venues.

In debates and project designs relating to sport, policy and statistical categories of 'inactive', 'sport-weak', and 'sport-passive' children were often glossed as 'associationless' or 'association-passive' children. In the Copenhagen Sports Policy Report, 'associationless' children were variously portrayed: as 'girls' who are not as inclined as boys to participate in competitive sports; as 'immigrant children' with massive social problems; as children who are 'foreign' to organised sports; and as children who drift because 'they cannot figure out how to show up at scheduled times' (*Idrætspolitisk redegørelse* 1998: 32–3).

'Associationless children' is, thus, a polysemous discursive construct, a keyword, in Williams' sense, widely used to evoke children who are physically and socially 'inactive' in organised civil spheres and thus on the margins of society, democracy and Danish culture. At the turn of the century, the term served as a 'mobilising metaphor' (Wright 1993, cited in Shore and Wright 1997: 18–20) and a call to action to bring children into the fold of associations. As a 'policy term', 'associationless children' was ripe with 'unwritten assumptions and images . . . about the "people" and the "problem"' (Wright 1995: 81), assumptions shored up by statistical studies of children's leisure habits, and played out with reference to adult experience with and images of children's lives.

Open Gym's loose children

In Vesterbro project-speak (Sampson 1996), 'associationless children' were glossed as 'loose children'. Coordinators of the Open Gym project defined loose children as children who were not members of a club or association, basically 'unattached' children who do not 'go to something' on a regular basis. The term conjured up prototypic images of socially passive children from burdened, low-income families; images of socially incompetent, stay-at-home TV and computer-freaks; and images of children who wandered the streets. According to Open Gym's coordinator, 'Danish' children living in Vesterbro were generally members of either after-school clubs or sports associations or both. Their leisure had, thus, considerable 'substance'. Consequently, the notion of 'loose children' merged with images of 'immigrant children',[4] who were a priori thought to be loose in several senses of the word. Of immigrant background, they were only loosely attached to the country and the culture, and they were 'on the loose' in the streets[5] and, thus, not properly lodged in local institutions. In the words of Open Gym's coordinator, 'loose children' were immigrant or ethnic children who wandered or drifted about without consideration for modern time coordinates.[6] They sauntered in when they felt like it. They did not choose one activity venue, but tried many, coming and going as they pleased. A handball coach described them as children who 'come and then, suddenly, they disappear'.

> It is difficult sometimes to go in and make a connection with the ones who come when they feel like it and come in groups. They can manage all by themselves; they don't need us grown-ups, right? If I say: 'Wouldn't you all like to try to improve your game or play with some others in a club', then it's just 'no way' and they move on, see? You can't get too close to them.
>
> (Project coordinator)

The elusiveness of some children's civil lives, seen from a public adult's perspective, perhaps partially explains the rhetorical use of herding and trapping metaphors in the project-speak of Open Gym and many similar projects. 'Loose children' were hereby metaphorically likened to evasive range animals and to wary birds or fish that must be carefully manoeuvred into more controlled quarters, a fold, corral, cage or pool, to organise ownership and make them relationally accessible. Adults spoke of 'capturing' and 'catching', 'roping in', and 'luring' children.[7] They spoke of 'bait', 'lures' and 'traps'.

It is interesting to note rhetorical discrepancies in this discursive domain. Images of children resourcefully evading entrapment and, thus, frustrating their would-be captors, contradict policy images of 'resource-weak', 'sport-weak', 'inactive', 'associationless' and 'passive' children. Conventional implications of involuntary marginalisation are overlaid with positive notions of freedom and negative misgivings about amoral sociality. The ambiguity is instructive because it suggests that descriptors such as 'inactive', 'passive' and 'weak' do not necessarily refer to a child's actual level of activity or conduct, but rather to his or her choice of spheres of civil interaction. Hence, I argue that policy descriptors actually refer to children who individually may be either 'weak' or 'strong', either socially 'passive' or 'active'. The common denominator from a policy and project perspective is that children are improperly attached to organised civil spheres and thus wrongly connected to local society.

Local children

Elsewhere I have argued that in Denmark the ideal public child is a local, civilly associated child (Anderson 2003). Here, I will briefly address the notion of 'local society' or community and the relationship between 'loose' and 'local' children. Open Gym was embedded in a matrix of national, municipal and organisational efforts to develop local society through association sports. Olwig notes that local society or community is a very complex concept although, in ideal form, it brings forth an image of correlation between 'a social entity' and 'a physical locality'. She cautions that from a research perspective, this image must not be taken for granted. Rather local structures and relations must be explored to determine how local society is defined and practised from a variety of perspectives, including children's (Olwig 2000: 13).

The concept of local society has particular resonance in Scandinavia (Olwig 2000). Here, it is an ideological and political concept charged with cultural values, a point Gullestad elaborated on in her article on Norwegian notions of 'everyday life', 'near environment' and 'local society' (1992). Gullestad suggested that these terms refer to the warm, close and secure life in a small rural community in contrast to the cold, anonymous and dangerous life of big cities.

For sports organisers in my study, the notion of local society encompassed the physical locality of Vesterbro and the social entity of all Vesterbro residents. The latter was imagined as a fragmented whole, at risk of falling apart due to resident mobility and social and ethnic diversity (Dengsøe 2000). Organisers assumed that local society, envisioned as an integrated social entity, could be created or, at least, shored up by projects established to produce social networks bounded largely by the physical locality. I am not concerned here with mapping these networks and their boundaries. Instead, I use Open Gym as a case for exploring organisers' understandings of resident children's places in the imagined order of local society. Hence, this is about how adults, envisioning local society, organise places for children with implications for how they are perceived, where they may go, and to whom they belong, where and when. I suggest that project objectives to 'anchor' loose children in the imagined entity of local society through sports associations led to a particular organisation of semantic and physical space. This was not a simple relation between sports and children, but involved broader understandings of bounded relations of inter-generational exchange, a complex process of bringing children and adults into proper relation in the civil sphere of association sport. Hence, joining local association sport and moving 'loosely' around the local neighbourhood constituted two different modes of being local children that had consequences for children's access to indoor sport facilities.

Open Gym – a temporary site

Open Gym took place in DGI-City's well-equipped facilities two afternoons a week between the hours of two and four. At Open Gym, children could choose quite freely between a wide variety of activities. The large gym was well equipped for badminton, basketball, floor ball or hockey, handball, football, volleyball, table tennis or just sitting on the bleachers, watching and chatting. Under supervision, children were allowed to use the climbing wall, as well as a smaller gym full of gymnastics equipment, including a popular inflatable air-track, a foam pit, and ropes, mats and foam plinths for swinging, jumping and tumbling.

As noted, Open Gym was meant to be a temporary venue for bringing Vesterbro children into contact with the new facility and channelling them into sports associations. Volunteers from various Vesterbro sports associations were to demonstrate their sports and entice children to join local associations. Making Open Gym a permanent attraction was not part of the design although the subject was sometimes broached at project-related meetings. There was general agreement that as a permanent attraction Open Gym was morally unacceptable. Organisers were afraid that a permanent open venue would teach loose immigrant children (and their parents) to expect associations and the municipality to provide all activities for free. Furthermore an open venue would not inculcate civil responsibility because it did not require children to commit themselves to an activity and to a group of people over a longer period of time. Open venues allowed children to access activities while remaining 'loosely attached' which amounted to rewarding unacceptable civil relations. Although moral arguments were foregrounded, there was also the fact that Open Gym, as set up by the project, was not administratively viable under current laws. An open venue did not conform to municipal allocation policies requiring groups receiving facility subsidies to be organised in associations.

Basically Open Gym was morally legitimate and economically viable only as a temporary site of transition. It was not considered a site where 'community' or 'local society' might unfold. Needless to say, witnessing the multitude of activities, the outpouring of energy and the diversity of people, both children and adults brought into relation through Open Gym, I found this stance rather paradoxical. Below, I address some of the basic patterns of social interaction unfolding among children and among adults attending Open Gym. My aim is to show that this activity might have been seen as a building block of local society, and yet it was not.

Eclectic clientele

As Open Gym got underway, my bi-weekly chats with the project co-ordinator repeatedly centred on attendance. She was anxious because the project would be evaluated in terms of whether 'enough' of the 'right' (local, associationless) kind of children showed up. 'The gym must not look empty; we have to show we can fill the gym', she explained. On days with low attendance, she offered reasons why this might be: 'the football boys are off riding go-carts', 'the children are celebrating Eid', or 'the weather has kept them away'. She and I and other adults involved with Open Gym were clearly relieved on days when many children filled the gym.

In general, Open Gym attracted an eclectic clientele that used the gyms as a well-equipped indoor playground. By eclectic I am referring to age, gender, ethnic and sporting diversity. Children who came were between the ages of 3 and 18; adults were between the ages of 20 and 60. There were males and females, 'Danes' and 'immigrants', 'sports freaks' and 'ordinary kids'. Generally, there were more children than adults and more boys than girls, whereas neither 'Danes' nor 'immigrants' colonised the gym as 'theirs'. Sports freaks often showed up in expensive sports gear and played only one sport while ordinary kids wore regular clothes and played more eclectically.

Adults attending Open Gym belonged to the following categories: parents, leisure-home or after-school club pedagogues, teachers, youth workers, project coordinators, project assistants, sports association volunteers and anthropologist. Children attending Open Gym were generally classified by adults as 'ordinary local children' and divided into subgroups of 'immigrant' and 'Danish'. Distinctions were also made between children who came in organised groups with after-school clubs or *væresteder*[8] and children who came on their own without adult accompaniment. Club pedagogues and youth workers accompanied the former whereas the latter usually arrived in groups of friends, classmates, siblings or collaterals. Some groups attended Open Gym regularly while others just 'happened by', like a group from a day-care institution in another part of town that stopped by after visiting an exhibition next door.

Activity flow

Most children attending Open Gym actively engaged in free play and games of various kinds. Children were encouraged to suggest what they would like to play and they soon found where balls, nets, game tables and tumbling mats were stored. The coordinator allowed children to help bring equipment out, set it up and put it away. Floor to ceiling nets divided the larger gym into sections to keep various games and balls separated. The smaller gym, used for tumbling and free play, was rarely divided and, thus active children often crossed trajectories as on any playground.

Children were generally willing to try different kinds of activities and moved spontaneously between venues whenever they saw opportunities for participation. Adults present did not usually try to organise more inclusive games, set up tournaments, referee games or supervise turns. They, too, moved with the general flow of play, fitting themselves into openings in different activities. Not all adults joined in the play. Some sat in the bleachers, talking with each other and with children, occasionally giving suggestions and occasionally sorting out differences if arguments persisted. Sometimes children called adults out on the floor to settle quarrels over scores or bets.

Not all children came to try different activities. Boys playing pick-up football or girls and younger children tumbling on the air-track and gymnastics equipment would remain glued to one activity for hours. Other children, seeking out particular activities, friends and 'the action' in general, shuttled back and forth between the two gyms. In general, activities flowed into and overlapped one another as children came and left, moved from one gym to the other or from one activity to another. As one girl enthusiastically explained to her friend who attended Open Gym for the first time: 'You can do all kinds of things!'

I was generally impressed with how well all children handled the open venue without adults directing the flow of activities or games. However, I do not want to paint too rosy a picture. There was a fair amount of bickering and some bullying of outsiders. Some adults felt that immigrant children caused most problems but my own observations did not bear this out. Groups of friends or classmates sometimes staked a claim around their games of badminton or football and expected others to remain at a distance. Children who crossed the lines of these games were told 'You can't play ball here!' or 'Stay out of the way!' Interestingly, most bickering and quarrelling went on among groups of friends or classmates who knew each other well. Some days they argued more than they played. Adults rarely explicitly controlled dominance among children based on age, gender, ability and group belonging. They intervened when called in by the children themselves or when they felt a real fight was brewing, but otherwise left children to sort out problematic relations by themselves. Serious fights were very rare and adult intervention was an exception to the rule.

Loose structure

The project coordinator was satisfied with Open Gym's ambience, but questioned the organisation. Should the large gym be divided into two or three sections? Should children be allowed total freedom to choose or allowed only two or three activities per afternoon? Should the air-track be closed down in order to gather children for sports demonstrations? Would children go home if it was closed? As the project progressed, the co-ordinator experimented with different models of organisation.

Organisers and club pedagogues who brought children to Open Gym were critical of the venue's unstructured play and street game mode. During an informal discussion, a pedagogue commented that Open Gym had been too 'loose'. She was looking forward to more structure in the coming season, so 'they would not just be twiddling around with three children'. She suggested that clubs share responsibility for arranging activities. Another pedagogue commented that it would be difficult for his club to collaborate in this manner because they made decisions contingent on the day, the weather and the children's immediate interests. Another club pedagogue noted lack of coordination between club groups: 'We're four adults down there, each with his own group.' He, too, felt that Open Gym did not work because it lacked structure: the children 'just played'. A youth worker noted that 'the children had steered things pretty well on their own'. The project coordinator, however, lamented that 'children were playing as they would on the streets or any playground'. She doubted that an unstructured flow of play and games could effectively channel children toward sports associations because free play did not equip children with 'a sport of their own'. She found it imperative to foster more direct contact between children and structured association sports. She explained that the local branch of DGI was not prepared to use resources on a permanent open venue and therefore 'the children must move on'.

Concerns about efficacy and legitimacy led organisers to merge Open Gym with efforts to establish a sport association (VIK) for Vesterbro after-school clubs. This was expected to produce more commitment among club pedagogues and youth workers to bring their children to Open Gym and, thus, create a more predictable and stable clientele. The coordinator met with club pedagogues to coordinate responsibilities and activities and plan when to invite local instructors to demonstrate sports. The second season was, thus, distinguished by efforts to bring in association volunteers, to create more structure, clearer short-term goals, more committed adults and greater attempts to share responsibility and coordinate activities. Yet despite these plans, activities and interaction modes did not change to any great extent. Open Gym maintained throughout an *ad hoc* quality, as organised activities could be, and often were, overruled in practice. Even with more adults taking part, children played games and tumbled, as in the first season, in a fairly informal, overlapping and flowing manner, except when an association volunteer came to engage them in a particular sport.

The purpose of this rather long excursion into children's interaction in Open Gym was to demonstrate the *ad hoc* and child-organised nature of Open Gym activities and to point out that, although interaction among children was not without dominance and conflicts, all in all there were no major problems. Children attending Open Gym played well amongst each other as they negotiated rules, teams, turns, equipment, space and social belonging. Furthermore, Open Gym supported a variety of both *ad hoc* and planned interfaces between children and other local activities and groups that might have, over time, created a community of users.

Open relations

Despite the influx of more after-school clubs, Open Gym remained a site of relatively open-ended relations for children and adults alike. The many relational possibilities, in turn, demanded much negotiation and created many small-scale social dramas. It is interesting to note that 'loose children' did not appear to be a relevant category for interactional negotiation for the simple reason that it was impossible to know for sure which children were indeed loose.

Loosely known children

Greater and more stable numbers of children brought by club pedagogues and youth workers appeared to support the presence of a greater number of children who came on their own. However, no adult involved with the project knew exactly which children in the gym on any particular day were indeed 'associationless'. Although the project coordinator knew many of the children from a local school, she did not know how they spent their leisure time. Pedagogues and youth workers knew their own group of children but rarely knew each other's in full. Some children connected to *væresteder* came on their own, making it difficult for most adults to tell 'whose' they were. Even two adults who attended regularly answered negatively when asked whether they knew which children were loose. I was often asked if I knew which children were 'loose' but, of course, I had as much trouble picking them out as other adults.

It was my impression that children knew better than adults who other children were and how they were interrelated because children knew each other through the overlapping networks and places of their everyday lives. Indeed, children's lives and networks cut across the institutional venues that placed and circumscribed adults as occupational kinds with limited access to the multiple venues children frequented. From a child's perspective, so-called 'loose' children might well be neighbourhood acquaintances, schoolmates, classmates, best friends, rivals, enemies, close or distant kin. For adults, whose relations with children at Open Gym were institutionally based, children fell into categories of 'my own', 'someone else's' or 'perhaps loose'.

I found it strange that a project set up to channel 'associationless children' into voluntary associations did not attempt to discover which children might actually fit this category. Organisers continued to speak of 'associationless' children despite little concrete information about their actual existence. This may, in part, be explained by the practice of glossing 'associationless' with the term 'loose'. The working understanding of 'loose children' at Open Gym was not 'associationless children' but rather 'children not belonging to any adults in the room'. In practice, then, loose children were children who belonged to domestic guardians not represented by any adults present. Thus, for organisers, the existence of 'associationless' children remained hypothetical, whereas 'loose' children provoked relational ambiguity every week.

Loosely collaborating adults

While associationless children remained loosely defined, adult organisers became more explicitly positioned as they met to coordinate Open Gym and the new sports association for clubs. Despite planning, collaboration was constantly renegotiated as programmed activities were commonly rearranged in practice. Lack of organisation, however, did not mean that club pedagogues remained passive while at Open Gym. They played football with groups of boys, joined in dance series with groups of girls, played badminton with children and with each other. But without customary routines and overall guidelines for collaboration, each new organised game required renegotiating space, teams, desire to play and reciprocal relations for adults and children alike. More frequent participation by clubs and *væresteder* created a more stable clientele, but automatically added relational tensions regarding which adults held sway over which children during what kinds of activities. To sort out this question of influence, it was necessary to be able to discern which children belonged to which adults and which children were on their own. Yet due to the open nature of Open Gym, the task was impossible.

I never witnessed dissent among adult organisers regarding plans to invite volunteer instructors to run introductory sessions. Yet when volunteer instructors did come to Open Gym, they were shown very little cooperation from adults present, as the following field observation illustrates.

> A volunteer from a local basketball club arrives to give an intro-ductory session to recruit players for the club. He does not receive much notice from adults and children alike. During the first half-hour, he shoots baskets by himself at one end of the gym while children play at the other end. He is basically ignored by all. Finally, the project coordinator contacts him, as does one of the pedagogues. Toward the end of Open Gym he starts a game of basketball with six of the younger children.

The purpose of the volunteer's presence was never officially announced. Thus, he spent more time shooting baskets on his own and talking to adults than he did introducing basketball to children. A similar scenario ensued during an experienced handball coach's session. Despite his ease with a large group of children, even he had problems when a project assistant did not shut down the air-track as planned and two club pedagogues sabotaged his efforts by playing football with their children during the introductory session. Orienting all of the children toward a 'childless' volunteer clearly required a joint effort by those adults who had children they could sway and yet their collaboration was not forthcoming.

The acephalous nature of Open Gym's organisation, where no one adult acted as official master of ceremonies,[9] may have contributed to the contingency of agreed-upon plans. No one adult was responsible for all activities, nor did anyone have explicit authority over all of the children and adults at any one time. Furthermore, there were no officially explicated rules of conduct. In this open relational setting, authority and rules were implicitly inscribed in diverse relations and *ad hoc* negotiations between adults and between adults and 'their' and 'others'' children. Moreover, despite project objectives to channel associationless children into association sports, no one adult was explicitly responsible for spotting and contacting this category of child. As noted above, no one had an overview of which children were indeed 'associationless', and 'loose' children fitted themselves into the open relational field without problems.

I contend that children generally had little trouble finding their role at Open Gym; they came to play and be with their friends. Adults on the other hand seemed sometimes at a loss to coordinate their positions of influence and authority. Adults frequenting Open Gym had many official statuses: club pedagogues, youth workers, project coordinators, project assistants, volunteer instructors and volunteer youth workers. In a sense, they were all feeling and picking their way through the many relational uncertainties thrown up by this open-ended venue, where there was a goal and a plan, yet no one person or group interested in directing it. For public caretakers, Open Gym remained a venue of relational ambiguity.

Open tensions

As noted in earlier sections, sports organisations and government policies emphasised the value of voluntary associations as sites of social fellowship, community building and democratic, 'Danish' socialisation. Furthermore, leisure funding policies privileged associations. In this context, Open Gym was an anomaly assigned temporary status to do the job of channelling children into proper public sociality in local sports associations. Below, I discuss dilemmas posed by sites of relational non-closure and free play such as Open Gym.

Essentially different worlds

Addressing the lack of cooperation at Open Gym among variously positioned adults, the project coordinator wrote in her evaluation report:

> The encounter between different milieux with different cultures has, however, not been without problems. For example, collaboration between professional institutional milieus and voluntary association life necessitates paying constant attention to and being constantly considerate of differences in the fundamental norms and values embedded in these two milieus.
>
> (Jørgensen 2000: 25)

She offers a cultural argument based on norms and values in milieus external to Open Gym to explain problems with organised contact and collaboration in the gym. A similar mode of explanation was invoked by Vesterbro's Sport Union chairman in his appendix to the same report.

> The coupling [from the after-school clubs] to the world of voluntary associations is not without hurdles and mutual understanding between the 'salaried' world of pedagogues and the 'voluntary' world of [sport] activities is perhaps not as obvious as one might expect.
>
> (Gorm 2000: 17)

His depiction of contact problems between club pedagogues and association volunteers likewise points to their belonging to two different 'worlds' here delineated on the basis of monetary compensation. He suggests that the distinction between 'salaried' and 'voluntary' work is significant enough to create barriers between the two categories at Open Gym. The project coordinator elaborates on the essentialising model in an interview:

> Children come to Open Gym with their club pedagogues and there they encounter other adults in the gym. If the pedagogue who came yesterday had been a schoolteacher he would have persuaded the boys to give floor ball a try. But he wasn't a teacher, he was a club pedagogue, so he says: 'You'd rather play football? OK, we'll play football then.' He agreed with them! And he starts to play football with them, even though there's a floor ball trainer standing there, whom he knows came on his own time for free to teach the children floor ball. And he says to the volunteer: 'You'd probably better leave, because the boys don't want to play.'

She explained that different types of institutionalised adults have different objectives with regard to Open Gym:

> As a club pedagogue, you're more or less just trying to pass time and do what the children feel like doing. You're not doing it because they should learn something – not trying to educate children or get them to join an association like the volunteers or youth workers from the *væresteder*. Pedagogues come down here to let their children romp and try all sorts of things. A volunteer doesn't have much time to waste, because he has to recruit some children before next season or his association won't be able to train in DGI-City.

Here, she claims that time plays a different role for volunteers and club pedagogues. The coordinator also argues that differently positioned adults have different aspirations with regard to educating children or letting them play.

Official interpretations dwelt on tensions between institutionalised differences embodied by individual adults. They did not address other forms of
contextualisation, such as the open relational nature of Open Gym or
personal behavioural differences cross-cutting institutional affiliations,
although these may have had explanatory value. Explanations implied that
institutional affiliation produces essential kinds of adults with different
values, norms, compensations, intentions and time frames. These differences were then used to understand the lack of collaboration between
pedagogues and volunteers that contributed to Open Gym's difficulties in
attaching loose children to local sports associations. I suggest that the
explanatory model used here demonstrates a cultural preference for collective
essentialisation. It provides a non-confrontational interpretative frame that
permits 'loose children' to remain unnamed and *imaginaire* and allows
uncooperative adults to stand forth as staunch representatives of different
institutional norms. It also produces a categorical conceptual field inhabited
categorically by children who either do or do not join associations and
adults who are nothing but institutional norms.

Preferred closure

I contend that despite embodying different institutional norms and values,
adults frequenting Open Gym had several things in common. First, all were
there as public caretakers of children. Second, no one adult took upon his
or herself to play the role of 'director'. All appeared to heed a sense of
limited access to 'other people's children' and, thus, limited influence over
'all of the children' at any one time. Third, all worked with children in
institutional settings defined in relation to public preferences for regular
membership and social closure. After-school clubs, voluntary associations
and even *væresteder* used social closure to promote group fellowship and
draw up clear lines of belonging and authority. Thus, all adults were used
to working with groups of children organised by age who were 'theirs' for
the duration.

Drawing on this common framework, I suggest that Open Gym's adults
were playing out shared understandings of exclusive inter-generational
belonging in the public sphere. While maintaining open 'acephalous'
relations, they were sorting out relational proximity and distance based
on personal rapport, collegiality, institutional and personal rivalry and
situational resistance. This was done implicitly by lending or withholding
support (and children) to activities and initiatives planned in common. For
adults, Open Gym represented an ambiguous, open-ended site of inter-
generational belonging affecting guardianship, tutelage and licence to sway.
Which adults held which relational rights to which children remained an
open question requiring much implicit and sometimes explicit negotiation.[10]

As mentioned earlier, sports policies, as well as national and municipal
laws privileging associations, made it difficult to establish Open Gym as a

permanent venue. Despite practical barriers, most arguments against permanency invoked issues of moral public socialisation. Open Gym was not considered a proper site of civil socialisation because it did not promote relations of social closure among peers and between generations. Arguments of this nature reveal understandings of preferred sociality based on social closure and show reluctance toward exploring Open Gym's potential as a site of community. Evidence that children managed 'open community' relations and actively enjoyed Open Gym was not addressed in this ideological mode.[11] This suggests that Open Gym was not just about encouraging children to join public activity spheres but also about ordering generational relationships of public belonging and identity.

Finding and losing 'associationless children'

To help plan the third and final season of Open Gym, the project co-ordinator and I conducted a survey to determine whether any of the children were, indeed, associationless. The month-long survey included 112 Danish and 'other ethnic' children between the ages of 3 and 16. Two-thirds of the children were immigrant children; one-third were Danish. In both groups, most of the children were male between age 10 and 14. Almost all children attended local public schools; approximately two-thirds were members of public after-school clubs, while about half were members of sport associations. The survey revealed fifteen 'associationless' children who were, from my observations, by no means inactive. All of these children were, as imagined, of immigrant background, but cate-gorical homogeneity stopped there. The children were between the ages of 8 and 16, some went to local public schools, some to Muslim private schools and one had finished school. Three had recently arrived in the country and were learning Danish in a reception class[12] at a local school. About half of these children frequented Open Gym, while the rest showed up only sporadically.

Informal interviews suggested that some of the children might be attached to civil spheres other than those used in this context to construct their 'looseness' but this lead was not pursued (see Lidén, this volume). Details of these children's lives, beyond club and sports association affiliation, did not seem to matter. But, then, neither did the survey. Before its results were known, Open Gym was restructured for a third time. Prime afternoon access was given to the clubs' new sports association, which was closed to non-members. Open Gym would be run one evening a week by volunteers from local sports associations organised by Vesterbro Sports Union. The resulting order was that the group of children who had little difficulty playing together in Open Gym were now categorically segregated in terms of membership and non-membership. On the other hand, club pedagogues and volunteer instructors, who had experienced difficulty negotiating authority and co-ordinating their efforts, were given clearly bounded spheres of influence.

The third and final season of Open Gym never got off the ground. According to the coordinator, this was because Vesterbro's voluntary associations were not 'geared' to taking over Open Gym (Jørgensen 2000: 26). The Sport Union's chairman noted that it was impossible to get local associations to take on Open Gym because of their narrow, goal-oriented focus on their own activities (Gorm 2000: 18). There were no ardent protests over Open Gym's rather abrupt demise. Referring to all children who participated in Open Gym, the Sport Union chairman asserted matter-of-factly: 'They were here, now they are gone!!; nothing won, nothing lost!!'(ibid.: 17). Despite Open Gym's objective of 'spotting the children and youth who do not have membership in a sport association or any other leisure activity' (Jørgensen 2000: 26), 'associationless children' remained more useful and more easily engaged as rhetorical figures than as live children.

Locating associationless children

No one knew what became of the fifteen 'associationless' children who had attended Open Gym; they literally disappeared back into their daily lives. Still, the category proved useful in a new project aimed at providing sports for marginalised groups in a newly renovated factory. From the start, there was general consensus that asociationless children belonged in Sport Factory. The project coordinator argued that although DGI-City was originally intended to house activities of this type, the facility had developed into a place for traditionally organised associations. Accordingly, it was difficult to insist that alternative venues with less stable clientele be allotted DGI-City's coveted time-slots (Jørgensen 2000: 3). The coordinator claimed that a supplemental facility was necessary to house activities for 'sport-weak', marginalised and association-less categories and argued that Sport Factory's smaller, more manageable layout was better 'geared' to loosely organised groups. She concluded by claiming that DGI-City – both architecturally and organisationally – did not belong to 'Vesterbro':

> If you stand and look at DGI-City's facade, the utterly natural contrast between these buildings and the rest of Vesterbro shows up very clearly. It is obvious that even though DGI-City is situated in Vesterbro, it is not especially 'Vesterbro-like'. [. . .] DGI-City will probably never really be a place for common Vesterbro residents, unless they are members of a sport association, which [. . .] many in Vesterbro are not.
>
> (Jørgensen 2000: 4)

Her discerning gaze indicates how physical segregation of social categories might 'just happen' despite political directives explicitly encouraging experimental activity in DGI-City and despite the fact that categories of loose, semi-attached and attached children had played quite well alongside each other at Open Gym.

Claims that DGI-City did not belong to 'Vesterbro' shored up counter-claims that the Sport Factory did and plans to reopen Open Gym at the Factory indicated that associationless children were particularly 'Vesterbro-like'. The move to Sport Factory placed associationless children among a cluster of categories such as physically handicapped, mentally ill, recovering alcoholics and drug abusers, Muslim women and weak elderly. Apparently, they all belonged in the manageable facility for 'real Vesterbroers' with a penchant for more informal organisation.[13]

The project coordinator acknowledged that Vesterbro children had been both willing and able to cross the line between 'Vesterbro' and DGI-City and that this border crossing had been valuable:

> But [DGI-City] also has its strengths. It is for example of great value to see children and youth, who are used to small apartments, small gyms and institutions get a chance to romp in strikingly different aesthetic and spacious facilities.
>
> (Ibid.)

Associationless children had clearly enjoyed themselves along with other local children in DGI-City even though they did not conceptually 'belong' to DGI-City's spacious and aesthetic surroundings. However, lack of club membership was enough to deny these children access to DGI-City's spacious facilities and relocate them in smaller, unpretentious, renovated facilities among marginalised categories of 'real Vesterbroers'. This suggests that for children, lack of membership in civil associations is considered a social handicap equivalent to mental and physical handicaps.

The distinctions played on here point to two conflicting images of being 'local', one based on the 'authenticity' of shared physical locality and low social status, the other based on universal social participation in 'local society'. In this contested field, associationless children were incorporated among 'real locals' and placed outside of 'local society'. In order to access DGI-City and local society, these children had only to join sports associations, after-school clubs or, at least, frequent a *værested*. The question remains why this form of organisation was so essential for a weekly romp in a larger, better-equipped facility. Why did children who were otherwise mentally, physically and socially fit end up as an authentic, local, clientised category for no other reason than lack of membership in clubs and associations?

Civil relatedness and child exchange

I have used Open Gym as a case to explore ideas of proper civil relatedness. Open Gym features images of children who lack proper civil relations and highlights ways in which concerned professionals and volunteers attempt to remedy their lack. For children and, perhaps, for citizens of any age, proper attachment to local society implies 'closed' relations of ongoing membership in civil groups pursuing various forms of physical performance, games and play.[14] To conclude my discussion I will briefly address adult frustrations over the elusiveness of associationless children and the lack of proper reciprocal relations with their parents.

Elusive children

The story of Open Gym is about public efforts to 'get hold of' loose children. Adults used herding and trapping metaphors when discussing how to draw these children in. It was frustrating work and adults vented their frustrations through anecdotes about children who 'come when they feel like it', 'do not come on time', 'show up once, withdraw and then expect to come back in again', and children who 'quit when they have to pay'. Such conduct clearly exaggerated and thus aggravated civil relations of social closure.

Open Gym was designed to accommodate and transform, but not condone this elusive behaviour. Nevertheless, as I have argued, Open Gym had its own contact problems. Difficulty telling whose children were whose made access to loose children uncertain and contact awkward. Club pedagogues and youth workers related most freely and openly with 'their own' children and vice versa. Volunteer instructors, only loosely attached to Open Gym, risked finding themselves 'childless' or left only with marginalised children when attempting to gather an entire roomful of children. Project assistants moved cautiously toward children via the children's pedagogues and youth workers.

The data, thus, suggests distinct patterns of adult–child relations. While project assistants and association volunteers risked 'childlessness', loose children, actually present in the room, were effectively 'nobody's children', or perhaps in effect 'everybody's children' and, thus, 'no one's'. Loose children lacked relational links that would connect them to specific adults, just as volunteer instructors lacked relational links that would connect them to 'all of the children'. That fact that no adult represented a link connecting 'loose children' to adults and 'loose adults' to children suggests that organised civil contact between adults and children is only relationally possible in well-defined groups.[15] As argued earlier, the notion of 'loose children' is perhaps best understood as children moving from place to place uncircumscribed by the dominant public generational order.

Non-reciprocating parents

Children's behaviour in public spheres is often imaged in terms of homes and parents (James 1998) and, indeed, 'loose children' embodied images of their parents' actions and priorities. Organisers commonly explained the phenomena of associationless children in terms of immigrant parents' lack of knowledge and understanding of 'Danish association life'. Equally as common were explanations based on parental priorities. Adults frustrated over the elusiveness of immigrant children exchanged moralistic anecdotes about the 'wrong priorities' of their parents. Anecdotes were related in the tone of righteous indignation invoked when insiders speak of outsiders who don't embrace the proper relations of social exchange (Rapport 1997: 74). The following story cropped up at an Open Gym evaluation meeting:

> An immigrant father who had not yet paid his son's association fees showed up at a game with a brand new video camera worth thousands of crowns. The father showed the camera to an assistant trainer and asked for help to figure out how to work it; the camera was new and the father was not yet familiar with all its features.

The anecdote revealed the father's effrontery. He clearly should not have 'flaunted' an expensive new camera when he had not paid his son's fees. Similar anecdotes portrayed parents who had enough money to buy 'large cars' or 'mobile phones for everyone in the family', but would not pay for 'quality leisure activities' for their children. Anecdotes are critical of parents who purportedly put a higher priority on status afforded by material goods than status afforded by participation in common social activities (cf. James 1998: 151).

While the focus here and in the anecdotes above is on parents not providing what is best for children, I want to suggest another relational link. The father in the story is clearly reneging on reciprocal relations of child-sharing and exchange between himself and the voluntary trainer. In Fortes' words, 'he had done his duty to hand [his son] over to society as a citizen' (1984: 118), but was now refusing (or delaying) payment of 'initiation' fees. The social identity of 'loose' children is thus ascribed through images of improper exchange between domestic and public caretakers and civil instructors.

'Loose' immigrant children attending Open Gym embodied 'condensed images' (James 1998: 149) of improperly reciprocating parents. To create 'Danish' children, properly attached to local society, parents must willingly, and through the sacrifice of fees, enrol their children in local clubs and associations, that is in 'closed' extra-domestic groups of age-mates and designated guardians. When parents do not, in Carsten's terms, 'give the gift of the child' (1991: 435), their children are regarded as relationally incomplete and, indeed, out of place.

Privileging association venues of social closure is a necessary feature of this exchange system. Only through closure is symbolic moral exchange between domestic and civil spheres of adult authority made possible.

However, by requiring membership, closed venues produce categories of 'associationless' children for non-member children to fall into. As we have seen, this has practical consequences. Loose children were phased out of DGI-City and relegated to a separate facility welcoming socially handicapped groups. McDermott (1993) has argued that children may be 'acquired' by categories and I suggest such a process is at play here. Locally active immigrant children, who were 'out in society' unaccompanied by public caretakers, were being acquired by the category of 'associationless children'. This left them beyond the reach of 'local society' and categorically embedded in a renovated factory with other authentically local, dependent civil individuals. Exclusion from other facilities was not based on the children's own conduct but rather on whether parents participated in the dominant system of child-exchange.

Conclusion

After two seasons of watching both 'attached' and 'loose' Vesterbro children use DGI-City's large gyms as an indoor playground, I was at a loss to understand why such a successful open venue could not be made permanent. When Open Gym was phased out in its third year, I searched my field notes for clues that could explain why this could happen so naturally. I have argued that there was nothing in the interaction between different categories of children that warranted closing the venue. It became clear, however, that the open, *ad hoc*, unstructured nature of this site posed problems for public caretakers whose relations to 'other people's children' depended on clear lines of belonging and influence afforded by social closure and reciprocal relations with parents. The open nature of the site was also a problem for organisers who received funding to convert 'associationless' children into 'members' and not vice versa. Thus, although all local children were invited to come by and play, Open Gym was never meant to be a 'place' in itself. It was not seen as a universal site of community but rather a temporary hall of transit and conversion.

Probing the history, legitimacy, activities and relations of Open Gym has revealed the contours of a dominant and politically supported form of child exchange between domestic and public spheres. I have argued that this exchange integrates children into 'local society', yet at the same time produces local social segregation. As envisioned by project organisers, local society was made up of bounded institutional entities between which children could move. The data shows that not being enrolled in this institutional system of shared child-rearing had consequences for where and with whom 'associationless' children were allowed to play. Remaining outside the system of civil exchange located immigrant children among marginalised social groups and effectively placed them outside the category of 'Danish children'.

Acknowledgements

This article has benefited from the helpful comments of Karen Fog Olwig, Eva Gulløv and participants in the Network for Cross-cultural Child Research workshop 'Children, Generation and Place: Cross-cultural Approaches to an Anthropology of Children', University of Copenhagen, 19–20 May 2001.

Notes

1 A report on sports provision in Copenhagen noted that Copenhagen's sports facilities were colonised by 'resource-strong', well-organised, mobile males and recommended that children, youth and other 'resource-weak' and 'association-passive' groups should be given priority access to any new facilities. The report also stressed that new facilities must be 'anchored' in local neighbourhoods to develop sport's social and health dimensions (Københavns Idrætsanlæg 1997).

2 In Denmark, public day-care and recreational institutions for children consist of *vuggestuer* (nurseries, age 0–3), *børnehaver* (kindergartens, age 3–7), *fritidshjem* (leisure-time homes, age 6–9), *fritidsklubber* (after-school clubs, ages 10–14) and *ungdomsklubber* (youth clubs, age 14–18). All require registration and fees, but after-school clubs and youth clubs do not require regular attendance.

3 That the category had conceptual force and political value, and thus could be exploited when applying for government and municipal funding, might explain some of its popularity.

4 Immigrant is a generic term used in Denmark to denote anyone of foreign background. Children of foreign-born parents or grandparents designated as 'immigrant' may themselves be born in Denmark and carry Danish passports.

5 This was a dominant image of immigrant boys. In contrast, immigrant girls were most often imaged as 'stuck at home'. They were, so to speak, not loose enough, and projects promoting girls clubs were set up to bring them out of their homes.

6 Even though project workers were well aware that that a semantic fusion between 'loose' and 'immigrant' did not pass closer inspection, this semantic merger remained dominant throughout the project.

7 'Loose children' were also metaphorically compared to fickle consumers, who must be enticed and tempted into the store by attractive offers.

8 *Værested* translates as 'a place to be'. The term refers to a municipal or project-funded place, for example a small storefront, set up like a club where a category of people (children, alcoholics, young single mothers), targeted by social workers, may come for free. Several *væresteder* were set up for 'loose' Vesterbro children to give them a supervised indoor place to socialise in their free time. Youth workers endeavoured to bring *værested* children 'out into society' through a variety of excursions and activities such as Open Gym.

9 It is difficult to say why collaboration was organised and expected to work without an official hands-on coordinator with the authority (of any Weberian kind) to sway either all children or all adults. I suggest, however, that 'acephalous collaboration' is a common figure in pedagogical venues, as I have also come across it in Danish school environments (See Anderson 1996, 2000: 86–98). When this form of open-ended, half-planned, half *ad hoc* collaboration fails to bring the expected result, blame is commonly placed on a category of persons –

teachers, pedagogues, loose children, sport volunteers – but rarely on the form of organisation. Therefore I contend that what I am calling acephalous collaboration is an orthodoxy in Danish pedagogical and educational domains.

10 In practice, association volunteers generally lost these negotiations because, having 'no children of their own' in this venue, they had to persuade 'others' or 'nobody's' children to join them.

11 However, in her final report, the coordinator argued in favour of considering making Open Gym a more permanent arrangement. 'It is difficult to convince oneself when standing in a gym filled with active and happy children that this [Open Gym] has no merit unless some of them subsequently join a local sport association' (Jørgensen 2000: 12). She recommended that local associations work together to run a permanent Open Gym.

12 A number of Copenhagen public comprehensive schools (folkeskoler) have 'reception classes' where newly arrived refugee and immigrant children learn Danish before joining regular classes.

13 This vision of who belongs where is an interesting example of how buildings may be used to represent social difference, to underscore social belonging and institute social segregation that, in turn, leads to constructions of locality and understandings of 'real' local identity (Cf. Carsten and Hugh-Jones 1995: 3, 41–4).

14 In Connerton's terms, this may be seen as a national *incorporating* practice (1989: 72). During fieldwork, I lent an ear to many adult memories of childhood experiences with both school and association sports.

15 I do not mean to imply that it was necessarily difficult to come into contact with differently related children in this venue. As an unknown observer, I had many opportunities to contact children, to ask questions, to guard shoes, hold jewellery, look after a little sister, lend my video camera, and conduct a survey. However, I do believe it would have been relationally impossible for me to gather all of the children for a common activity or keep a group of children focused for any length of time on an activity of my choosing.

References

Anderson, S. (1996) *Chronic Proximity and the Management of Difference: An Anthropological Study of the Danish School Practice of* klasse, Specialerække 69. Copenhagen: Institute of Anthropology, Copenhagen University.

—— (2000) *I en klasse for sig.* Copenhagen: Gyldendal.

—— (2003) *Civilising Children: Children's Sport and Civil Sociality in Denmark,* Ph.d-række nr 23. Copenhagen: Institute of Anthropology, Copenhagen University.

Carsten, J. (1991) 'Children in between: Fostering and the process of kinship on Pulau Langkawi, Malaysia', *Man* 26(3): 425–44.

Carsten, J. and S. Hugh Jones (1995) 'Introduction: About the house – Lévi-Strauss and beyond', in J. Carsten and S. Hugh-Jones (eds) *About the House – Lévi-Strauss and Beyond.* Cambridge: Cambridge University Press.

Connerton, P. (1989) *How Societies Remember.* Cambridge: Cambridge University Press.

Dengsøe, P. (2000) *Hverdagsliv på Vesterbro – fra folkeligt kvarter til moderne bydel.* Ålborg: Aalborg Universitetsforlag og Forlaget ALFUFF.

DUF (Danske Ungdoms Fællesråd) (2000) *Welcome to the Association: Information for Parents About Good Free-time Activities for Children and Young Adults*. Copenhagen: DUF.

Fortes, M. (1984) 'Age, generation and social structure', in D. I. Kertzer and J. Keith (eds) *Age and Anthropological Theory*. Ithaca, NY: Cornell University Press.

Gorm, P. (2000) 'Project Vesterbro set af Vesterbro Idrætssamvirke', in M. Jørgensen, *Projekt Vesterbro – 'Fra sidelinie til førerfelt': Et tre-årigt idrætsprojekt under DGI Storkøbenhavn*. Copenhagen: DGI-Storkøbenhavn.

Gullestad, M. (1992) 'The transformations of the notion of everyday life', in *The Art of Social Relations: Essays on Culture, Social Action and Everyday Life in Modern Norway*. Oslo: Scandinavian University Press.

Holstein, B. (1997) 'Motionsvaner blandt børn og unge', in *Idrætten i København går nye veje*. Referat af idrætspolitiske konference, May 1997.

Idrætspolitiske redegørelse (1998) Fremlagt af Kultur – og Fritidsudvalget, Københavns Kommune, July 1998.

James, A. (1998) 'Imaging children "at home", "in the family" and "at school": Movement between the spatial and temporal markers of childhood identity in Britain', in N. Rapport and A. Dawson (eds) *Migrants of Identity: Perceptions of Home in a World of Movement*. Oxford: Berg.

Jørgensen, M. (2000) *Projekt Vesterbro: 'Fra sidelinie til førerfelt': Et treårigt idrætsprojekt under DGI Storkøbenhavn*. Copenhagen: DGI Storkøbenhavn.

Københavns Idrætsanlæg (1997) *Idrættens Vilkår i København. Oplæg til idrætspolitiske konference*. Copenhagen: Københavns idrætsanlæg.

McDermott, R. (1993) 'The acquisition of a child by a learning disability', in S. Chaiklin and J. Lave (eds) *Understanding Practice*. Cambridge: Cambridge University Press.

Olwig, K. F. (2000) 'Børn i lokalsamfund – børns lokalsamfund', *Barn* 3–4: 5–22.

Ottesen, L. and B. Ibsen (2000) *Børn, Idræt og Hverdagsliv – i tal og tale,* Working paper. Copenhagen: Copenhagen University, Institut for Idræt.

Rapport, N. (1997) 'The morality of locality: On absolutism of landownership in an English village', in S. Howell (ed.) *The Ethnography of Moralities*. London: Routledge.

Sampson, S. (1996) 'The social life of projects: Importing civil society to Albania', in C. Hann and E. Dunn (eds) *Civil Society: Challenging Western Models*. London: Routledge.

Shore, C. and S. Wright (1997) 'Policy: A new field of anthropology', in C. Shore and S. Wright (eds) *Anthropology of Policy: Critical Perspectives on Governance and Power*. London: Routledge.

Wright, S. (1995) 'Anthropology: Still the uncomfortable discipline?', in A. Ahmed and C. Shore (eds) *The Future of Anthropology*. London: Athlone.

Chapter 8

Changing place, changing position

Orphans' movements in a community with high HIV/AIDS prevalence in western Kenya

Erick Otieno Nyambedha and Jens Aagaard-Hansen

Omondi

Omondi, a Luo boy living in western Kenya, lost his mother in July 1998. At the time of his mother's death he was 15 years old and attending fifth grade at a local primary school, but he dropped out immediately afterwards. When we visited him, he was living with his 67-year-old father, who had a severe drinking problem. His eldest brother, who was 26 years old, lived in a house adjacent to a local shopping centre with the other siblings, three boys who were 17, 11 and 6 years old respectively. They had also dropped out of school, as there was no one to pay their fees. Later, the 17-year-old brother went to go and stay with a cousin in Nairobi. However, the two remaining young brothers stayed with Omondi's eldest brother. Nobody in the family would look after them, because Omondi's parents had had a strained relationship with this family, and at one stage Omondi's father accused members of the extended family of being responsible for Omondi's mother's death through witchcraft.

Omondi started to look for work opportunities within the locality in order to feed himself and his father, who was of no help whatsoever. Eventually, he joined other orphaned children within the area to form a *saga,* a group of boys who work collectively. As he continued to work for pay, Omondi carefully spent his money partly on buying foodstuffs and other basic needs, partly on purchasing what he needed to return to school. After a while, close members of Omondi's patrilineal kin became concerned about his way of life, as it was not a traditional practice for such a young boy to be left to fend for himself when other adult relatives were around. A younger brother of his father's, who had just returned from Nairobi, decided to take Omondi into his house, but this was against his wife's wishes. By then Omondi had acquired the basic necessities for school (such as textbooks, a uniform and funds for school fees) and managed to go back to school. After some time in his uncle's house, Omondi had to move out because his uncle's wife did not want him living there. Omondi then contacted another paternal relative, a relatively rich, elderly man of his paternal grandfather's generation. He agreed to take Omondi into his house and even to pay for his schooling, provided that Omondi help with household chores. Omondi therefore ended up living in the home of a paternal relative who was a classificatory grandfather according to Luo kinship terminology.

Omondi's story gives an outline of the social problems that face many Luo children who lose one or both parents. It shows how the children themselves negotiate their livelihood strategies, in the process moving to new places and assuming new social and economic responsibilities. Young Luo children were traditionally supposed to be cared for by paternal relatives and only gradually incorporated into the world of adults. Thus, when Omondi had to drop out of school and work in order to support himself and his father, members of his paternal kin became embarrassed about the situation and stepped in to help him. The plight of Omondi and his brothers is not unique. There are many orphaned children in situations of deprivation, lack of parental support and diminishing protection from kin, and constant changes in both physical and social places such as the one Omondi faces. This is particularly relevant for communities that have been seriously ravaged by the HIV/AIDS epidemic, as is the case in this Luo community in Bondo District, western Kenya. Such situations present us with a new set of parameters for understanding Luo childhood and the various places for being an orphan in western Kenya.

Throughout the local community, as in other parts of Africa, children are losing their parents because of the AIDS epidemic. This has not just meant that much of the parental generation has disappeared, but also that caring for and raising children, which is closely embedded in the kinship system, has changed dramatically. As a result, many children no longer undergo a process of gradual introduction into the adult world, but are to a great extent left on their own, as their relatives are either bound by previous perceptions of who is expected to take care of them, or else seek to take advantage of the situation.

In this chapter, we describe the traditional institutions for socialising children among the Luo and show how they have been affected by the unprecedented increase in the number of orphaned children. We discuss how children adapt by inventing new strategies for pursuing their livelihoods, while at the same time drawing on the traditional cultural norms and social structure. Omondi's story provides a picture of a child who loses his social place as a child when he assumes the position of an adult carer in order to feed himself and his father, but who manages to regain his former social place by changing physical place, moving first to his uncle's and later to his 'grandfather's' place. We are therefore examining change in traditionally recognised social and physical places for children, as well as how categories of orphan-carers influence children's occupation of these places. We also examine the social implications of this change and the ways in which children have developed networks of relationships within the community to enhance their survival. The chapter finally investigates how these relationships have changed the generational order and grounded children in the new physical places and social positions that have removed them from the insulation of traditional places that are associated with child-rearing in this community. The chapter therefore considers how the social structure, children's agency and power relations work to place children in various positions in this situation of turbulence.

Traditional places of child-rearing among the Luo

Like many other African peoples, the Luo, who form one of the largest ethnic groups in Kenya, have a patrilineal kinship structure and are polygynous (Hauge 1974). This implies that places of belonging for children are defined according to the rules of the patriline (descent traced through the male line). The Luo have two categories of intra-familial relationship. The first exists within the homestead and immediate locality or lineage (*kakwaro*). The second exists outside the patriline, in other words is connected with a man's matrikin and affines (Whisson 1964).

Among the Luo, the *kakwaro* is conceptualised as the largest social space in which children and adults can interact. In studying orphanhood, *kakwaro* provides an important key to our understanding of the space of childhood, and is important for our analysis of the various places for and of children in the homestead. The concept of *kakwaro* is equally important in conceptualising notions of kinship, insulation (that is, the protective role of certain members of the lineage towards children), physical location, integration, hierarchy and the various places traditionally available to children. It is from the vantage point of *kakwaro* that children's negotiations of place can be analysed. All the rules of places of belonging and social position in this community are organised around the principles of *kakwaro*, which determine patrilineality and the regulation of discipline in the domestic space in the traditional set-up of the homestead. This symbolises the close interrelationship and interplay between the physical, social and cultural conditions of life for Luo children.

A *dala*, or homestead, is a cluster of households where up to three generations often cohabit: the elderly couple, their sons and their wives, and finally the sons' children. The *dala* was the traditional framework for the *duol*, the places where homestead members and other members of the lineage ate collectively and where children in need were catered for (Ocholla-Ayayo 1976: 71–2). These were also places where the elderly gathered to discuss important matters of the lineage.

Traditionally, Luo children grew up within the patriline and were ascribed specific physical and social places within the household, homestead and clan area according to their age and sex, in accordance with the generational order. In a typical polygynous homestead, young children stayed with their biological mother in a separate household adjacent to the households of her co-wives and their offspring (their half-siblings), and interaction among the children of the co-wives was encouraged. Young children slept with their mother in the house, and children's physical movements were tightly controlled by the adults, especially patrilineal relatives. Likewise, children's mobility in relation to various social positions was determined by genealogical rules as well as by their age and sex.

The social position of the girls was lower than that of the boys, until they got married and increased their access to the various places and resources of their husband's patriline. Right from birth, a female child was traditionally seen as someone who would one day leave the community to get married elsewhere, and who therefore potentially belonged to unknown physical places where she could go. In return for her leaving, her parents would be rewarded with some cattle as bridewealth, which officially sealed the marriage and also gave her firm rights to take up her social position in the new home. This arrangement obliged the other party to accord her a position commensurate with that of a wife in the home and to assign the children of that union their rightful place in the community. Thus we can see the role of bridewealth in defining both physical and social places for girls who married and for the issue of the marriage in this community. Although girls were assigned social positions at their places of birth, these were of low status because their positions were potentially waiting for them in their future places of marriage.

Unmarried and recently married boys were assigned social positions of lower status than the older men, who were in charge of decision-making in the community. But this also sometimes depended on the lineage hierarchy, so that those who stood at a higher point in the hierarchy occupied higher social positions than men who might be older. However, overall husbands occupy higher social positions than their wives, who in most cases are supposed to obey them.

In terms of income-generation, children were not allowed to engage in or negotiate work opportunities with adults. They could only engage in income-generating activities on behalf of their parents, who were responsible for the negotiations concerning the work and decided how the income would be spent. Children's needs were supposed to be met by the adults. This signified the insulating role of the traditional kinship system in this community, which is manifest in its ability to insulate the children against forces that may hinder their normal development into responsible adults in the community. For example, in this community children were not allowed to handle money of their own, as this was seen to 'spoil' them and lead them astray from adult teachings.

After reaching puberty, the girls started to sleep in a *siwindhe* (the girls' dormitory) with a woman who had reached menopause (Ocholla-Ayayo

1976: 73). 'From the age of fourteen, the education of girls was continued at a higher level . . . at the grandmother's house, which the senior girls used as their dormitory, *siwindhe*' (ibid.: 64); 'the girls continue life at *siwindhe* until they are married' (ibid.: 73). Traditionally, these were places where the girls were reared in preparation for adult responsibilities and taught how to lead a proper life in marriage. The young girls were also taught how to relate to other young people of the opposite sex, especially boys from other lineages, who might be their future husbands. Boys attended the *siwindhe* between the ages of about 7 to 13 or 14, together with the girls (ibid.: 73). After this the boys moved into the *simba*, the boys' dormitory, which was (and still is) a free zone, in the sense that it is a place of intra-generational interactions with minimum adult control, where the senior boys exercise limited authority over the younger members (ibid.: 83).

In the *siwindhe*, children were taught the customs and manners of the community, as well as its history and religion. Grandparents were the main agents of transmission of this knowledge to the young. This was supposed to be done through story-telling in the grandmother's house before the children fell asleep in the evening. This required a loving atmosphere, in which grandparents were expected to pamper the grandchildren, and not quarrel with them. Children were taught traditional knowledge of the community's value system and prescribed modes of behaviour regulating patterns of interaction between children and adults. According to Ominde (1952) these regulations were believed to come from the ancestors.

However, it sometimes happened that mothers sent their children to live with their maternal grandfather or grandmother. The rationale was that the child should assist the older relative with practical tasks, such as performing household chores, while the parents retained their financial obligations towards the child. This was done in situations where such old people did not have grandchildren from their sons (i.e. from within their own patriline) to assist them. Most often the adults, especially the elderly men and women, were not comfortable with the idea of children from their lineage going to stay with maternal relatives in distant places. It was even more unacceptable for male children to stay with their brothers-in-law. But it was less objectionable for girls to stay with their married sisters. However, patrilineal relatives were always keen to retain children so that they did not move away, because the practice of children going to physical places controlled by other patrilineages and other relatives was considered to be a reflection of the inability of patrilineal relatives to provide adequate support.

The rules outlined above reflect the ideal, traditional ways of the Luo. Though there have always been exceptions to the rules, many of them are still practised (e.g. the *simba*), whereas others have been abandoned (e.g. the collective feeding arrangement of the *duol*). At the present day, as

Cohen and Atieno-Odhiambo describe (1989: 97), an increasing number of the children of children are being born out of wedlock, then being known as 'the children of daughters' or 'pregnancy of *simba*'. *Simba* are the traditional places where all unmarried boys who have reached puberty sleep and also entertain their visitors. In these places of interaction between youths, young girls who have reached puberty also visit their boyfriends, which sometimes leads to pre-marital pregnancies. This is a recent phenomenon, however, and children from such relationships do not acquire appropriate places of belonging unless their mothers marry and take them to their husbands' place of residence, to which they move upon marriage. Traditionally, such children, if their mother did not bring them to their husband's patriline upon marriage, remained with the mother's patriline where she grew up, but under the rules of patrilineality they do not have the same social position or access to resources as sons' children. The parents of the pregnant girl often tried to identify the father of the child so that his or her physical place of belonging could be determined. However, such children face discrimination in the maternal grandparents' place and are considered to belong to distant places. They are discriminated against because traditionally they do not have inheritance rights in the maternal grandparents' kin network and belong to distant physical places, where their fathers, formerly their mothers' boyfriends, belong. Therefore, children from such informal associations do not fit into the generational order of the patriline and are difficult to incorporate into local society.

Traditional views of domesticity can still shed a great deal of light on issues concerning the routine ordering of domestic space, and how this generally defines conceptions of childhood and the whole question of child–adult relationships in the traditional Luo community. Although these structures seem to represent the typical situation of childhood in this community, there is a need to examine how they are played out under varying socio-economic circumstances. As Prout states (2000: 3), childhood should be 'hailed as a social and cultural phenomenon marked by spatial and historical variability'. Holland *et al.* (1998: 17) also emphasise the importance of turning from the analysis of culture as an objectified and abstract system toward analyses of the ways in which cultural forms develop through the constant improvisation and renegotiation of cultural rules in the light of ever-changing social and material conditions. This view seems relevant when examining orphaned children such as Omondi, who are attempting to establish new networks of relationship in the community in order to relate to the changed social structure. Of particular significance is how the efforts of Omondi to work for pay and his assumption of responsibility for feeding his drunken father are interpreted by his extended kin network, and how this network is reacting to his efforts. It is therefore important to look at the network of connections through which children's agency is produced and to investigate the changes that have occurred in the traditional notions of lineality, domesticity and its traditional protectionist role for children in difficult circumstances, as is explained by Mbuya (1965). In this analysis, we are using the term domesticity to refer to the wide range of obligations, rules and regulations that govern the interactions of individuals within the wider domestic space of the homestead (*dala*) where *siwindhe*, *duol* and *simba* are found, and to the ways in which the various people in the homesteads interact within the wider framework of relations defined by the *kakwaro*.

We acknowledge the recent and important theoretical insights gained in the understanding of human conditions by emphasising the continuous, dynamic processes at the interface between personal agency and structural blueprints. These processes are especially dramatic in this context (e.g. structural hierarchies, cultural norms, socio-economic conditions) given the radical changes in the whole age structure. In the following, we shall look at the disruptions to some of the basic relationships and power balances as epitomised by movements of children – their change of physical place and social position within this community.

The setting

This study was conducted in the Nyang'oma division of western Kenya, which is located along the shores of Lake Victoria (Nyambedha 2000; Nyambedha *et al.* 2001). The local economy is mainly based on subsistence farming, though other activities, such as fishing, small-scale mining, labour migration and minor trading, are important as well – a reflection of what Ocholla-Ayayo called a 'pastoral-agrico-fishing' society (1976: 18). The climate is characterised by scarce and erratic rainfall, which makes agriculture unreliable. To a limited extent, people earn a living as teachers or employees at the local Roman Catholic mission. The Catholic Church, however, has successfully barred children's participation in the wage economy at the mission, while at the same time giving children access to the Catholic schools that are now widely regarded by the locals as vital learning places for children and that have systematically replaced traditional educational institutions.

There are several primary schools in the area, mainly sponsored by the Catholic and Anglican Churches, though they do not discriminate on the basis of religious affiliation when admitting pupils. The only requirement is that, while they attend school, they adhere to certain Catholic doctrines. Though the government pays the teachers' salaries, the guardians still have to cover a number of expenses for children attending school. These expenses may seem petty in the more affluent parts of the world (approximately US$10 per year in school fees), but they are often prohibitive in the local context. As a result, many children lack educational opportunities entirely. Inability to pay school fees has affected children's access to these places of Western-style education, and orphaned children, who form a third of the children within the study area, seem to be the most affected. But some of these children have renegotiated their participation in such new places of learning in other ways, as we saw in Omondi's case.

Livelihood strategies

For many generations, Luo children have been involved in various kinds of manual work contributing to the upkeep of the extended family. Children engaged in weeding or harvesting the family's fields, herding animals belonging to patrilineal relatives or performing household duties such as cooking or washing, which was part of raising practices. It can be argued that some fundamentals of these traditional raising practices have laid the ground for children's initiatives, which is now evident in their ability to negotiate their own opportunities to earn an income during times of economic difficulty.

Orphaned children who participated in the study engaged in various income-generating activities to meet the cost of food and other necessities. In order to achieve this goal, they took a number of initiatives. Those who were still interested in schooling but could not obtain their carers's support reported doing business, which was confined to selling petty things such as fruit or unrefined sugar at school to buy what they needed for school, while others reported burning charcoal or working for other people in the village who could pay them some money. Part of this money they would give to their carers, while some of it was used to satisfy some of their requirements for both schooling and domestic use. Some carers appreciated these initiatives and encouraged the children, whereas others did not approve of the idea of children working for money. Like Omondi, some orphans also formed collective work groups (saga) to undertake agricultural production, which considerably helped reduce the work load, especially for elderly carers. Thus, a good many orphans displayed a sense of concern for both their siblings and carers, as they were constantly engaged in negotiations with adults in the community to obtain work for payment or credit facilities in cases of food shortage or sickness, as a number of them did with 'over-the-counter' sellers of medicines in cases of illness.

Some orphans sought help outside the local community among relatives living elsewhere. They might, for example, leave temporarily of their own accord to stay with a relative living in a neighbouring locality during times of scarcity, returning when the harvest was ready. They usually did this after completing the agricultural work, and only went on such visits as a way of obtaining relief from the hard work of searching for food during times of scarcity. This type of change of physical residence was particularly noticeable in some of the households that were headed by adolescents.

Migration to urban areas was also observed among orphans who wished to look for wage employment. Some of them could decide on their own to stay with school friends to look for wage employment, without consulting the carers. There are cases where orphans have moved elsewhere to obtain accommodation in friends' relatives' houses, or even secured work opportunities by networking through friends at school. This happened especially when orphans realised that they did not have any further opportunity for schooling, and working presented itself as a feasible alternative. Thus, poverty was pivotal in changing physical places and residential arrangements, and moving usually took place in response to local factors, such as the availability of casual work on the beaches at Lake Victoria, and sometimes in the small-scale mines nearby.

The children working on Lake Victoria went out with the fishing boats, helping pull in the nets, whereas those working in the small gold mines participated in the actual digging for gold. These children usually work under terms determined unilaterally by the adult owners of the fishing vessels or the mines. In these places of work, the adults seem to take advantage of the difficult situation of the orphans to compel them to work on their own terms. In such circumstances, orphaned children become victims of these public workplaces, where they only serve the interests of adults. The children's presence and power is therefore invisible in these places, and their agency is somewhat disempowered by the exploitative nature of adults controlling social relations and resources. There is a mixed perception of how children look at themselves as children in relation to adults who are also their employees, and how they perceive themselves as children being employed by adults in these workplaces. While there is the traditional demand that children respect adults while receiving assistance from them in return, children in these particular work circumstances find it confusing to remain children. This is because they sometimes have to argue with their adult employers when they feel aggrieved, even though this may be interpreted as disrespect. But at the same time adults in these workplaces find it appropriate to take advantage of the inherently low social position of the children in order to exploit them. This has introduced some confusion and conflict in the relationship between children and childhood in these places of work.

In some cases, children's involvement in these activities and the places where they were conducted led to strained relations. The carers (and especially the grandparents) felt that the beaches and the mines where some of the children worked were not ideal places for bringing up children because of the activities that took place there, while the children felt they needed the income to make up for what their grandparents and other carers could not provide. In such cases of conflict, the adult employers along the beaches and in the mines offer the children shelter and even feed them as long as they are working for them. But this did not go down well with local community leaders, especially the beach leaders, locally elected leaders and the local administration, who would prefer the children to be in school. Thus children's engagement in these places creates conflicts in different quarters, which reflects conflicts among individuals and the traditions of the land in a rapidly changing community.

Children's migration to urban areas takes place largely within a network of relations within the extended family or *kakwaro,* in which orphans and their carers negotiate work opportunities through their relatives' network in urban areas. By working through family networks, relatives also ensure the safety of children who are moving out of their original place of birth to remote places, particularly in urban areas, where close relatives may not be able to monitor them. While the extended family, the *kakwaro,* formerly provided a safe local environment in which children might grow up, today a primary role of this family has become the offering of a network of relations extended in space that may provide work opportunities for children. It is, for example, common for the more affluent members of the extended family network to offer domestic work to disadvantaged children who are related to them, rather than to give assistance to these children so that they may remain in school. This represents a complete departure from traditional modes of raising children, as presented in earlier Luo ethnographies by Ominde (1952) and Ocholla-Ayayo (1976).

The situation in urban areas appears to offer the orphans new possibilities for agency and for the construction of new places, which has influence back home. Such influence is manifested in the control that urban working children have over what the parents they have left behind, who depend on their remittances, do at home in the rural areas. While, in the modern environment, the children, mostly working as household help, have exercised autonomy over how they spend the money, their social position is raised because of the influence they have over their parents, thus changing the balance of the traditional generational order.

Change of place could be significant in another way as well. There were cases where orphans had lived with their deceased parents in town but now had to migrate to the countryside after the death of their parents to live with new, patrilineally related carers. Orphaned children from urban areas did not find it easy to integrate themselves into the rural extended family network. This is because they were often used to an individualistic life-style and the less demanding physical labour in urban settings. A number of orphans from urban areas found it strange to share meals with other people outside their grandmothers' households, thus removing the few remaining traces of the notion of collectivity, which in the past served to assist vulnerable children and place them in their right positions (Whisson 1964; Ocholla-Ayayo 1976; Nyambedha *et al.* 2003a). Such notions of collectivity were based on the egalitarian mode of livelihood, where children shared meals in a group at the *duol* or old man's house and *siwindhe* or old woman's house. In both cases, all the children and adults ate, regardless of whether one's mother had prepared a meal or not (Mbuya 1965), thus ensuring food security for all members of the household. But, as we have argued in the case of children who have been brought up in urban areas, this mode of livelihood does not exist in the urban environment. When children change their places of residence from urban to rural, it takes them some time before they become accustomed to the life style in the rural environment, where there are a few traces of an egalitarian mode of life, such as the sharing of meals by all members of the community.

The social implications of children changing places

As already noted, Holland *et al.* (1998) suggest that subjects are not completely free to shape their lives and identities but are decisively influenced by the locally dominant socio-cultural constraints. Giddens similarly observes that the notion of human agency cannot be adequately explained without the notion of structure, and that agency and structure influence each other (1979: 255). Structure thus influences the realised possibilities of orphaned children to act upon their world and remake the world in which they live, as Inden would put it (Inden cited in Holland *et al.* 1998: 42).

In our study of this community, we documented many and varying instances of orphans changing their place of residence, both within and outside the study area. Some children changed residential arrangements by moving from one household to another within a homestead, whereas others were forced out of their paternal homesteads because of the interest some relatives had in their deceased parents' land. For example, we came across a situation where three orphaned children had been forced by their own paternal relatives to demolish their deceased parents' houses and vacate their home, because the relatives argued that the piece of land the houses stood on was in dispute and did not rightfully belong to their deceased parents. The children were forced to move out of the community to their maternal grandparent, who lived far away. Cases of adults dispossessing widows and children of their inheritance rights have not been uncommon. Some widows reported situations in which their brothers in-law have taken away their property, thus forcing them and their children to find survival strategies other than the traditional mainstay of agriculture. These are some of the typical cases, where structural limitations and power relations within a kin system can impose severe limits on the orphaned children's agency.

The places to which the orphans moved varied according to the social position of the carers in the kinship system. Because of the rule of clan exogamy, staying with matrikin or in-laws was likely to imply that the orphans had to move out of their clans' territory to places located anywhere between 10 and 80 kilometres away. Whatever the circumstances, the consequence for the orphans staying with different categories of carers was usually that they had to move to new places of residence, and sometimes to different social positions.

Orphaned children do not just move between different geographical locations: they also move within family networks in search of better living conditions. As the case of Omondi shows, they also constantly change their social positions within the community where they are living, being socially and economically defined as children under adult supervision at one moment, and as adults caring for various dependents the next. Data from the community reveal situations in which children start by assuming the positions of their dead parents, some dropping out of school in the process, while others retain their place at school as well. Later, as in the case of Omondi, those who have dropped out of school may return there, partly on their own initiative, but also partly with the aid of members of the extended family, who, due to their increased sense of responsibility, decide to take orphaned children into their homes. When children find themselves placed under the direct control of adult members of the extended family, they return to the social position of being children responding purely to the demands of childhood. Children's places in such situations are seen as processes that are firmly grounded in social interactions, available support networks and opportunities within the community. Orphaned children therefore move back and forth between different places within the community, as their material and social conditions change. Social relations play an important part in moving between places and orphan carer categories. In our study, as Omondi's case shows, there may be a deliberate lack of support from members of the extended family because of the strained relations that may have existed between the living and the dead, and the counter-accusations preceding the death of a member of a lineage. Such strained relationships are common when a member of a particular lineage dies and some people within the extended family are accused of being responsible for their deaths through witchcraft. These accusations, which are common in Africa, are a manifestation of underlying tensions between people of same lineage. The quality of such relations therefore has direct consequences on children's ability to negotiate and obtain access to different places for themselves.

Our data suggest that the social position occupied by orphaned children in this community may resemble that of adults in traditional society. This places these children at the centre of the politics of adult life. When children become socially and economically active, for instance in group activities, group members cease to treat them in terms of the social position of the deceased parents, but rather according to how the children, now orphaned, themselves engage in group activities following their parents' death. For example, we participated in group activities where members of the group went to see orphaned children in their deceased parents' houses just as they would visit an adult group member living in their own homes, and they even raised money to help satisfy some of the pressing needs in the orphans' households. In such situations, children are judged alongside other adults in the group and compete for the group's attention. Recently, when one of us attended the funeral of one of our informants, a widow, most of the people who gave eulogies praised her for having been active in the local church group's activities even when she was terribly ill, but at the same time they also praised her eldest son, then 17 years old, for having assumed his mother's place when she had been overwhelmed by illness. In fact, the boy was actively encouraged to take his mother's place, as this would also offer him security in the future. But in other instances, children received little attention from members of the extended kin network because of the bad relationships their deceased parents had had with their surviving relatives, which, of course, placed them at the centre of the conflicts between their deceased parents and those relatives.

In his study of the Azande of Sudan, Evans-Pritchard (1976) explained that there is inherent rivalry between co-wives as a function of their struggle for their common husband's attention, as well as for family resources, this readily being reflected in the way other adults in the community relate to the children of the rivals. Early Luo ethnographies by Whisson (1964) have demonstrated the existence of similar situations. Children therefore have to rely on their knowledge of the surrounding environment to find survival mechanisms and come up with new social positions that guarantee them minimal survival. Their agency in this new social position is only shown by their skills in making decisions, cultivating social relationships and taking actions that change their life worlds, as well as those of their siblings and other members of their households. This change has worked to situate them in their unique places within the community, which contradicts recognised processes of socialisation that are traditionally understood in many African communities. Such initiatives have transformed the traditional social position of children. The situation of orphans and grandparents is of particular interest in relation to changing places. The grandparents now find themselves parenting, which sometimes calls for the strict supervision of the duties and responsibilities that are delegated to various members of the household, including the grandchildren. In a number of cases, orphaned children had strained relationships with their elders. In a few instances, the latter, especially the grandparents, reported having sent the orphans away because they did not satisfy the conditions of household production that we have described elsewhere (Nyambedha et al. 2003b). The new positions of the grandparents and the grandchildren vis-à-vis one another affected their mutual power and status relations. More specifically, it altered how the grandparents were supposed to convey the traditional knowledge and norms of the Luo to their grandchildren, as had been practised down the years. Circumstances had transformed the relationship into a stricter 'parent–child like situation' that was not conducive to the cosy atmosphere of story-telling and conveying Luo mores in the *siwindhe*. Furthermore, some grandparents became emotionally disturbed, so that they hardly enjoyed the peace of mind necessary for story-telling. Thus, the traditional position of the old as providers of knowledge also came to be challenged in this fluid situation.

Conclusion

In this chapter, we have discussed how orphans shift physical and social places with changes in their fortunes within the community. The central theme in the construction of these places is the children's agency, which has been exhibited in the social interactions and relationships that have continuously changed. But this chapter has also presented cases where children's agency has been disempowered or severely limited by poverty, traditional structures, especially in respect of children's participation in public places of work, as well as circumstances leading to their changing physical places.

In terms of social place (position), new relationships materialise, for example, an elder sibling taking the position of the household head and catering for his or her younger siblings, or the redefinition of conventional relationships, such as the tie between a grandchild and a grandparent being recast from a traditional close and enjoyable bond to a child – parent-like relationship, with stronger disciplinary tensions. At the same time, orphans are forced to cater for themselves to a greater extent than before by adopting various sorts of income-generating activity. In this process they often assume greater independence and power, in disharmony with the ascribed roles and steep age hierarchies of former times. We expect that, as orphans develop new places for themselves, this may lead to a reconfiguration of the proper places for children and adults in society (Olwig and Gulløv, introduction).

Acknowledgements

The authors are indebted to the Institute of African Studies, University of Nairobi, for assistance in developing the proposal. Many thanks go to the Danish Bilharziasis Laboratory (DBL) for financial support, without which the fieldwork would not have been possible. Special thanks also go to the Kenyan–Danish Health Research Project (KEDAHR) for practical support and the people of Nyang'oma for their hospitality and willingness to participate in the study. We are also grateful to Dr Pia Haudrup Christensen, Professor Allison James and, not least, the two editors for their valuable input during the writing process.

References

Cohen, D. W. and E. S. Atieno-Odhiambo (1989) *Siaya: The Historical Anthropology of an African Landscape*. Nairobi: Heinemann Kenya; London: James Currey.

Evans-Pritchard, E. E. (1976) *Witchcraft, Oracles and Magic among the Azande*, Oxford: Oxford University Press.

Giddens, A. (1979) *Central Problems in Social Theory: Action, Structure and Contradiction in Social Analysis*. London: Macmillan.

Hauge, H. E. (1974) *Luo Religion and Folklore*. Oslo: Scandinavian University Books.

Holland, D., W. Lachicotte Jr., D. Skinner and C. Cain (1998) *Identity and Agency in Cultural Worlds*. Cambridge, MA: Harvard University Press.

Mbuya, P. (1965) *Luo Customs and Beliefs*. Kendu Bay: African Herald House.

Nyambedha, E. (2000) 'Support systems for orphaned children in Nyang'oma Sub-location, Bondo District, Western Kenya', unpublished MA Dissertation, Institute of African Studies, University of Nairobi.

Nyambedha, E. O., S. Wandibba and J. Aagaard-Hansen (2001) 'Policy implications of the inadequate support systems for orphans in western Kenya', *Health Policy* 58: 83–96.

—— (2003a) 'Changing patterns of orphan care due to the HIV epidemic in western Kenya', *Social Science and Medicine* 57(2): 301–11.

—— (2003b) '"Retirement lost": The new role of the elderly as carers for orphans in western Kenya', *Journal of Cross-Cultural Gerontology* 18(1): 31–48.

Ocholla-Ayayo, A. B. C. (1976) *Traditional Ideology and Ethics among the Southern Luo*. Uppsala: Scandinavian Institute of African Studies.

Ominde, S. H. (1952) *The Luo Girl: From Infancy to Marriage*. London: Macmillan.

Prout, A. (2000) 'Childhood bodies: Construction, agency and hybridity', in A. Prout (ed.) *The Body, Childhood and Society*. London: Macmillan, pp. 1–18.

Whisson, M. (1964) *Change and Challenge: A Study of the Social and Economic Changes Among the Luo*. Nairobi: Christian Council of Kenya.

Part III

Place as a source of belonging

Local communities, national identities, global relations

Sweet and bitter places

The politics of schoolchildren's orientation in rural Uganda

Lotte Meinert

The educational policies of the Ugandan state and its international donors are increasingly promoting the ruralisation of primary education with a view to equipping children with the skills relevant to sustainable, agriculture-based rural livelihoods. Faced with rural poverty and population pressure, policy-makers want to prepare children, through schooling, to improve rural living conditions and avoid the large-scale urbanisation that often goes along with urban poverty in sprawling slum areas in developing countries. On the other hand, rural children hope that going to school will eventually remove them from dependence on agriculture and thus improve their social status and life chances. In school, children learn to see themselves as citizens of a nation state and an international community, and some start longing to move away from their locality, its limitations and its horizons. Even though only a few families and children actually experience other family members enjoying urban success, urban places often come to symbolise children's hopes for the future and for another social status.

This chapter focuses on the conflict inherent in these different perspectives. In this tension, what role is the primary school intended to play, and what role do children experience the school to play in orienting them towards future places? How do place, social status and gender relate to each other in this conflict?

As Levinson and Holland point out on a more general note, 'schools interject an educational mission of extra-local proportions' (1996: 1), and modern schools may be among the most densely globalised institutions of our times. Yet what school means locally and where it is perceived to take people varies greatly (e.g. Lorimer, this volume; Niewenhuys, this volume). Schooling initiatives like the Universal Primary Education programme in Uganda build on 'modernisation theories', which assume that schools are the most significant institutions for promoting economic growth, development and modernisation in third-world countries (e.g. Inkeles 1974). However, as many scholars have pointed out, there are reasons for problematising this approach, because modernisation and education are not unidirectional, homogenising processes producing social leveling. Schooling systems often work as a conservative force reproducing class structures (Bourdieu and Passeron 1977) and other social inequalities. Education may advance some under-privileged groups economically, but at the same time it creates new hierarchies (Fuller 1991).

Anthropological studies have long shown that the politics of placing children in social space can be intense and that, in most societies, they have an outspokenly normative character. Some studies have shown how the placing of children is regarded as crucial in controlling and socialising new generations into social structures (Raum 1940; James *et al.* 1998: 38–9). Other studies have highlighted how place is central in creating what is regarded as 'proper childhoods' (Boyden 1997: 197–202; Niewenhuys this volume). A third approach shows how placing children is considered strategic in a socio-temporal perspective (Evans-Pritchard 1940: 247–56; Reynolds 1996: 6–7; Jenks 1996: 13–15; James and Prout 1997: 239–41). Relatively recently, anthropologists and other scholars have also started researching children's own perceptions and experiences of places, of being placed, and of placing themselves (e.g. Hart 1979; Olwig 1987; Halloway and Valentine 2000; Lidén 2000).

In this chapter I attempt to combine the latter two approaches, namely the socio-temporal approach and an experiential approach, by examining the intersection between larger-scale educational changes in Uganda and children's life-worlds. In particular, I discuss the contradictions between rural Ugandan children's striving for social mobility, including a life 'away from the village', and the Universal Primary Education programme that was introduced in 1997, which has doubled the enrolment of children in schools and promotes local farming in attempting to orient children towards a positive rural future. I argue that the school in Uganda has a pivotal role in orienting children towards different future places. However, due to the history and significance of schooling in Uganda, schools play a different role than that intended by policy-makers. At the same time, the well-intended, rational attempts of educational policy to direct schoolchildren towards rural agricultural futures are not welcomed in the local community I describe, where schooling is associated with the wider world, social mobility, urbanity and modernity.

Places of fieldwork

I describe and discuss the above-mentioned conflict on the basis of fieldwork conducted in 1997–8 among children in a rural area called Kwapa in eastern Uganda. I lived in this village for one year and followed a group of school-aged children (5 to 18 years) in their homes, schools and other places.[1] Later (2000–2) I returned to Uganda, staying in the capital, Kampala, but also paying frequent visits to Kwapa and other places where the children, teenagers and grown-ups now live, so as to follow their various life courses over a longer period of time. Some of those who were 'children' at the time of my earlier fieldwork now came to visit me in Kampala, providing opportunities to discuss livelihoods, life-chances and the limitations of different places. Here I draw mainly upon a series of interviews with children about their lives, education and future wishes held in Kwapa in 1997 and relate these to some of the stories they gave me in 2002.

Kwapa sub-county is part of Tororo District in eastern Uganda, which is considered to be a fertile part of the country, despite unpredictable rainfall. People depend mainly on subsistence farming, but although most crops can be harvested twice a year, the soil has been eroded, resulting in declining yields. The area is characteristically rural, but is still densely populated, with over 230 people per square kilometre (Kaharuza *et al.* 1998), and given the very high population growth rate (2.6 per cent) (Uganda Bureau of Statistics and ORC Macro 2001), families are experiencing having less and less land to feed more and more mouths. The unpredictability of the weather and prolonged dry seasons have resulted not only in periods of hunger, but also in feelings of uncertainty and frustration with agriculture.

Children participate in farming, herding and household activities in the family from an early age. Together with women, children do most of the agricultural work in the family. Their fathers own the land, and their mothers are commonly in charge of cultivating it. In some families, boys in their teens are given a small plot of their fathers' land to cultivate their own crops. Some older girls, especially in better-off families, are occasionally given a basket of millet from which they brew and sell beer. In this way, children contribute to the household economy and take care of some of their personal needs in respect of soap, clothes, exercise books and pencils.

The Iteso people who inhabit Kwapa sub-county have a reputation for brewing some of the best millet beer *(ajono)* in eastern Uganda, and beer-drinking is an important part of everyday social life, as well as of ritual occasions. However, alcoholism, especially among younger men, and the distilling of local alcohol *(waragi)* is perceived to be on the increase, with subsequent social problems and the breakdown of family and kinship ties. Kinship among the Iteso is patrilineal and virilocal, in which the children belong by definition to the father's clan, or more precisely to the man who has paid bridewealth for the woman who gave birth to them. Clan membership and family networks are important providers of social security and of access to resources. Clans are usually closely related to a piece of land named after the clan or lineage. As clans are exogamous and virilocal, boys learn that they will stay on that land, or at least have close ties, rights and responsibilities with and in the clan and on the land where they grow up. Girls, on the other hand, learn that they are supposed to leave their homes and join a different home when they marry, and they will give up their parental clan membership in favour of their new husband's clan. Being familiar with relatives, clan mates, their homesteads and pieces of land is considered a fundamental part of childhood socialisation.

Children are used to family networks stretching far distances, and it is not uncommon for children to go and live with relatives in another village or town for longer periods of time. In some cases children, especially girls, go and stay with busy and better-off relatives to help out with household chores. In other cases children are sent to stay with relatives because schooling possibilities are better or cheaper in the area. In fact schooling constitutes a major factor in child and youth migration in Uganda. Families who can afford the fees often choose to send their children to boarding schools, sometimes far from home. The quality of education in boarding schools and town schools is considered significantly better than that in 'village schools'. Furthermore parents often mention that it is good for children to have 'exposure to the outer world'.

Urbanisation, rural development and schooling

Uganda is still regarded as one of the least urbanised African countries, with an estimated 83 per cent of the population living in rural areas (Uganda Bureau of Statistics and ORC Macro 2001). Yet the gap between rich and poor is widening, which is an important reason why many young people are attracted to the towns and cities, where the symbols of modern wealth are concentrated. Urbanisation is believed to be increasing at an accelerating rate. It has been estimated that, by the year 2015, 27 per cent of the population in Uganda will be living in urban areas (Uganda Bureau of Statistics 2001), even though small-scale farming in rural areas is being imagined as the backbone, and future, of the Ugandan economy. Policy-makers are alarmed by this prospect and are therefore attempting to counteract urbanisation with development programmes in rural areas. Agricultural modernisation and rural trans-formation are regarded as crucial in eradicating poverty, in building the national economy and for security in the country (Ministry of Finance 1998). However, resources for and interests in rural development are evidently not sufficient to change the situation in the countryside to an extent that attracts younger generations into wishing to stay there. A programme for the modernisation of agriculture, followed by a change in the primary-school curriculum to focus on improving agriculture, are examples of initiatives that aim to develop rural areas as productive and attractive and to prevent urbanisation. Yet many young people living in rural areas are less optimistic than the policy-makers that this will actually change living conditions and life opportunities for the next generation in these areas.

Poverty is bitter

During my fieldwork, and when following some of the children from Kwapa in the years thereafter, I was often struck by their desire to move away from the village when they grew up, their eagerness to go to a school in town, and their hopes that this would change their lives and future possibilities. At the same time, they also wished to come back to the village and build a house for their family, which would also be a status symbol demonstrating their wealth. My subsequent visit and the conversations held then induced me to reflect on how children and young people in rural Uganda come to imagine that life in town is better, and how government initiatives are trying to counteract this tendency.

When I first met Orieba, he was 16 years old and was about to finish his primary education in the nearby village school. He was then determined to go to secondary school and hoped the family could afford to send him to town to study. However, neither the finances nor the exam results allowed Orieba to go to a school in town, so he had to continue in the secondary part of the village school, of lower cost and standard. After a year he dropped out due to what he described as 'lack of fees and too many problems'.[2] When I asked him why he did not return to the village school to finish his studies, he replied:

> I am not going back to a school here in the village. The conditions are really harsh. I want to go to a boarding school in town, if my family can afford it. Then of course if I get good results, and fees are there, I want to get a course and find a job in town. Life in town is sweeter. . . . If you get stranded here in the village, you will work very hard, but life is just bitter.[3]

It is undeniable that life in rural eastern Uganda is marked by poverty, seasonal food shortages, land shortages and high rates of illness and death for the majority of people living there. However, labour migration from this area to the capital has been relatively low, and it is rare that someone who has gone to town to seek prosperity comes back satisfied. Orieba's older brother, who finished secondary school, left the village many years ago to look for a job in the capital, but has still not been very successful. Occasionally Orieba goes to visit his brother to ask for financial help for the family, only to return empty-handed to report the brother saying that he has nothing. Yet Orieba appears to be impressed with the urban life-style and, like his brother, he hopes that he will one day have the luck to taste some of the 'sweetness of town'.

In order to understand this vision of a better life in town, which is shared not only by Orieba and his brother, but also by many children and young people in Kwapa, let us look at the perceived links between place and prosperity, and the significance of schooling and discourses of modernity in this link, via a brief historical digression.

Seeking wealth

Wealth in this part of Uganda is perceived as multiplex and includes land, cattle, children, health and social networks, as well as consumer goods such as radios, bicycles, and cars (Meinert 2001: 122–4). The kinds of wealth that can be bought for money usually come from the nearby towns, the capital, Kampala, or abroad. To obtain 'smart looking things from other places' in honest ways, one needs to have trade skills or a salaried job, for which a formal school background is one of the prerequisites. The importance attributed to schooling in Kwapa is closely related to religion, modernity and wealth, and has strong historical roots. The first formal schools to be established in the area as part of colonisation at the start of the last century were catechist training centres aiming at Christianising and civilising the population. Those who became 'Christian readers' were given special privileges in the colonial structure and opportunities to acquire wealth. Since then, the school, closely tied to the Church, has been one of the major motors of modernity and nation-building in Uganda. By going to school, children aim to be regarded as 'proper, modern, and religious citizens' and hope to be able to advance in wealth and social mobility by eventually getting a job.

What Whyte writes about the neighbouring Nyole is probably valid for much of rural Uganda:

> Religion and education form important parts of Nyole people's lives and sense of themselves in the context of modern Uganda. To be a citizen of the nation is to be a 'reader', to share in the universalist values of the religion of the book. But religion and reading have more specific relations to the pursuit of prosperity; parents hope that education will help their children not to be totally dependent on the hoe.
>
> (1997: 44)

According to the older generation of teachers in Kwapa, education was 'the key to success'[4] in the old days. Individuals who had been to school and had a formal education were able to obtain jobs as civil servants in town, where they found prosperity, and some of them came back to 'develop the home'. A handful of families in Kwapa served as prototypes in the entire community for the success of education. They assumed the position of a local elite who had invested in children's education by sending them away to urban boarding schools, and later receiving returns in the form of wealth. Children and young people who had gone to urban educational institutions and developed urban connections became a national kind of 'been-to' in Hannerz' words (1992: 228–31), who had better chances to claim positions of privilege in social structures both locally and nationally.[5] With this development, the majority of children from Kwapa who stayed in the village were increasingly being categorised derogatively as backward village kids, associated with the primitive and the 'bush'.

Most families in Kwapa tried to send at least some of their children to school, even rural schools. But with the relatively high school fees, before the Universal Primary Education programme was introduced in 1997, many children dropped out before they finished primary school. Children who stopped schooling after primary level or only had a few years of primary schooling were commonly regarded as 'failures', because the education system was geared towards advancement to the next academic level and ultimately obtaining a salaried appointment.[6]

The political crises in Uganda of the 1970s and 1980s brought predatory regimes to power, including that of Idi Amin. During this period, the functioning of the state was severely undermined and the economy wrecked by civil war and conflict. After this period, education did not automatically provide people with jobs and material success. Teachers in Kwapa said that this had made some parents lose confidence in education, so that they kept their children at home. Yet the popularity of registering children for the free Universal Primary Education programme in the late 1990s strongly indicates that people again assume that primary education is worthwhile. Most of the rural poor regard obtaining free access to schooling a life chance in Dahrendorf's sense[7] (1979), which cannot be dismissed, even though parents are aware that the dream of obtaining a job might not materialise for the majority of students. But many parents still hope that their own children will be 'the lucky ones' to advance through the schooling system and ultimately find a job.

Success in a person's educational life is defined by the ability to proceed in the system from primary to secondary school and so forth, and thus move away from the local, rural environment into paid employment and be able to return to, or at least pay visits to, the rural home 'with something' (money or consumer goods). With education, people hope to be able to tap into the resources of modernity that they see as flowing from the urban centres.

Schooling: a life chance, or a moral, rural trap?

Pushed by the Structural Adjustment Programme (SAPRI 2001) and President Museveni's election campaigns, universal primary education was launched in Uganda in 1997. The government pointed out that the universalisation of primary education was presently the chief priority of the education sector (GOU 1997). The rationale for this priority is the SAP-fuelled belief that an 'early, high share of spending on high quality primary education accelerates economic growth and poverty alleviation' (GOU 1997: 28). Through access to and equity in primary schooling, the government hopes to 'enhance jobs and income-generating opportunities for the poorer families and help better income-distribution and overall well-being' (ibid.). However, the Universal Primary Education programme and the new focus on agriculture have not yet worked as intended, and problems that are well known from other African countries that have implemented Universal Primary Education programmes are now becoming obvious in Uganda as well.

With a point of departure in the Zambian experience of universal primary education, Serpell sharply criticises these programmes:

> The project of 'universal primary education' has captured the imagination of politicians and social planners in many if not all nations in the Third World in the twentieth century. Yet the project is confronted with a moral trap. . . . Stated in its simplest form, the trap is for the school to find itself in the business of producing failures.
>
> (1993: 10)

This is because the majority of children who start primary school do not, for a combination of reasons, make it through the system into secondary school, which is a minimum criterion for success. The trap Serpell describes lies in the structure of the system of formal education: children are structurally squeezed out of school but perceive themselves as 'failures who did not have the brains'.

In Uganda a moral educational trap also lies partly in the structure of the education system, because only a minority of pupils will be able to find a place in a secondary school, even though universal secondary education is being planned. Moreover, it is also experienced as an existential and rural trap for some children, because the morality and competences that schooling aims at promoting do not rhyme well with children's wishes for their future.

Children in Kwapa do not go to school with the aim of becoming better farmers. Instead, they hope that, by going to school, they will have a chance to move away from the village, like Ochuna, 15 years old, who said in conversation about his future:

> When I finish primary school, I want to continue straight in secondary school. I cannot stay in the village, it is so difficult and boring. Maybe I will start in Asinge [a village secondary school] and then later my brother can take me to another school in town. I will try to save some of my cotton money [from the cotton harvest] for school fees, because I know my father cannot afford this. He is just a poor farmer. [. . .] For me, I have seen that with farming you will just stay poor even if you

work very hard. I will study hard to become a businessman who can move in town to buy and sell things.

School is experienced by some young people as a place of hypocrisy. Historically it has promoted the 'modern way of life', making young people long for further education and a life in town, yet with time it has become increasingly obvious to rural populations that most children will not have access to this. Paradoxically, when the Ministry of Education in Uganda started promoting vocational education and focusing on agriculture and local development to make education relevant to children's rural lives, many young people felt that they were being lured into a trap which was meant to keep them in the rural areas, depriving them of the 'sweet life' in towns, which those who already had a job were wanting to keep to themselves. The following is an excerpt from a conversation with a boy from one of the local primary schools about favourable and less favourable subjects in school.

Lotte: Why do you say you hate agriculture?
Peter: Because they make us go to the garden and dig.
Lotte: Why is that bad?
Peter: Because we have already been digging at home and it is a very tiresome job.
Lotte: But don't they teach you to do better farming which will not be as tiresome?
Peter: Heh, (laughing) yes, about improved seeds, adding fertiliser and that, but we don't have those things here, so digging is still just hard.
Lotte: Why do you think the Ministry of Education want to teach you agriculture?
Peter: I also don't know. Maybe they just want to punish us for no reason. They want us to become farmers just and keep the nice jobs and things in town for themselves.

Pupils, parents and many local teachers were unenthusiastic about agricultural lessons in school for different reasons. Pupils like Peter did not see the point in practical cultivation in school because it was no different from farming at home, and they felt it was a way of directing their education towards rural lives, which they expected to be poor and 'bitter'. Parents considered garden work in school to be a punishment for pupils who had committed a crime, because manual tasks have usually been used in schools for disciplinary purposes. The following incident in one primary school shows how agricultural work in school is considered a punishment, and how it often creates conflicts in terms of who will harvest the fruits of the work.

One morning, as I was watching a class having a practical lesson on how to plant sweet potatoes (a skill that most people in the area obviously already have), one parent came by and saw his daughter working in the school field. He quickly walked up to the teacher and asked him why he was punishing all these children. When the teacher replied that it was not a punishment but part of the new agricultural lessons, the father frowned and said he did not see what new things they were learning, adding crossly that he hoped that the potatoes would taste bitter on the teacher's tongue.

Suspicion and mistrust of teachers did not characterise school–parent relationships in Kwapa in relation to agricultural lessons alone. Teachers had long had access to children's labour as a form of payment for the lessons. This was more or less tolerated by parents and children because teachers often had to wait for their very modest salaries, if they received them at all. However, after the intensive promotion of universal primary education as free of charge and the policy that no child could be sent away from school, parents and children resisted the exploitation of children's labour to a greater degree. Parents did not see 'garden work' as part of the new educational programme, but rather as a continuation of old forms of punishment and labour exploitation.

'We don't want local skills': resistance to ruralisation

The hope of achieving social mobility through schooling adds strength to the traditional academic focus in Ugandan schools on obtaining good exam results in order to pass on to the next level of the school system. A revolution in education away from academic learning and 'the diploma disease' towards 'vocationalisation', as proposed by the Education Commission of 1989 (Kajubi 1991) and several initiatives since then, obviously faces obstacles.

Some of the discrepancies between local and national ambitions with respect to school education became clear to me in a seminar on universal primary education and 'basic education' held by the District Inspector of Schools for head-teachers and school-management committees in Kwapa sub-county in May 1997. The inspector's objective in holding the meeting was to promote the idea of 'basic education as minimum learning needs for the survival and benefit of the local communities'. He emphasised that basic education should 'focus on skills, and not on academic knowledge'. 'Negative attitudes to manual labour and children's wishes to stay in towns and migrate to other places was a problem', he said, and so was 'children's lack of values for caring for public and private property'. Continuing his moral tale, the inspector instructed teachers to educate 'job-makers, and not job-takers in this country'. On the other hand, when participants from the schools were asked to voice their expectations to the meeting, their first concern was to improve their knowledge of the academic subjects in the syllabus, especially in the sciences.

The paradoxical discourses in this meeting are characteristic of the current dynamics in the education sector in Uganda: planners, represented by the inspector, who are interested in education on a national and strategic level, argue for a focus on local skills. Teachers and management committees are concerned about education from a local tactical level, where parents and children are striving for academic knowledge in order to get away from the local skills and 'minimum learning needs for survival'. From the planners' point of view, 'local skills' are regarded as empowering local people. From teachers' and parents' point of view, the focus on local skills is interpreted more like a degradation, depriving people of the hope that education can take them away from local miseries and provide opportunities for economic and social mobility.

The 'ruralisation' and 'vocationalisation' of the image of the educated person as suggested by Ugandan school programmes were not appreciated locally, and teaching practices did not seem to change for both practical and ideological reasons.[8] The local cultures of schooling keep stressing academic learning and the importance of 'looking proper' and 'smart' in a school uniform, as opposed to the image of the dirty 'village child' or 'primitive farmer', because the school is still regarded as a place that prepares children for a non-rural, modern future. It is striking how these differently situated national and local discourses on the future place of children slip past each other without further notice or discussion.

Gendered placing

Although Kwapa children's ambitions about their place in the future are similar in many ways, a more differentiated analysis can be attempted. Looking more carefully at the conversations I had with children about their futures, gender, age and social class emerge as important factors in shaping children's urban or rural orientations. Some of the gender differences are clear from the following excerpts.

Emejje Steven is 16 years old, goes to primary school and comes from a family that he describes as neither poor nor rich. He says about his future wishes: 'I want to become a doctor: if I study very hard, I want to open a clinic in town so that I can help people when they are sick. Later, if there is money, I can also open a clinic here in the village and help the relatives here'.

Amusugut Grace is 9 years old, attends class three and comes from one of the poorer families in the village. She said about her future: 'I want to study and become a teacher in my area. [. . .] I wish to marry a kind man from here who can help the family.'

Muruga Godfrey is 14 years old and goes to class six in the village school. His father is in the army and his mother does the farming in their home. About his future he said: 'I want to continue schooling from Kampala and become a policeman or an engineer. I also want to build a house in the village for my mother when I grow up.'

Olusa John is 13 years old and attends class five; he lives with his mother and siblings in a small house, as his father has left the family. When I asked him about his future wishes, he replied: 'In the future I don't wish anything because I don't know if I will be able to complete my studies or not. [. . .] If I don't finish my studies I will just have to remain here in the village like that'.

Dorothy is 16 years old, goes to a secondary boarding school in town, and comes from one of the wealthier homes in Kwapa. She said about her future plans:

> I am serious in school because I want to go all the way to university. I want to become a doctor or a lawyer [. . .] and I wish to have a husband who is well-educated, and who is not yet married to another woman. I don't want to live in a polygamous home. There are too many problems. But I will not marry until after school. I want to become rich, so that I can help the needy, my sisters, brothers, the parents and grandparents. I would like to be able to pay for some of my sisters' and brothers' education and if possible build a good hospital and a school for them in the village.

It was noticeable, not only in these interviews with children about their hopes and wishes for the future, but throughout conversations during my fieldwork, that boys' visions of their future always included further education, and almost always involved a journey, if not a permanent move to town. Girls also wished keenly for more schooling in urban centres, but after that they mostly desired to enter a monogamous marriage with an educated man from a wealthy and friendly home. Girls in most families in Kwapa are socialised and recognised as successful in the community if they manage to finish primary school, get married to a (potentially) wealthy man and have children. Girls are brought up knowing that when they marry they will go to their husband's family home, and that will be the place of their future. They hope that the general economic status of the new home will be better than where they come from. However, they also know that the status of a daughter-in-law, which they will acquire by marrying, is a relatively low one. Many girls also hope that, by staying in the vicinity of their parental home, they will be able to receive moral support from there and to redistribute some of the wealth they hope to have access to from their new families. A couple of girls from better-off families said that they wished to stay in town when they married, away from their in-laws, in order to avoid the everyday burdens and conflicts of being a daughter-in-law.

In Tanzania, Stambach describes similar strategies among young women, referring to so-called 'city-sisters' who orient themselves towards an urban and independent life, as opposed to becoming stay-at-home mothers (2000: 187ff.; 2000: 61ff.). In Uganda too, it is remarkable that young people's desires to place themselves in an urban or rural context are not only part of generational change, but are also intersected with – perhaps mainly young girls' – wishes for changes in gender and kinship relations.

As they grow up in Kwapa, boys know the status of their families' home, which is supposed to be their future home as well in this patrilineal and virilocal system. Boys are allotted a piece of their fathers' land, usually near the homestead, to live on and cultivate with their future families. If they do not see much opportunity or future in their paternal home – and many do not, due to shortage of land – the longing for town and other avenues to prosperity increases.

With few exceptions, the gender aspects of the educational anthropology of the developing world have tended to focus on the importance of girls' education (Bloch et al. 1998; Anderson-Levitt et al. 1998; Stromquist 1998; Stambach 2000). However, as we have seen here, schooling in Kwapa may work in different ways in terms of boys' and girls' aspirations to placing themselves, and not least for the urge of educated boys' to go to town or their feelings of being failures.

Longing for a different place; longing for a different social status

The gender differences in children's wishes for their future lives indicate that the importance attributed to location is overruled by the importance attributed to status. This resonates well with the words of the geographer Yi-Fu Tuan, cited in the introduction to this book: 'the primary meaning of place is one's position in society rather than the more abstract understanding of location in space' (1974: 233, cited in Olwig and Gulløv, this volume). When children and young people in Kwapa long to go and live in town, they may be attracted by the specific features of these places, but more importantly they are longing for a different position in society.

There has been a longstanding debate over where schooling leads people, and what schooling means for children's spatial orientation is discussed in many of the newer educational ethnographies and anthropologies of migration, as well as in two other chapters of this book, which I would like to discuss briefly. In a study of the Caribbean island of Nevis, Olwig shows how children orient themselves outwards to relatives living overseas, towards out-migration and professional futures beyond the island, despite the schools' and other political attempts to orient future generations towards the island, the nation and local agriculture. Nevisian children have a negative impression of the relative economic value of local agriculture as opposed to migratory work, and in general agriculture has low social prestige in Nevis. For this reason, the school systems' attempts with agriculture fail (1987). From this Nevisian study, it is clear that factors beyond the school strongly influence where children and their families orient themselves.

This is also an important point in Lorimer's study (this volume). She shows how Kuku-Yalanji children in Australia try to make sense of school by moving between their homes, relatives and schools in their attempts to weave a social support net. Based on children's varying school attendance, the school may seem to play a peripheral role in these children's lives. However, this is necessarily so because schools are placed outside Aboriginal communities, where children do their 'place-making' in order to belong to them in the future. Here, schools do not seem to play the role of orienting children towards mainstream society: rather they appear to reproduce the Aboriginal category as outside Australian society. In a similar vein, using Augé's concept of non-place, Nieuwenhuys (this volume) describes government schools in Poomkara, India, as 'non-places' of childhood in the sense that these schools do not help children to build the necessary social relations and identities that will benefit them in the future. It is noteworthy that in these two studies the significance of schooling appears to have been studied from a perspective outside the schools themselves. From a study perspective inside school, the institution may take on different meanings for children. From a study based in both school and community, Levinson shows how secondary schools in Mexico are important places of identity work and are used to create social relations that are perceived to help students beyond the school (1996: 211–32).

What is striking from these different studies is the variety of meanings schooling is perceived to have for children's social mobility and future possibilities or limitations in local, national and international arenas.

I agree with scholars who argue that the influence of schooling is significantly absent in many anthropological studies, and yet school penetrates (or attempts to penetrate) everyday life in ways that few other state institutions can, provoking (successfully or not) individuals, families and communities to structure expectations and practices according to specific temporal patterns and socio-spatial horizons (Levinson and Holland 1996; Levinson 1996, 1999). However, as we have seen here, factors beyond the school also orient children temporally and socio-spatially. What is interesting is how schooling plays together with other social, historical and political factors and institutions that mould people's identities, possibilities and orientations, and how schooling works in different ways for different persons.

The glimpses I have presented here of children's hopes with schooling and place in eastern Uganda and national schooling initiatives illustrate that large-scale attempts to place and direct children for the future often do not have the outcomes anticipated. School plays a significant role in Ugandan families' endeavours, but the Universal Primary Education programme in Uganda and the attempts to ruralise the curriculum have taken on their own meanings in children's lives in Kwapa. In the conflict between rural and urban ambitions, the primary school becomes an ambiguous place because it is intended to prepare pupils for rural futures, but rural teachers and parents do not appear to support these intentions. Instead they keep promoting schooling as a place that prepares children for white-collar jobs, upward mobility and thus, in effect, urban futures.

Divergences in Uganda about *where* school education should be leading children are clearly part of a political game that has international, national and local stakeholders. Each category wishes to influence the future by directing children to certain places 'for children's own good' as well as 'for the common good'. These stakeholders' perspectives vary greatly from political concerns about urbanisation and economic growth, development and equity, to local families' experiences with poverty and hopes not to be entirely dependent on agriculture in the future, young boys' longing to taste some of the 'sweetness of town', and young girls hoping to improve their social status while still being able to visit, and return some wealth to, their families.

Acknowledgements

The fieldwork on which part of this chapter is based was made possible by a grant from the Council for Research in Developing Countries under the Danish International Development Agency, and it was also supported by the Danish Bilharziasis Laboratory.

I am grateful to the editors of this volume, as well as to Michael Whyte and Anton Baaré, for their useful comments in the process of writing the paper.

Notes

1 For an in-depth description and discussion of methods and methodology, see Meinert 2001: 23–48.
2 One of the problems he was facing was that he had impregnated a girl, which is considered a reason for expulsion from school. Boys are usually allowed to stay in school, but with a recent 'defilement law' in Uganda, young boys have become particularly vulnerable. If a man or a boy has sex with a girl under 18 years he can be prosecuted for committing a capital offence. At present the great majority of inmates in prisons and remand homes are there for 'defilement'. Most of these young boys and men are accused of impregnating young girls, while the girls' families often hope to be able to negotiate economic compensation. Paradoxically, what was meant to protect young girls is turning out to act against both young girls and boys.
3 Metaphors of sweetness and bitterness are common in Uganda. In Kwapa old people described the times of war and Amin's regimes as bitter in a

metaphorical as well as a literal sense because there was suffering and loss and also no sugar to buy. Another example from more recent times, when people are discussing abstinence as a form of AIDS prevention, is the saying: 'Love without sex is like tea without sugar'; consequently some relationships are described as 'just bitter'.

4 'Education is the key to success' is a popular motto of primary schools in Uganda. In some schools mottos are written in large letters on the buildings.

5 The rural home, family and kinship context is still an important nexus for people who migrate to towns. It is in the rural home that people strive for recognition for being modern, having been to town, and being successful, helpful and wealthy.

6 The proportion of boys completing primary school (class 7) fell from 90 per cent in the mid-1980s to 35 per cent in the mid-1990s. The completion rate for girls dropped from 50 per cent to 25 per cent over the same period (GOU 1997: 3).

7 Dahrendorf describes life chances as 'more than the total sum of opportunities offered to the individual by his society, or by a more specific position occupied in society' (1979: 28). 'Life chances are opportunities for individual action arising from the interrelations of options and ligatures. Both options and ligatures are dimensions of social structure, that is they are given as elements of social roles rather than as random objects of people's will of whim' (ibid.: 34).

8 Rockwell describes a similar reaction in schooling programmes in rural Mexico and points out that 'teachers fashioned a practice that did not wholly resemble the official mandate. Rather it was a blend of their knowledge of local custom and language, the pedagogical common sense they had inherited from their childhood mentors, and a progressive outlook they had absorbed during official training. The mixture of these educational uses and meanings was what actually shaped the local cultures of schooling' (1996: 317).

References

Anderson-Levitt, K. M., M. Bloch and A.M. Soumaré (1998) 'Inside classrooms in Guinea: Girls' experiences', in M. Bloch, J. A. Beoku-Betts and B. R. Tabachnick (eds) Women and Education in Sub-saharan Africa: Power, Opportunities, and Constraints. Boulder and London: Lynne Rienner Publishers, pp. 99–130.

Bloch, M., J. A. Beoku-Betts and B. R. Tabachnick (eds) (1998) Women and Education in Sub-saharan Africa: Power, Opportunities, and Constraints. Boulder and London: Lynne Rienner Publishers.

Bourdieu, P. and J.-C. Passeron (1977) Reproduction in Education, Society and Culture. Beverly Hills: Sage.

Boyden, J. (1997) 'Childhood and the policymakers: A comparative perspective in the globalization of childhood', in A. James and A. Prout (eds) Constructing and Reconstructing Childhood. London and Washington, DC: Falmer Press, pp. 190–229.

Dahrendorf, R. (1979) Life Chances. Chicago: University of Chicago Press.

Evans-Pritchard, E. E. (1940) The Nuer: A Description of the Modes of Livelihood and Political Institutions of a Nilotic People. New York and Oxford: Oxford University Press.

Fuller, B. (1991) Growing up Modern: The Western State Builds Third World Schools. New York and London: Routledge.

GOU (Government of Uganda) (1997) *Education Strategic Investment Plan 1997–2003: Strategic and Programme Framework*. Kampala: Education Planning Department, Ministry of Education.

Halloway, S. and G. Valentine (eds) (2000) *Children's Geographies*. London and New York: Routledge.

Hannerz, U. (1992) *Cultural Complexity: Studies in the Social Organization of Meaning*. New York: Columbia University Press, pp. 217–67.

Hart, R. (1979) *Children's Participation: The Theory and Practice of Involving Young Citizens in Community Development and Environmental Care*. London: Earthscan.

Inkeles, A. (1974) 'The school as a context for modernisation', in A. Inkeles and D. B. Holsinger (eds): *Education and Individual Modernity in Developing Countries*. Leiden: E. J. Brill, pp. 7–23.

James, A. and A. Prout (1997) 'Representing childhood: Time and transition in the study of childhood', in A. James and A. Prout (eds) *Constructing and Reconstructing Childhood*. London and Washington, DC: Falmer Press, pp. 230–50.

James A., C. Jenks and A. Prout (1998) *Theorising Childhood*. Cambridge: Polity Press.

Jenks, C. (1996) 'The postmodern child', in J. Brannen and M. O'Brien (eds) *Children and Families: Research and Policy*. London: Falmer Press.

Kaharuza F., D. Bagenda, F. Scheutz and S. Sabroe (1998) *The Maternal and Child Health Baseline Survey Report*. Tororo Community Health (TORCH). Kampala: Child Health and Development Centre.

Kajubi, W. S. (1991) 'Educational reform during socio-economic crisis', in H. B. Hansen and M. Twaddle (eds) *Changing Uganda*. London, Kampala, Athens and Nairobi: James Currey, pp. 322–33.

Levinson, B. A. (1996) 'Social difference and schooled identity at a Mexican *secundaria*', in B. A. Levinson, D. E. Foley and D. Holland (eds) *The Cultural Production of the Educated Person: Critical Ethnographies of Schooling and Local Practices*. Albany: State University of New York Press.

—— (1998) 'Resituating the place of educational discourse in anthropology', *American Anthropologist* 101(3): 594–604.

Levinson, B. A. and D. Holland (1996) 'The cultural production of the educated person', in B. A. Levinson, D. E. Foley and D. Holland (eds) *The Cultural Production of the Educated Person: Critical Ethnographies of Schooling and Local Practices*. Albany: State University of New York Press.

Lidén, H. (2000) 'Barn – tid – rom –skiftende posisjoner. Kulturelle læreprocesser i et pluralistisk Norge', Dr. Polit avhandling. Fakultet for samfundsvitenskap og teknologiledelse. Socialantropologisk institutt. Trondheim: NTNU.

Meinert, L. (2001) 'The quest for a good life. Health and education among children in Eastern Uganda', Ph.D. Thesis, Institute of Anthropology, University of Copenhagen.

Ministry of Finance, Planning and Economic Development (1998) *Vision 2025, Prosperous People, Harmonious Nation, Beautiful Country: A Strategic Framework for National Development*. Kampala: Ministry of Finance, Planning and Economic Development.

Olwig, K. F. (1987) 'Children's attitudes to the island community: The aftermath of out-migration on Nevis', in Jean Besson and Janet Momsen (eds) *Land and*

Development in the Caribbean. Warwick University Caribbean Studies. London: Macmillan Caribbean, pp. 153–70.

Raum, O. F. (1967 [1940]) *Chaga Childhood: A Description of Indigenous Education in an East African Tribe*. New York: Oxford University Press.

Reynolds, P. (1996) *Traditional Healers and Childhood in Zimbabwe*. Athens, OH: Ohio University Press.

SAPRI (Structural Adjustment Participatory Review Initiative) (20 May 2001) Report of the information team on World Bank-supported structural adjustment programmes in Uganda. The National Steering Committee of the structural adjustment participatory initiative. http://www.worldbank.org/research/sapri/uganda/forum.htm

Serpell, R. (1993) *The Significance of Schooling: Life Journeys in an African Society*. Cambridge: Cambridge University Press.

Stambach, A. (2000) *Lessons from Kilimanjaro: Schooling, Community and Gender in East Africa*. New York and London: Routledge.

Stromquist, N. (1998) 'Agents in women's education: Some trends in the African context', in M. Bloch, J. A. Beoku-Betts and B. R. Tabachnick (eds) *Women and Education in Sub-saharan Africa: Power, Opportunities, and Constraints*. Boulder and London: Lynne Rienner Publishers, pp. 25–46.

Taun Y.-F. (1974) 'Space and place: Humanistic perspective', *Progress in Geography* 6: 211–52.

Uganda Bureau of Statistics and ORC Macro (2001) *Uganda Demographic and Health Survey 2000–2001*. Calverton: UBOS and ORC Macro.

Whyte, S. R. (1997) *Questioning Misfortune: The Pragmatics of Uncertainty in Eastern Uganda*. Cambridge: Cambridge University Press.

Chapter 10

'Imagined communities'

The local community as a place for 'children's culture' and social participation in Norway

Anne Trine Kjørholt

Introduction

> My name is Toralf Petersen, and I am 8 years old. I attend second
> grade in Strandvik school. I want to start a club. This club is about
> drawing, painting, books, carpentry, sewing, trips and much more.
> All these things Bird Island can take part in.

This text is an excerpt from an application addressed to the administrative
authorities in a town in northern Norway. The 8-year-old boy is living on
Bird Island, an island with approximately 1,100 inhabitants about 50 km
from the town where the municipal administration is located. Toralf
wanted public funding to start a club in the small local community where
he was living. He wanted to take part in a participatory project for
children and young people run by the Norwegian Council for Cultural
Affairs in eleven different municipalities in Norway in the early 1990s. The
main aim of the project, called Try Yourself, was to empower children as
social participants in their local communities. By providing the children
with funding for cultural activities that they had developed themselves, the
project was intended to give them the opportunity to act on their own in
society. The emphasis on 'children's own culture' was a key aspect of the
project. As noted by the initiator, the main aim of the project was: '. . . to
give children status based on their own qualifications and needs, and to
promote children's own culture' (The Norwegian Council for Cultural
Affairs 1988: 2).

The formulations on Toralf's application form illustrate how brilliantly
he manages the text genre of 'public applications'. He addresses the letter
correctly to the cultural administration in the municipality, he presents
himself by name, and he elaborates on his idea about the planned project.
In conclusion, he informs the authorities of his own postal address, where
they can send their reply.

The text may be interpreted as an illustration of how Toralf positions
himself and creates an identity as a kind of 'fellow citizen'[1] in his local
community. He is thus placing himself in contemporary and powerful

discourses on 'children and participation,' which are prevalent within Norwegian child policy and construct children as autonomous subjects with particular participation rights in society. Since the early 1990s, many participatory projects aimed at realising children's and youths' rights to have a say in matters that affect their everyday lives have been launched in Norway by public authorities, NGOs and others placed at various levels of society, including the national, regional and, in particular, local level of society. These projects have been carried out in different places – for instance in leisure organisations, schools, city halls and 'community buildings' – and within community settings in general (Kjørholt 2002).

The focus of this chapter is the local community as a site for children's social participation within a participatory project entitled Try Yourself. On the one hand, I examine how the discourses on children as autonomous subjects with particular rights of participation in society that informed the project placed children in the local community and enabled their actual participation as citizens in society. On the other hand, I investigate how, through their texts on application forms and the social practices they developed, the children contributed to creating new *places of visibility for children* in public spaces, in the process inscribing themselves as social participants in their local communities in new ways. In doing so, I argue, children also reaffirmed narratives about the local community as a power-ful symbolic place of belonging, equality and democratic participation. The children and the project Try Yourself thus contributed to revitalising particular Norwegian notions of localities as 'imagined communities' (Anderson 1983; Rose 1995) of equal, autonomous subjects. However, by focusing on children's communicated experiences as participants in the project, I also wish to discuss certain paradoxes and contradictions that are connected with the realisation of the particular construction of 'children as social participants' that is embedded in the project. My analysis is empirically grounded in texts about the different ideas for projects formul-ated by children in their applications for Try Yourself, as well as in semi-structured, individual interviews that I carried out with them in connection with an evaluation of the project. The interviews had a narrative approach, aimed at letting children tell stories about their ideas and social practices as participants in the project. I shall here focus in particular on narratives related by two girls, Guro and Line, aged 10 and 11 at the time.

Local community as a social and cultural landscape

Local communities are often regarded as important places for adults' and children's everyday lives. The concept of place, in this sense of the term, does not refer to a physical and fixed entity, but to socially constructed entities committed to multiple meanings. Rodman (1992: 641) asserts that places 'have multiple meanings that are constructed spatially' in the course of social relations and practices. She notes that: Places are not inert containers. They are politised, culturally relative, historically specific local and multiple constructions (ibid.).

The concept of local community is a good example of the socially and culturally constructed nature of place. Thus the term entails a certain ambiguity concerning the particular combination of the two terms 'local' and 'community'. As Olwig notes (2000), the term 'local community' often refers to an implicit idea that a specific physical place coincides with a particular social group sharing the same cultural values and notion of place. All local populations, however, will vary internally according to such factors as age, gender and social position, and they will accordingly have different experiences, and related notions, of local community. Olwig therefore suggests that studies of local communities need to consider how different forms of life experiences lead to the emergence of specific conceptions of local community connoted with particular cultural meaning. She argues especially for a focus on how, through their social practices, children develop different notions of place, in the process contributing to the reconstruction of local communities.

Whereas 'place' often refers to practices and relationships that define a specific physical and geographical locality or area, the concept of *space* refers to the spatial location and extent of social relations. Through the particular meaning that is ascribed to space, we can say that new places are created that are not necessarily restricted to physical places, but rather to spaces that are given a new symbolic meaning. Instead of being rooted in a specific and geographically defined locality, place is given a spatial dimension. What identifies the place is therefore not its physical limits, but the symbolic and cultural meaning that can be identified as a particular 'place in space'. Based on this, one could also argue that local communities today do not refer to definite physical localities, but are rather places with fluid, flexible and changing boundaries, identified through symbolic and cultural meanings.

From the perspective of discourse theory, local communities are places constituted by discourses. By the term discourse, I do not just mean speech and text in a narrow sense. Using Michel Foucault as a reference point, I conceive of discourses as including social practices and materiality. According to Foucault, space is discursively constructed and can be described as a history of the spatial distribution of power and knowledge. Places are then also places for different subject positions (Foucault 1972). Analyses of the meaning of different places in a Foucaultian perspective therefore include historical analyses of social processes connected to power and knowledge in which places and spaces are given meaning. These processes allow for certain actions, subject positions and social practices, while prohibiting others.

Narrating local community

Place is more than location and more than the spatial index of socio-economic status: it also refers to one's position in society (Tuan 1974). Although a particular place comes into being through social practices, places are also constituted through texts in a more narrow sense, through written and spoken words. Tuan argues that 'speech is a curious gap in the extensive literature on place', and he asserts that it is important to focus on how places are constructed through spoken and written words (Tuan 1991: 684). Narratives and texts become increasingly important as constitutive of places. Furthermore, places are described as narratives:

> In this sense, places not only feature in inhabitants' (and geographers') narratives, they are narratives in their own right: a place comes explicitly into being in the discourse of its inhabitants and particularly in the rhetoric it promotes.
>
> (Berdoulay 1989: 135, quoted in Rodman 1992: 642)

Following this line of argument, one might suggest that texts and narratives are important elements in the process whereby people constitute particular localities as significant cultural communities . I argue here that the participatory project Try Yourself can be read as a narrative that contributed to revitalising Norwegian local communities as significant places for democratic participation. As participants in the project, children contributed to this particular construction through both their written texts on the application forms and their social practices in connection with the project.

During the 1970s and 1980s, ethnic and local communities in the Western world reconstructed their boundaries on a symbolic foundation as a response to massive political attacks on the old structural boundaries of these communities, favouring the homogenising logic of national and international political economies (Cohen 1985). In a situation where the idea of local community as an important cultural place is threatened, the importance of narratives and texts increases. While the particular physical and geographical locality of a community is often taken for granted, the local community as a space connoted with symbolic and cultural meaning is not always openly discussed.

Valentine asserts that local communities are normative and moral landscapes that are produced in public spaces (Valentine 2001). In Norwegian society, the term 'local community' is often used to refer to close relationships between people tied together by physical structures, cultural history and local dialects (Gullestad 1978, 2001). The local community where you were born is called the *hjemsted* or 'home place', and is associated with rootedness, belonging and close social relationships (Gullestad 1992, 1996). Home operates as a metaphor for local communities, symbolising care, support and common interests within a group of people living close to each other in the same physical area. These local relationships are highly valued and are regarded as being based on informal equality. The idea of social relations as egalitarian implies a denial of social differences such as class divisions (Barnes 1954; Gullestad 1992). This is related to the notion of egalitarian individualism that has characterised Norwegian democracy (Eriksen 1993; Berggreen 1993; Gullestad 1997). Egalitarian individualism points to a close relationship between the individual's right to self-realisation and self-determination on the one hand, and equality and collectivity on the other. The rural local community of the past operates as a symbol of vital and autonomous local societies geographically dispersed around the country and practising self-determinination – *sjølråderett* – and egalitarian individualism.

Children and local communities are both associated with important Norwegian values revolving around the importance of people living in a pact with nature, exercising autonomy and self-determination, and having a 'culture of their own' (Gullestad 1996, 1997). In Try Yourself, children were placed in particular discourses that constructed them as *equal* to adults, as autonomous subjects with certain participatory rights in society, but also as *different*, belonging to a specific age-group with their own particular culture (Kjørholt 2001). This discourse may be seen as a proto-type of egalitarian individualism. Children were at the same time constructed as both equal and different. By bringing discourses on 'children and participation' together with discourses on sustainable local communities, traditional Norwegian discourses on egalitarian individualism were reconstructed and renewed (Kjørholt 2002).

Placing children in public spaces: paradoxes of being different and equal

Within this particular participatory project, children were, in many ways, placed in discourses constructing new social positions for children as autonomous subjects within their local communities. Children were given access to public spaces in their municipalities in new ways. From the age of 7, they were allowed to address public authorities in order to apply for public funding to realise their own ideas about leisure activities, without having to obtain their parents' permission. Through this independent access to public funding and public authorities, I argue, they were positioned as a kind of 'fellow citizen' by being placed as subjects in public space. This position is quite different from that described for children in many modern western societies, in which they have been characterised as being mainly subjects belonging to the family in the private sphere and to different institutions with professional care and teaching in public space (James *et al.* 1998; Lee 2001).

The local community was chosen as a site for realising children as social participants in the Try Yourself project. The project was initiated by the Norwegian Council for Cultural Affairs in the early 1990s and was funded for a three-year period. It was inspired by a similar project in Denmark. However, whereas the Danish project was administered by state authorities, the Norwegian project was run by local authorities. As part of the process of promoting children's rights as social participants in the local community, those behind it stressed that the children's projects would be totally separate from any kind of institutional or organisational affiliation or other forms of adult control. Rather, children were to develop their projects 'on their own terms', without any interference from adults. In each municipality, one person was appointed to be in charge of the project locally.[2] The initiators wanted to avoid ordinary bureaucratic procedures so that the application process would be 'child-friendly'. The children were merely asked to write a short text on a simple application form concerning the activities they were planning and what kind of economic support they needed to realise them. The people in charge of the project locally were responsible for awarding the children the money, and they were able to issue the funds requested as soon as the children had submitted an application. It was emphasised that no strict rules or normative (adult) opinions concerning the value of the children's projects should prevent children from receiving funding (Kjørholt 1993). Though the project was planned for a limited period of time, the overall intention was to institute a permanent practice in the municipalities of earmarking a certain amount of money for 'children's own culture' performed by the children themselves.[3]

An important aim of the project was to create a place for children's activities in public spaces. This place was mainly intended to be for 'children's culture'. A quote from one of the many articles on the project in the Norwegian newspapers – an interview with one of the initiators – illustrates this point:

> This deals with the issue of having trust in children, to look at them as resources, to have confidence in them and give them responsibility. Now children up to 14 years are going to apply for public funding – for their own cultural activities. The Norwegian Council for Cultural Affairs has decided to use half a million Norwegian kroner[4] in three years for a project that places 'children's own culture' in the centre [. . .] The project will initially be carried out in 11 geographically dispersed municipalities.
>
> (Ny Tid, 6 April 1988, translated by ATK)

Even though the initiators intended Try Yourself to be a participatory project 'on children's own terms' by constructing certain subject positions for children while prohibiting others, the discourses connected with the project defined very specific ways in which children were thought to be able to act on their own. The subject position from which children were expected to engage in their own cultural activities was closely related to a public narrative[5] concerning what I have called 'Children as an endangered people' (Kjørholt 2001).[6] In this narrative, children are placed in a particular position in the generational structure as a special group of people who are preoccupied with playing and practising 'their own culture'. The idea of an egalitarian community or *fellesskap* among children is a core theme. The Norwegian concept of *fellesskap* is not exactly the same as the English concept of community, which, according to McDowell, refers to 'a fluid network of social relations that may be, but are not necessarily tied to, territory' (McDowell 1999: 100).

The Norwegian notions of *barns egen kultur* ('children's own culture') and *barnefellesskap* ('children's community') refer to the existence of a sort of 'imagined community'[7] among children who are affiliated with a common culture. This is anchored in moral values of friendship and play among equal individuals belonging to the same age group. The concept of 'imagined commmunities' is defined by Rose as: 'A group of people bound together by some kind of belief stemming from particular historical and geographical circumstances in their own solidarity' (Rose 1995: 426).

The 'imagined community of children', however, is not anchored in any particular geographical area, but in a notion of childhood constructed within particular historical and cultural circumstances. The public narrative of children as belonging to a distinctive and endangered culture is analogous to the description of endangered species and indigenous cultures. This narrative is an illustration of what Stephens (1995: 9) describes as 'a growing concern in recent decades with the domain of childhood as threatened, invaded and "polluted" by adult worlds'. The 'natural and playing child with its own culture' is generally placed in the private sphere or in public institutions run by professionals. Nature and outdoor life are presented as important places for children's play and the practice of 'their own culture'. Children are first and foremost constructed as *different* from adults and are inscribed in a particular cultural group based on belonging to a specific age group. In recent years, a new dimension has been added to these discourses. This concerns children as active participants in society. It is therefore the *different, playing children*, and collective groups of peers, that are given the right to social participation in their local communities (Kjørholt 2001). This notion of children is similar to what James *et al.* have called 'the tribal child', a reference to a conceptualisation of children found in some of the new social studies of childhood that emphasise children's difference and relative autonomy (James *et al.* 1998: 29).

The Try Yourself project strongly opposed discourses that placed children in a subordinate position vis-à-vis adults and thus in a marginal social position associated with limited agency and power when compared to adults. The project drew on new discourses that construct children as competent social actors and tried to remove them from inter-generational relationships characterised by the unequal distribution of power, with adults being in a position of control and dominance. At the same time, however, the project was initiated and controlled by adults with particular ideas of what it means to be a child, and it was therefore inevitably associated with certain forms of adult control and dominance. Children were recognised as a kind of individual autonomous citizen with the right to apply for money from public authorities in their local communities, but at the same time they were maintained in a position *as children*. They were allowed to apply for public support because they belonged to the social category *child*, and only on behalf of a group of individuals belonging to this same social category, which was essentialised as consisting of creative and playing social actors. Yet, when examining the actual ways in which the children experienced participating in Try Yourself, it was apparent that their agency was greatly influenced by their ability to draw on inter-generational relationships between individual children and adults in the local community.

Children's places: inter-generational relationships

During the three years that the project lasted, nearly 1,700 children aged 7–14 (and even older) engaged in various activities such as dance, music, making a newspaper or setting up clubs to look after cats, produce eggs, clean local water, etc. Each and every one of these projects had its own characteristics with respect to both the chosen activities and the social processes that developed among the persons involved. Social relationships and practices among the participants constituted a variety of social land-scapes, which were characterised by different social groupings and defined various borders between the categories of *us* and *them*. However, these categories and borders were blurred by the networks of inter-generational relationships in which the children were placed.

Guro and Line, who as noted were 10 and 11 years old when they participated in the project, were close friends living in the same rural district and attending the same class at school. They wanted to start a music band together with three other girls, – the youngest being 9 years old and the oldest 12. Many other peer groups in the same small local community, mainly boys, had already received funding from the Try Yourself project to organise various bands. Guro's narrative about her experiences as a participant in Try Yourself opens as follows:

> It was a poster at the school, then. A Try Yourself poster. Then, in a music class, then I said as a joke: 'Let's start a band, we too.' Then we went to Nils [the principal of the school] and then we called Tone [the

local contact person in the project]. . . . We had never been involved in music activities before we started in the fourth grade. Like played on guitars and drums and things like that. We didn't even know they had instruments like that at our school before they showed them. It was Olav who had moved to the island [who made this possible]. Then there was a lot of music! Then we were saved from having to play that boring recorder all the time.

As this text illustrates, Olav, the music teacher at the school, played an important part in generating an interest in starting bands among the children in this local community. According to the interview with Guro, children's creative activities were closely related to the inspiration and support they received from adults. Instead of the existence of 'children's own culture' consisting of distinct and separate cultural activities, Guro's statements point to the importance of dynamic interaction between children's activities and the adults present. The girls' subject positions as children playing in a band were made possible primarily by Olav's contribution. They thus inscribed themselves as social participants into an inter-generational relationship involving mainly Olav, the music teacher who recently had moved to the island and inspired them to play music. Whereas the public narrative of 'children as an endangered people' constructs children as belonging to an age-related social order, inhabiting a particular culture of their own that has to be protected from adults' intervention, the girls placed themselves within an inter-generational social order, emphasising how the social practices they initiated within the project were inspired by an adult teacher. Furthermore, whereas the children were placed as autonomous subjects within discourses of an age-related social order that emphasises disrupture and discontinuity between different generational age-groups, Line and Guro's band demonstrated the importance of inter-generational continuity by drawing on cultural forms and practices that were generated by other age-groups. Line and Guro were not the only ones to be inspired by the music teacher: indeed, several children wanted to participate in Try Yourself by starting a band, and many bands were funded in this local community.

The school, and the teachers associated with it, all played a key role in the implementation of the project in this community. The principal, for example, allowed the children to use the school building in the afternoon to play the instruments, which were rented for a certain amount of money, and he, or a teacher, was available in the office if the children needed support of any kind. Furthermore, the local anchor person for the project was a teacher. The importance of the school is apparent in Line's account of how they got involved in the project, which starts as follows:

There was a poster about Try Yourself. The idea just came. We had to buy the instruments, eh, and we did not have money. Then we went to the principal, and he said we could call Tone. And then we got seven hundred kroner from her [. . .] We gave four hundred kroner to the guy who coached us, and three hundred for renting the instruments. The principal got this money.

In her narrative, Line reveals that participation in the public project enabled the children to create subject positions both as employees and as employers. Thus Line relates how she and the other girls in the group used the public funding to hire a coach to teach them to play music. This coach, as will be seen, turned out to be a 13-year-old boy, who acquired a position as a music teacher being paid for his services.

Being different – paradoxes of the 'imagined communities of children'

As noted, public discourses operate with a notion of an imagined community of children who share a common culture of childhood. Yet, an important theme in the stories of their participation in Try Yourself that the children related concerned their desire to demarcate themselves from other children by creating smaller groups, or special communities of children, who had a special identity of their own. The children's projects therefore involved processes of boundary-making between 'us' (those who took part in particular projects) and 'them' (the other children). The girls' ideas about the community that they wanted to construct seem to be anchored in beliefs and imaginations of a unique collective group identity that they wanted to develop and give a particular expressive form to. The expressive group identity they wished to realise may be seen as a kind of symbolic identity united with feelings of belonging to an imagined collective group of people, in the case of Guro and Line the members of the music band.

Guro's narrative about the girl band stresses in different ways the importance of constructing a distinctive and original identity as a band that is different from other bands. An important element in this identity construction involved finding a special name for the band. Line explained that they first decided to call the band 'Fiasco', but then they changed the name because:

Tone [the adult local contact person] didn't like the name Fiasco. She thought it was strange. Then we decided on the name: 'Funny Girls'.

The name Funny Girls is not a translation from Norwegian, for the girls actually gave their band this name in English. Guro's construction of an identity as a 'funny girl' included positioning herself within a community of girls who made up a music band together. In her dialogue with me, she talked a lot about writing texts and composing the melodies, and the fact that they managed to do this all by themselves. A central part of this construction of a particular collective identity was, for Guro and Line, to be unique. Line's statement illustrate this point:

> We have composed the music ourselves. This makes it more difficult for others to do the same – to be exactly like us. I'm sure nobody will manage to find out what our new songs are like.

By constructing a collective group identity, the girls sought to assert themselves as being *different* from other groups of children who were engaged in similar activities. Because of this desire to project a special image of themselves as a unique music group, the children displayed little tolerance of children who might threaten their special identity. Thus Line explained that one 9-year-old girl had been excluded from the Funny Girls because 'she did not have a good singing voice'. Furthermore, when the Funny Girls discovered that another group of girls had started a similar band, they were very displeased about it:

> There has been a little dispute with the girls in the fifth grade who started a band after we did. We were disappointed that they also were going to start a band. We didn't like it, because they were actually going to start a bath club, but they didn't. Then we heard they were going to start a band, and then we quarrelled. Then they said: 'Why did you copy the girls in the seventh grade?' But we didn't even know the seventh graders had started a band. It was disgusting to us.
>
> (Guro)

Many of the children's narratives of their experiences in Try Yourself high-lighted their efforts to create a unique project that was different from any other project. They explained that the steps in their dances were genuine, the melodies original compositions, the pictures artistic and so on. The *play* itself and the *processes* involved in creating the cultural product, seen by adults as as having great value in themselves within the separate place of 'children's culture', did not seem to be of any significance for most of the participants. Rather, the children wanted to create an expressive identity for themselves in special groups that could be recognised by others. This meant excluding certain children and establishing boundaries with respect to other groups of children.

This emphasis on individual self-realisation is closely aligned with contemporary cultural values. According to Gullestad (1997), 'being oneself' is a core issue for parents in modern Norwegian society in today's child-rearing practices (ibid.). This particular social construction of child-hood, which emphasises children's rights to 'find themselves', is powerful and prevalent in inter-generational relations in Norway, as well as in institutional contexts such as after-school programmes and child-care institutions in Nordic countries (Gullestad 1996, 1997; Højlund 2000).

A duty to decide for themselves

The idea of Try Yourself was to support *groups of children* practising 'their own culture'. The Norwegian Council for Cultural Affairs thus created a place for 'children's culture', and also emphasised and communicated the need for adults to let the children decide without adult intervention. This place, however, imposed major restrictions on children's possibilities to act as social participants in their local communities as individual fellow citizens. Some of the funded projects collapsed due to conflicts among the children that they were not able to resolve by themselves. Others suffered because the children experienced difficulties in realising their planned activities on their own. Children working on projects that involved a range of activities, such as choreographing new dances, making film strips or building huts, said that they needed assistance from adults. Some of the applications even included adult participants, such as the following, written by a group of teenaged boys who needed funding to run a tinkering club or *mekke-klubb*:

> We need tools and what one needs to repair a car. We have a 73 Crysler that is nearly complete in Pål's garage that we are allowed to screw on, for instance scrape rust. We are 5–6 boys who are doing this every afternoon. The oldest among us is 43 years old.
>
> (Trygve, Terje Pål and Even)

The desire to involve adults in the children's project was also apparent in Line and Guro's accounts. They, like many of the other children, said that they would have liked help and support from adults in carrying out their planned activities and ideas, and they thus challenged the public narrative that saw adult involvement as a threat to children's 'own culture'. Funny Girls did receive important help from Olav, the music teacher, in the initial phase of the project period. However, when they asked him to teach them music and help them decide on a music programme he refused, being obedient to the idea of Try Yourself that children were to carry out their activities on their own without intervention from adults. The girls solved the problem by appointing Roger, a boy aged 13 in the sixth grade, as a helper instead of the teacher:

> It is more fun now, because Roger teaches us a bit more. He decides a bit more, too. . . . But Olav [the music teacher] he didn't decide anything. 'It's you who decides', he said.
>
> (Guro)

This clearly illustrates one of the paradoxes of the project. An important aim was to empower children and give them support 'on their own terms'. However, as it turned out, the adults laid down these terms by virtually 'forcing' the children to decide for themselves, in the process prohibiting them from using adults as important resources of expertise and skill, even when they wished to do so. By prohibiting the children from seeking help from adults when they wished to do so, so that the children might develop their projects on their own, the adults in effect prevented the children from carrying out the projects on their own terms. The adults, in other words, asserted their control and power over the projects. The contradiction between the adults' position of control over the project and their formulated aim of letting children realise themselves 'totally on their own terms' illustrates that the discursive practices connected with Try Yourself also represent certain forms of adult control and power in relation to children. The fact that Guro and Line changed the name of the band because the local contact person did not like this name is another clear example of adult intervention. The name Fiasco did not match the adults' vision of Try Yourself as a successful realisation of children's culture. The constructed places for children's participation in their local communities are not places where asymmetrical relationships between adults and children are removed. As Keith and Pile assert, 'all spatialities are political because they are the (covert) medium and the (disguised) expression of asymmetrical relations of power' (Keith and Pile 1993: 38).

Making places of visibility in public spaces

While the narratives of the Funny Girls challenged the public narrative in certain ways, the girls did corroborate the idea that public funding meant support for and recognition of children. They appreciated that, as participants in Try Yourself, they were given access to public places, like the school, in subject positions other than that of being a pupil. They were allowed to use the school in the afternoon without direct control by teachers, although there was a teacher in the office who had the ultimate responsibility for project activities. However, by giving children access to the school in order to use it for the activities they had initiated, the school was tranformed in the afternoon into a public place where children were allowed to be active social participants in new ways.

Through their narratives, the Funny Girls constituted themselves as subjects who acted in public places in the local community. First and foremost, it seems that by assuming subject posistions as *project participants with public funding*, to some extent they inscribed themselves as 'fellow citizens' and social participants into the public community. Furthermore, the children were able to take part in concerts, exhibitions and other events organised by the local project leader at the community hall in the centre of the local community. In Line's story, the music band's participation in different concerts was a central theme:

> It wouldn't have been the same to be in a music band without participating in Try Yourself. Because it wouldn't have been that fun. They don't make that many entertainments [. . .]. It's no use just sitting here on the island. We usually just perform at the end-of-term celebration and at school concerts and the like.

For Line to be on a stage playing music to an audience of local people was clearly a highlight in her involvement in the project. Without the project events, the community was a place of inactivity, with neither fun nor value: 'It's no use just sitting here on the island.' This statement clearly illustrates how places are constituted by social practices and written and spoken words (Tuan 1974, 1991). The meaning of the place is related to activities and social relations, revolving on this occasion around performing on stage and receiving social recognition for the performance. Performances at school concerts and the like were not as attractive as playing in front of larger audiences, for instance at the community hall. It seemed to be important for Guro and Line to be visible and recognised not only by people whom they knew well in their close surroundings, but also by larger audiences in the public space. The focus on expressivity in this connection is remarkable. Line continues:

> We really loved the concert at 'Hill' [the centre of this local community with a community hall]. That 'Babyrock' thing [the title of a particular piece of music they had created] – we didn't think we were going to be applauded for that. It seems a bit childish, perhaps. We didn't expect applause from Gunfire [a band of older boys]. They are much better than us.

Line here clearly illustrated her awareness of social differentiation among children and groups of children. Different music bands had different positions according to certain norms, and being 'childish' was obviously not related to social recognition according to social values that were prevalent in the social network of which she was part.

To a large extent, my empirical data confirm the notion that the construction of identities in public spaces seems to be important to children. Try Yourself opened a discursive field of 'children as social participants', operating in new ways in public spaces. For many children, the identity of a 'project participant' seems to be transformed into a kind of 'fellow citizen' identity. This identity meant working on relationships among the friends in the music band, but mostly with other people and the public society in general that they came into contact with as a band.

One of the applications, written by two girls aged 8, vividly illustrates the importance of being visible as subjects in public spaces. The girls wanted to be *passepiker*, that is, babysitters who take care of babies in the neighbourhood during the afternoon, a common practice in Norway among young girls (Gullestad 1995). A *passepike* usually goes for a walk for an hour or two with a baby or a toddler, the latter often in a pram, and she is usually paid for this activity, which is recognised as a kind of work. A *passepike* often looks after the same baby, for instance, for one or two days a week over a long period, through an agreement between the girl and the baby's parents. This is a practice that does not need any funding. Nevertheless, Tine and Tonje wanted to be participants in Try Yourself and wrote the following on the application form:

> We want to take care of small children (to be *passepiker*).
> *Write down what you need in the way of materials and other things in order to get started:*
> Nothing, really.

> (Tine and Tonje, 8 years old)

A similar example is an application from three boys aged 11, who wanted public funding to form a detective club. This club had been established one year previously, and the boys had been playing together, acting as detectives in the forest near their homes. They applied for support to buy a rope, but one of the boys told me that they did not actually need this rope. However, by sending this text to the public authorities in their local community, they inscribed themselves as social participants in public spaces, making themselves visible as subjects who were recognised by other people in the local community. *Visibility in public spaces* seemed to be part of the children's construction of identities as social participants in their local communities. Competition to obtain favourable social positions within a differentiated network of children in the same age-group is an important part of their construction of identities as social participants.

As part of this construction, the possibility of 'being seen' in public spaces is of the greatest importance. As noted, for the Funny Girls, the concert in the community hall was the highlight of their narrative about being project participants. Tor and Pål, two 10-year-old boys living in the same local community, similarly emphasised the opportunity to assert themselves in public in their narratives. They participated in the project by starting a photo club together, taking subjects from nature and their local community. I quote from Tor's narrative:

> It was exciting taking pictures, and then it was really exciting to see how beautiful the pictures were when they were hung up on the wall. And the Try Yourself exhibition . . . a huge amount of people arrived and photographed us . . . the newspaper and everything. . . .

Children's texts on the application forms indicate that relationships with someone outside the family, their peer-group and private places were an important theme in the texts. Realising themselves within peer-groups through different kinds of activities such as dance and music did not seem to be of major importance in and of itself. Inclusion into an inter-generational order, however, by being recognised as contributing social participants by people *outside* their peer-group – adults, youth or the public society in general – is a key theme in narratives of children's experiences as project participants.

Since the local community was the framework for the Try Yourself projects, it came to be narrated as a place for the practice of democracy by children. Local newspapers played an important role in the marketing of the Try Yourself project in general by writing about the various projects carried out by children in their local communities. For many children, the overall aim of being part of Try Yourself seemed to be being photographed and having their names and pictures published in the newspapers along with stories about their activities. This allowed them to express their particular identities, but also to demonstrate their agency.

Recognition as contributing social participants

Through the texts they composed for the application forms, the children inscribed themselves as social participants in their local communities, becoming visible social actors in public spaces who contributed to society. Money can be seen to be an 'act of recognition' by public authorities of the children's identity as a kind of fellow citizen. Many of the children's written texts on the application forms demonstrate this. Thus for some children, the ability to engage in useful work that would allow them to earn money was an important goal of the planned activities. I quote from three different application forms to illustrate various forms of work:

Two boys, 11 years old:

> We apply for funding to run a bicycle workshop to repair bicycles for others. We need an oil can, repair kit, cycle pump, large and small screwdrivers, wrenches, toolbox, gear cable and brake cable, that is, 800 kroner or more. We'll probably earn some money, but it depends on how many people are going to get their bicycles repaired.
>
> (Ole and Per, 11 years old)

A girl, aged 10:

> We have planned to make an animal club. We'll try to make a newspaper about animals, and we'll teach a girl to ride, to take care of animals (maybe provide a good home). We need money to buy a

photo. We'll try to make a newspaper that is going to be called: 'The Animal-newspaper'. About 3–4–5 kroner for each.

A girl, aged 8:

We are going to build a hut. Then we plan to sell coffee, cakes and lemonade. We need planks, nails and then we need just a few things – 500 kroner all together.

However, many wanted to contribute to society without earning money, and many applications, from girls in particular, were for social activities, like caring for others. These projects involved various activities, such as removing rubbish, repairing the football ground, cultivating small lakes, establishing clubs to organise activities for younger children, etc. The application below is one of many received from girls who wanted support to engage in different kinds of charitable activity:

We want to sing and make music cassettes, and if we are allowed to, we want to travel around, and that is going to be to the benefit of the cancer association.

(Elisabeth, Linn, Trude and Bjørg, 9–11 years old)

'Children's culture' and localities as threatened communities

In Norway, both local communities and 'children's culture' may be regarded as moral and symbolic landscapes produced in public spaces (cf. Valentine 2001). Children's culture and local communities have both been seen as coming under threat in recent decades (Kjørholt 2001, 2002). The particular construction of Try Yourself narrated and renewed both these places as powerful 'imagined communities', thus reconstructing significant cultural values in Norwegian society in different ways. Children's texts on application forms narrated and reconstituted cultural ideas of the local community as a place for realising egalitarian individualism. 'Authentic voices' from children were thus removed from private places and made visible in public spaces. Notions of autonomous subjects and participatory democracies revived their symbolic vitality. The various and creative social practices children developed within the project demonstrated a particular combination of individual self-realisation, creativity, autonomy and community *(fellesskap)*.

An important aim of Try Yourself was to revitalise 'children's own culture', interpreted as the expression of egalitarian communities based on creativity, play, nature and participation on 'children's own terms'. These egalitarian communities were placed within local communities as a social and public space. The particular construction of children as both equal and different in the discourse points to visions of democracy that also embrace *difference*. Social inclusion and the recognition of individuals who are understood as being different from the majority in one way or another represent a major challenge to modern democracies.

The Try Yourself project documented how the particular construction of children as social participants belonging to a separate 'children's culture' connected to the project represented several paradoxes and dilemmas for the children who were participating in the project. The construction of a place for children's participation in the local community was a place loaded with particular symbolic and cultural meaning. The discourses created a space for children's creativity and culture, in other words, a place for making certain ideas of 'childishness' visible. These particular cultural ideas of 'childishness' represented forms of adult control that restricted children's possibilities to act and to be integrated into inter-generational relationships and practices. As Line's and Guro's stories show, their project was not the realisation of this 'childishness'; rather, they wished to establish a place of visibility for themselves in public spaces as contributing and equal social participants. Some children also wanted to create spaces of social action that were not just restricted to their local communities.

Qvortrup asserts that one of the main paradoxes of modern childhood is that, whereas social relationships between children and parents are valued, children spend more and more of their everyday lives separate from adults (Qvortrup 1995). One might argue, and rightly so, that Try Yourself offered a new way of positioning children in their particularity and making new separate places for them as 'playing citizens' in public spaces. The opportunity to be positioned as individual subjects in public spaces was limited by the fact that the children were positioned in the discourse first and foremost as *groups of creative children*. The challenges many children met in coping with moral ideas of individual self-realisation and the development of a collective, authentic community among children reveal the complexities connected with this particular construction of children as social participants.

I have shown, however, that Try Yourself also opened up possibilities for children to be visible as contributing social actors in their local communities in new ways. Yet this place of visibility for children was not 'on children's own terms', but a construction of a particular normative and moral landscape in public spaces, anchored in particular cultural notions of childhood and local community.

Notes

1 The term 'fellow citizen' is used by deWinter (1997) and is a reference to children as citizens in the making, emphasising the importance of giving

children and young people social space in which to practise their participatory rights as part of their education in democratic citizenship. My use of the term refers to children's rights to social participation in society in respect of being human beings, not only as part of education into citizenship. However, according to traditional, liberal theories of citizenship, children are not citizens in the formal, political sense of the term.

2 Their professional status varied. Most of them worked in the cultural or social administration in the municipality; a few were teachers or connected to other professions. Their duties were first and foremost to inform children about the possibility to apply for money, besides distributing the money itself.

3 The Norwegian Centre for Child Research was given the responsibility both to be in charge of the project nationally, and to evaluate it.

4 Thirteen Norwegian kroner correspond to one British Pound.

5 Public narratives are defined as 'those narratives attached to cultural and institutional formations larger than the single individual, to intersubjective networks or institutions, however local or grand, micro or macro stories' (Somers 1994: 619).

6 This narrative is further elaborated and discussed in Kjørholt (2001).

7 This concept is used by Benedict Anderson to describe the nature of national identity in modern societies, taking the form of a more abstract and symbolic identity and feelings of solidarity and belonging to a certain imagined collective group of people (Anderson 1983).

References

Anderson, B. (1983) *Imagined Communities: Reflections on the Origin and Spread of Nationalism*. London: Verso.

Barnes, J. A. (1954) 'Class and committees in a Norwegian island parish', *Human Relations* 7(1): 39–58.

Berdoulay, V. (1989) 'Place meaning and discourse in French language geography', in J. Agnew and J. Duncan (eds) *The Power of Place*. London: Unwin, Hyman, pp. 124–39.

Berggreen, B. (1993) 'A national identity in person: The making of a modern Norwegian', in A. C. Kiel (ed.) *Continuity and Change: Aspects of Contemporary Norway*. Oslo: Scandinavian University Press, pp. 39–54.

Cohen, A. (1985) *The Symbolic Construction of Community*. London, New York: Routledge.

Eriksen, E. O. (1993) 'Norwegian social democracy and political governance', in A. C. Kiel (ed.) *Continuity and Change: Aspects of Contemporary Norway*. Oslo: Scandinavian University Press, pp. 131–48.

Foucalt, M. (1972) *The Archaeology of Knowledge*. London: Routledge.

Gullestad, M. (1978) 'Lokalsamfunnsbegrepet og dets anvendelse i studier av bysamfunn', in T. Thuen and C. Wadel (eds) *Lokale samfunn og offentlig planlegging*. Oslo: Universitetsforlaget, pp. 37–62.

—— (1992) *The Art of Social Relations: Essays on Culture, Social Action and Everyday Life in Modern Norway*. Oslo: Universitetsforlaget.

—— (1995) 'Barn som aktive samfunnsdeltakere: Passepikens virksomhet', in *Kultur og hverdagsliv*, Oslo: Universitetsforlaget, Det blå bibliotek, pp. 67–87.

—— (1996) *Everyday Life Philosophers: Modernity, Morality and Autobiography in Norway*. Oslo, Copenhagen, Stockholm, Boston: Scandinavian University Press.

—— (1997) 'A passion for boundaries: Reflections on connections between the every-day lives of children and discourses on the nation in contemporary Norway', *Childhood* 4(1): 19–42.

—— (2001) *Det norske sett med nye øyne*. Oslo: Universitetsforlaget.

Højlund, S. (2000) *Childhood as a Social Space: Positions of Children in Different Institutional Contexts*. Paper presented at the conference 'From Development to Open-ended Processes of Change' Institute of Anthropology, University of Copenghagen, 7–7 April.

James, A., C. Jenks and A. Prout (1998). *Theorising Childhood*. Cambridge: Polity Press.

Keith, M. and S. Pile (1993) *Place and the Politics of Identity*. London: Routledge.

Kjørholt, A. T. (1993) *Prøv Selv: Kulturprosjekt og visjoner om barndom*. Rapport 29. Trondheim: Norwegian Centre for Child Research.

—— (2001) 'The participating child – a vital pillar in this century?' *Nordic Educational Research* 21(2): 65–81.

—— (2002) 'Small is powerful: Discourses on children and participation in Norway in 1990s', *Childhood* 9(1): 63–82.

Lee, N. (2001) *Childhood and Society: Growing up in an Age of Uncertainty*. Buckingham, Philadelphia: Open University Press.

McDowell, L. (1999) *Gender, Identity and Place: Understanding Feminist Geographies*. Cambridge: Polity Press.

Norwegian Council for Cultural Affairs (1988): *Barn kan* – notat. Oslo.

Ny Tid (1988) Norwegian newspaper. Oslo: 6 April.

Olwig, K. Fog. (2000) 'Børn i lokalsamfunn – børns lokalsamfunn. Introduksjon til temanummer', *Barn* 18(3&4): 5–22.

Qvortrup, J. (1995) 'Childhood and modern society: A paradoxical relationship', in J. Brannen and M. O'Brien (eds) *Childhood and Parenthood: Proceedings of ISA Committee for Family Research Conference on Children and Families, 1994*. London: Institute of Education.

Rodman, M. (1992) 'Empowering place: Multilocality and multivocality', *American Anthropologist* 94(3): 640–56.

Rose, G. (1995) 'Place and identity: A sense of place', in D. Massey and P. Jess, *A Place in the World? Places, Cultures and Globalization*. Milton Keynes: Open University; Oxford: Oxford University Press.

Somers, M. (1994) 'The narrative constitution of identity: A relational and network approach', *Theory and Society* 23: 605–49.

Stephens, S. (1995). *Children and the Politics of Culture: Rights, Risks and Reconstructions*. New Jersey: Princeton University Press.

Tuan, Y.-F. (1974) 'Space and place: Humanistic perspective', *Progress in Geography* 6: 211–52.

—— (1991) 'Language and the making of place. A narrative-descriptive approach', *Annals of the Association of American Geographers* 81(4): 684–96.

Valentine, G. (2001) *Social Geographies: Space and Society*. Harlow: Prentice Hall.

Winter, M. de (1997) *Children as Fellow Citizens: Participation and Commitment*. Oxford, New York: Radcliffe Medical Press.

Chapter 11

Children's places of belonging in immigrant families of Caribbean background

Karen Fog Olwig

Children in migration processes

Children are usually seen as playing a key role in migration processes because of their particular place in the inter-generational order of cultural transmission. Whereas adult migrants have been regarded as steeped in the cultural values and social relations they knew from their country of origin, their descendants, whether they migrated while they were still young or were born in the migration destination, have been viewed as important agents of integration into the receiving society. Migrants' children have therefore constituted an important focal point of study in research on the integration processes of migrants. Much of this research has examined migrants' children in relation to their place of origin and various social and economic indicators of their levels of integration into the society of the receiving country. However, there has been relatively little interest in investigating migrants' children as actors in their own right, capable of developing different ties and places of belonging that reflect their understanding and interpretation of their everyday lives, wherever they live.

This study focuses on migrants' children's experiences by investigating the places of belonging that emerge in life stories related by children who have grown up in families where one or more parents or grandparents have migrated from the Caribbean to North America or Europe. My analysis suggests that children's making of places of belonging does not refer primarily to a geographical or ethnic identity associated with the nation state of their ancestral place of origin, nor to the geographical or national identity connected with the nation state of their destination as migrants. Rather, children's place-making involves the creation of different social sites of belonging connected with the various spheres of life that children encounter in their everyday lives. Indeed, the development of a particular ethnic or national identity may not be of key importance to the children, as their lives straddle a host of places of belonging that are identified with the local, national and transnational relations in which they are engaged. An analysis of children's making of places of belonging therefore offers an important corrective to research on integration processes among migrants, which to a large extent has focused on migrants' relations to their country of origin on the one hand, and to their new country of adoption on the other.

The place of children in migration research

A central topic of concern in migration research has been the integration of migrants into the receiving society. This focus on the making of new citizens out of immigrants is related to the fact that most migration research has been carried out by scholars in the receiving countries, whose research agenda has been influenced by domestic political issues concerning the integration of immigrants into society.

There has been a particularly close relationship between national development, immigration policies and migration research in the United States and Canada, where immigrants have provided a critical source of population growth (Olwig and Sørensen 2002; see also Olwig 2001).[1] In this migration research, children have been an important topic of investigation, because they are believed to provide a good indication of the level of integration of their families in the receiving country. Migration research has therefore traditionally tended to examine the integration processes of migrants in terms of generational stages of adaptation, where each new generation of children is expected to display progressively more successful forms of integration into a receiving country, reflected, among other things, in their upward socio-economic mobility. It has been common to operate with a three-stage model of integration, which, in the American context, has been regarded as having been completed when immigrants adapt to 'an ethnic culture that facilitates combining the American and the immigrant social systems' (Waters 1999: 194; see also Thorne et al. forthcoming). This model of integration has been used especially in relation to European immigrants, who dominated North American immigration well into the twentieth century. Since the Second World War, migratory patterns have changed considerably. Population movements are now dominated by migrants from the developing world, and Europeans no longer comprise significant migration groups. On the contrary, Europe has become an important destination, along with North America, for migrants from the developing world, who are looking for social and economic opportunities in the North. This has led scholars of migration to re-examine established models of integration. During the past two decades, a number of studies have critically re-examined the unilinear three-step model of integration and suggested that integration may be more pluralistic than hitherto assumed (for a review of the literature, see Zhou 2001). They argue that, because many immigrants today come from the non-Western developing world, they experience difficulty integrating into modern, white, middle-class society in the developed world. Many children of migrants therefore undergo a process of 'segmented integration' and end up in marginalised ethnic sub-groups in society (for a Caribbean case study, see Waters 1999).

Responding to the contemporary interest in the post-national, global society, some scholars have challenged the very notion of progressive levels of integration. They point out that, even after several generations of upbringing in a migration destination, some children grow up within communities of strong diasporic or transnational ties rooted in a country of origin of migrant ancestors, and therefore never become fully integrated into their country of residence. Rather, they learn to regard their country of origin as their homeland and true place of belonging. In this research, to some extent the notion of integration has been replaced by concepts of transnationalism and diasporic links to homelands. These concepts suggest that migrants may remain closely attached to their places of origin, either through actual transnational economic, political or socio-cultural activities (Sutton 1987; Schiller et al. 1992; Basch et al. 1994; Mahler 1998; Portes et al. 1999; Vertovec 1999), or through diasporic communities that celebrate a specific homeland for generations (Clifford 1994; Tölölyan 1996; Cohen 1997; Schwartz 1998).

With the introduction of the concepts of transnational and diasporic identities, it seems that migration studies have changed their interpretive approach entirely. Whereas in earlier migration studies children were viewed as the agents of integration into a new country of opportunities, today they are often seen as the guardians of identities rooted in a distant ancestral homeland that continues to be of importance in their adopted country of residence. Furthermore, whereas earlier migration studies examined migrants' social and economic relations, there is now a greater interest in more institutionalised and public forms of diasporic or transnational identities. These include a broad range of expressions of cultural identification in the form of, for example, literature, music, the arts, museum exhibits and cultural festivals, as well as ethnic, homeland or transnational political organisations. However, they share a common characteristic of being what Arjun Appadurai has called 'marked culture', in the sense that they do not display the 'virtually open-ended archive of differences' to be found in the world today (1996: 13), but rather emphasise a particular 'subset of these differences', which can be 'mobilized to articulate the boundary of difference' that is believed to demarcate the cultural identity of the makers (ibid.: 14–15). This shift of focus in migration research has been particularly apparent in North America and Britain, where a large influx of post-Second World War immigration from Latin America and Asia has occurred. This can be tied to the emergence in the United States, Canada and Britain of ethnic politics or policies of multiculturalism, which in turn can be related to attempts to downplay monocultural nationalism in favour of global integration that seeks to improve the social position of immigrant minorities by working for the recognition of a particular cultural background tied to their country of origin (Baumann 1999).

Institutionalised and public forms of culture may say a great deal about the cultural politics of the society in which migrants and their descendants live, but they do not reflect the broader 'unmarked' cultural activities of migrants' everyday lives. Nor do they represent the varying social relations and cultural identifications that migrants and their descendants develop through time as they negotiate a place for themselves in society. This is particularly apparent when examining inter-generational changes in migrant communities. This observation leads me to question the overall interpretive framework of migration processes and the role of children in them, as it has developed to serve first the interests of models of national identity construction, and then those of globalisation and post-nationalism. What would this picture look like, I am led to wonder, if we examined the role of children in immigration from the point of view of actors who are not engaged in grand nationalist or post-nationalist projects, but who are rather creating a place for themselves at different levels of society?

Here, I shall examine the relationship between the cultural categories of identification established in the wider society and promoted in official institutions, such as schools, and the multiple and shifting forms of identification developed by children reflecting ongoing inter-generational socio-cultural changes through time. My research suggests that the contemporary emphasis on multiculturalism, where identities tied to a distant homeland are seen to be of continued importance and to inform the lives of the descendants of migrants, may bear a limited relationship to the sort of lives that the children of migrants lead and to how they view themselves. This chapter presents a particularly clear case of the difficulty of applying a multicultural or ethnic approach to the study of integration processes, because the families I studied are of middle-class Caribbean background. This means that the children have grown up in families sharing many modern middle-class values concerning the importance of obtaining an education, having a good career, preferably in the professions, and living in a nuclear family based on a companionate marriage. Furthermore, most of the children were of mixed racial and ethnic background. Having to choose a public identity based on their African-Caribbean ethnic background was therefore experienced as restricting the possibilities for multiple identities offered by their family background, rather than as an expression of their true roots. The children's perspective adopted in this analysis suggests that ethnic or multicultural policies, introduced by some national governments to accommodate immigrants' supposedly strong identification with their country of origin, may be rather too unidimensional in relation to the complexly interwoven identities of many different dimensions that can be found among migrants' children.

Places for children in immigrant societies

During the late 1990s, I undertook life-story interviews with members of three dispersed family networks, each consisting of a group of siblings and their descendants.[2] The three sibling groups had been born and reared in the Caribbean islands of Jamaica, Dominica and Nevis respectively, but virtually all of them had lived for a number of years outside these places of birth, and many of their descendants had been born, reared and lived all their lives outside the Caribbean islands of origin of these particular family networks. Most of them were living in the United States, Canada or Britain. When interviewing family members, I asked them to tell me their life stories and did not particularly ask them about their migration experiences or ties to a place of origin outside their place of residence. Family members were therefore free to tell me about any topic they deemed to be of importance to the lives they had lived. Most informants related a fairly brief summary of their life story to me, lasting anywhere from a few minutes to an hour, and during the rest of the interview I would ask follow-up questions that were directed towards exploring in greater depth the topics of concern that different family members had brought up. Toward the end of the interview I asked specific questions concerning identity issues, where the family members had not already made reference to this subject themselves.

Out of the approximately 150 persons that I interviewed, 31 were children or young people aged 20 years or less. The children's recounting of their life stories tended to be rather brief in comparison to the life stories related by their adult parents and grandparents. Generally speaking, however, the children seemed to enjoy talking about themselves and the lives they had led. All but three of the children belonged to the family originating in Dominica and Jamaica, and I will therefore here concentrate on these two families. These families were of Caribbean middle-class background, and many family members had become well educated and settled in solid middle-class neighbourhoods abroad. A few, however, were less well educated, and some were residing in less privileged immigrant neighbourhoods. Whereas the middle-class areas tended to be primarily White, the immigrant neighbourhoods were characterised by large numbers of recent immigrants from the developing world. The cultural diversity of these immigrants has been emphasised in the multicultural and ethnic policies that have been introduced in recent decades, most notably in Canada, where an official multicultural policy was established during the 1970s (Mackey 1997). This has led to a heightened awareness of the significance of immigrants' cultural backgrounds in their place of origin, and the classification of people according to ethnic group, rooted in a particular place of origin, is common in all three countries.

In Canada, most family members lived in the Toronto area, which has received a large number of immigrants in recent decades. They represented three generations in the family network that had emigrated from Dominica. The oldest generation was born in Dominica, the second in Canada, England and Dominica, and the third in Canada. Despite the fact that the family had lived in Canada for several generations by the late 1990s, family members were still expected to identify themselves with reference to a place of origin outside Canada. Indeed, at school the children were taught to represent themselves in this way, as this excerpt from my interview with a 9-year-old girl, Laura, three generations out of Dominica, illustrates:

> On the first day of school we had to tell where we are from and stuff. We don't do this every year, but some years. Last year in grade four you had to stand in front of the classroom and talk about yourself.
> What did you say?
> I said, 'My name is Laura Lewandowski, I am 8 years old, I am Canadian, I was born in [. . .] Hospital. My mother is English.' We only do this with some teachers.
> Is it important to know where people are from?
> No, it is important that they are nice, that they share – their snacks and their books.

Although the children were probably expected to introduce themselves according to the place of origin of their parents or grandparents, Laura opted to claim that she was from Canada, having been born in a local hospital. She added, however, that her mother was English, a place of origin that, as I shall discuss later, may be rather unexpected, given her appearance as a person of colour. Thus she opted not to mention her deceased father's Ukrainian background, or for that matter her mother's Caribbean background. While this choice was probably rather strategic, it seems likely that an essential aspect of the school's teaching of respect for people of different cultural background was the lesson that origins in and of themselves do not matter. Thus Laura explained, when I asked her about the significance of knowing where people are from, that this is not as important as children being nice to one another and sharing their things. In this way, place of origin and the ethnic label that went with it were highlighted as important means of identifying people, but one that said little about them as individual persons.

By the time children leave school, it seems to have become self-evident to them that Canada is populated by people who originate in many different places. Thus when I asked Laura's 20-year-old sister Brenda, who was also born and reared in Toronto, how she identified herself, this question triggered a long response concerning the multiracial and multicultural character of Canadian society, which included this description of her workplace:

I am the only black person in the office. The secretary is from Thailand, one girl is Italian, one is just Canadian, another is from Hungary, one is from the Czech Republic, one from the Philippines. So we have the world.

What is 'just a Canadian'?

A white person from Nova Scotia or Newfoundland.

Are you not Canadian, then?

I am Canadian. For a lot of people their background and race are more important than their nationality. We are all one family, but we are so different. I have two friends from Canada, one is Jewish and the other is Korean, and I am West Indian Canadian.

It is apparent that identifying people according to place of origin is a rather complex matter, and that varying origins have different implications for the sort of Canadian identity that people acquire. Thus Brenda starts by describing herself as the only black person at work, thus apparently adopting a racial identity, but then goes on to contrast this with various identities rooted in countries of origin in Asia and Europe. However, she also operates with an unmarked Canadian identity, based on origins in the Atlantic provinces settled by early white colonists, and explains that this Canadian identity is different from the apparently racialised identities of people of, for example, Korean, Jewish or West Indian background.

Behind her complicated manoeuvres in the ethnic and racial landscape of Canada, one can detect the imprint of the Canadian version of multiculturalism. In a study of Canadian cultural politics, Mackey (1997: 138) notes that despite a 'mythology of pluralism, white English-speaking Canadians have economic and cultural dominance'. Canadians therefore operate with three major groups in society: the 'First Nations' of Native or Aboriginal people; the 'Founding Nations' of the English and the French; and the 'Ethnocultural' groups of the later immigrants. Furthermore, 'white Anglophone Canadians often consider themselves simply "Canadians" or "Canadian-Canadians", whereas other groups are marked by difference from this implicit norm' (ibid.: 138–9). This distinction between 'real' Canadians and somewhat deviant Canadians is apparent in Brenda's description of her work mates. Moreover, she distinguished further, within the third category of 'Ethnocultural' groups of late immigrants, between those who are racially different and those who are not racialised:

You have got the feeling that you share the same heritage, but a lot we don't share. We have the same nation and country. [But t]his is a racist society – everything is part to me. I am Canadian, but not the same kind of Canadian.

This awareness of the importance of appearing different corresponds to the notion of 'visible minorities', an official term introduced in Canada to refer to 'persons who are non-white in colour or non-Caucasian in race, other than Aboriginal people', who may need special protection through affirmative action (Synnott and Howes 1996: 137). The visible minorities are significantly sub-divided into smaller groups, including 'Blacks', 'Filipino' and 'Koreans', terms that Brenda uses in her description of employees at her work place. Brenda's self-description in terms of ethnic identity therefore closely corresponds to the ethnic categories established in Canada's multicultural policy and associated minority programmes.

Brenda seemed to accept the ethnic and racial distinctions because she lived in Toronto, where most people carried some sort of label, and the 'Canadian-Canadians' were a minority. Such distinctions were more troublesome to her 18-year-old cousin Nicole, who lived in a small, white-dominated town outside Toronto. Here my question about identification led to the following exchange:

> Do I have to identify myself in any particular way? [Somewhat apprehensive]. I say I am a person.
> Do you ever identify with the Caribbean?
> I never say I am Caribbean.
> You prefer not to have a label?
> Yes, I am just me.

Nicole's ethnic labelling appears to have been occasioned entirely by her physical appearance as a person of some colour. Indeed, she had grown up and gone to school in the small town she was living in when I interviewed her, and was well acquainted with the local community. Furthermore, her father, who was of British origin, belonged to one of the oldest families in the local community, and Nicole lived with her parents in a large, venerable wooden house in one of the better parts of town. In a small-town context dominated by a white majority, being singled out as of a particular ethnic background was tantamount to being labelled as not really belonging in the local community and the national community of unmarked 'Canadian-Canadianness' that such a white Anglophone community represented (see Mackey 1997: 151). However, Nicole chose to attribute this emphasis on cultural homogeneity to the ignorance and lack of culture of the local community:

> So you have gone to school here. How do you like it?
> It is boring, being in a small town, there is not much culture. It is the same kind of people. No culture at all. No Asians, blacks, just mostly white.
> This is a problem?
> Yes, it makes people narrow-minded. They are only used to one kind, they become biased, they have a small-town mentality.

She therefore redefined multiculturalism to mean a richness, rather than a plurality, of culture, as opposed to the poverty of culture to be found in communities where people were all of the same kind.

Ethnic categorisation based on places of origin also figured as an important concern in the life stories of children interviewed in the United States. Laura's 13-year-old cousin, who grew up in a predominantly white suburban neighbourhood north of New York City, expressed annoyance that friends asked him about his background:

> I don't know what I am. What am I? I am what I am. I don't care what they think. The same people asked me twice. I don't know why they ask.

His 11-year-old brother had settled on identifying himself as West Indian, but worried about the connotations of the term:

> Friends ask sometimes about my origin, but not often. I say that I am West Indian. I say that I am not a native American. They may think so because of the Indian in West Indian.

His 15-year-old brother Keith had also decided on a West Indian identity, but he was wondering what the meaning of his ethnic label might be:

> Close friends have asked whether I am black. Like if I am from Africa or something. I don't know what to say. I say that I am West Indian. [. . .]
> What does West Indian mean?
> Being black. I know I am black. I am not sure what I am. People say they are Polish, so I say I am West Indian, just to say something. It means little.

In their study of identity among inner-city youth in the United States, Heath and McLaughlin note that 'Ethnicity seemed, from the youth perspective, to be more often a label assigned to them by outsiders than an indication of their real sense of self' (Heath and McLaughlin 1993a: 6). And they add: 'Ethnicity takes on both subjective and objective meanings, both as an internal assignment for the self and, more often in the United States after the 1980s, as a label given by external sources' (1993b: 14). These boys were prepared to deal with ethnicity as an externally imposed identity, but they were clearly more reticent about adopting it as a personal identity, having little knowledge of or personal experience with the place of origin to which it referred. Still, they recognised that they had a tie to the area through their parents, if not through their own experience. The 13-year-old brother thus replied, when I asked him whether he had special ties to the Caribbean:

No, I have gone to Barbados, and it was OK, I can't remember
Dominica. If I went now I could answer the question.
What about the relatives there?
I know that I have relatives there. I met them from Dominica. They
came here, uncles and aunts.
So you feel you are an American?
Yes, but not 100 per cent, because my parents are from somewhere else.

Whereas the children living in the United States and Canada were
subjected to external ethnic categorisation, most of the children in Great
Britain did not have this experience because they looked 'white'. Thus 18-
year-old Phyllis explained, when I asked how she identified herself:

If people talk, I tell them the long story about my Jamaican, English,
Scottish, Norwegian background. It is quite a mix. If I fill in an
application form I just put white.
English?
Yes, I think so. Before, if I said that I was partly Jamaican, I was told
that I don't look that way.

Like their phenotypically 'black' relatives, they were therefore not able
to choose the part of their background they wished to identity with, but
had to adopt an identity that suited their appearance.

Children's place-making

I have argued that in immigrant societies, where notions of ethnicity and
multiculturalism have become a dominant mode of structuring social
relations, places of origin do not necessarily represent a self-chosen mode
of identification. By identifying people according to the one place that has
been particularly salient in the public debate, that is, an often distant place
of origin, other kinds of places that may be of greater significance in the
lives of people and provide important sources of identification in their
daily lives tend to be ignored. It was apparent that the children I interviewed were engaged in various kinds of place-making that involved
playing with externally imposed categories, as well as creating entirely
different frameworks of identification. My interviews with the children
showed that the younger ones especially, who have not as yet internalised
adult social categories, operated with a variety of different places of
importance, corresponding to a much more culturally complex position in
society than the dominant multicultural order of things recognised.
    My interview with Laura showed that she identified with a number of
local physical sites and social positions. When I began my interview with
her by asking her to tell me about herself, she replied:

I go to a school by the name of [. . .] The teachers there are very nice, but I do wish there was a playground. Sometimes I get into fights with my friends. I share. Mostly I go into split classes. That's pretty much all.

The school was clearly a primary place of identification for Laura, which was hardly surprising, given that she spent a great deal of her time there. Dominica, her 'place of origin', did not figure at all in this introduction, however, probably because it was a distant place that played a fairly minor role in her everyday life. When I asked her later in the interview what she could tell me about Dominica, she explained that she had been there twice and summed up her impressions in three short sentences: 'It is very hot. I have some friends there. You've got to go swimming.' This does not mean that she was not aware of the significance of places of origin. I suggest, however, that she was playing with different kinds of places of identification of varying significance to her.

In the self-presentation for the class that she did when she had to tell 'where she was from and stuff', as already mentioned she said: 'My name is Laura Lewandowski, I am 8 years old, I am Canadian, I was born in [. . .] Hospital. My mother is English.' In this presentation, following her name, the first element of identification was her age, an important distinguishing feature among children (Gulløv 1999). This was followed by her mentioning her nationality, but this somewhat abstract nationality was then made concrete by localising it in a particular hospital. In her local universe of school friends, being able to point to a local hospital where one was born may have presented a way of distinguishing the Canadian-born from those who were born abroad, but it also localised the Canadian-born in a particular place of birth. In her self-presentation, she then went on to claim an English origin for herself by stating that her mother was English. This was entirely correct to the extent that her mother had been born in England and lived there during the early part of her childhood. But since her mother was the offspring of black migrants from Dominica, it is rather questionable whether this assertion of English origins would be accepted in a society in which people from Britain are expected to be white and are associated with the original settlers of British Canada, the 'Canadian-Canadians.' I wonder how Laura's classmates reacted to her claims, as a black person, to English origins. It may be that places of origins were still rather abstract entities in their universe, where having good school-mates was a much more pressing concern. It may also be that for these children distant places were mostly places of imagination where anything was possible. Thus towards the end of the interview, when I asked her whether she liked where she was living, Laura replied: 'I like it here, but I do wish I was in Las Vegas, where all the superstars are.' It may also be that Laura had not yet learned to order places into hierarchies of relative significance, but still referred to various different places according to their importance in particular situations.

The strong identification with the local community as reflected in personal affiliations with local institutions such as the hospital and the school, the playful presentation of ethnic background and the description of the Caribbean place of origin in terms of personal experiences rather than ethnic roots were important themes in many of the interviews with the children. The local community figured as the most important frame of reference in the children's description of themselves in the life-story interviews. Children described their lives with reference to such local places as the houses where they had lived, the schools they attended and the clubs where they played different kinds of sports. Indeed, for those children who had moved from one local community to another, or even within a local community, the moves, and the ways in which they had changed their lives, constituted an important organising principle in the life stories. This was perhaps most evident in 14-year-old Jeanette's life story, where she described being born in Florida and then moving to the outskirts of a city in Texas, where her family had had a succession of homes. She tied these moves to important events in her life, such as her attending various schools, getting to know family and friends, and engaging in various activities. Thus in her life story she related having moved to 'a duplex' by her grandparents' home; 'a trailer by the lake, close by where the school is', coinciding with her parents taking in a foster brother, who stayed with them for some years; 'a green house' in a new part of the city, where she attended first and second grade; 'next door to a friend's house', which they 'painted and fixed up', and where she attended third grade; a home in a new part of the town, where she attended another elementary school and seventh grade in middle school and got to know her best friend; and finally to the present home, where she had begun high school and was 'starting cheer-leading and dance classes'. Jeanette seemed to have taken all the moves in her stride, but other children related having been worried about losing their friends and not being able to adjust to the new community.

Whereas the local communities were important frameworks of life for the children, ethnic identity was experienced as a rather more abstract entity that was not clearly related to their everyday lives. Nevertheless, children learned that ethnicity played a role in the wider society and that they had to deal with this. Many responded by taking a rather pragmatic approach to the issue of ethnic identity. As already noted, Keith decided to call himself West Indian, 'just to say something', when others enquired about his ethnic background. Thirteen-year-old Lisa, a third-generation member of the family of Jamaican origin, who lived in an affluent, mostly white town outside Los Angeles, California, explained that she sometimes opted for her European identity in order to find a common ground of identification vis-à-vis her school mates:

At school there are only three to four kids of my race; most are white. Everybody else is Scottish, Irish and so. So I say that I am Scottish too, so that I can relate to them a little. They see my dark skin, and they think about African slaves. It is a shock to them that I am also Scottish. They only see the Black part. Some who are of Scottish background say, 'Oh, wow!' Whenever I see my mom's picture downstairs of the original Scotsman, I am reminded of it.

This flexible approach to ethnicity was also apparent among the children of British–Greek parents studied by Michael Anderson (1999). He found that the children of these mixed marriages identified themselves as Greek or British, depending on the social context in which they found themselves. As was the case with the children of British and Greek parents, the children I interviewed had a mixed ethnic background, and it was therefore difficult to settle on one particular ethnic identity. They seem to have taken pride in being mixed, and some, like this 14-year-old girl living in Miami, displayed considerable knowledge of her particular background. She solved the problem of ethnicity by regarding her mixed Caribbean identity as part of a more general identity as black, viewing her black identity as a common human identity overriding all the other identities that she could claim for herself:

> You should be proud of what you are and where you are from. I classify myself as black, and sometimes as multi-racial. I am black more than anything else.
> Why are you multi-racial?
> Because of my white heritage. Sometimes they don't have the multi-racial category. I don't like the 'other', it is like being an animal.
> What white background do you have?
> Grandfather is black, my grandmother she is white. [. . .] And dad is also mixed. Both his parents are mixed. His mother's father was German, the mother Jamaican. And dad's dad's dad's mother is from Portugal, her husband a Jamaican. I think everybody is from Africa, it is the mother country, where creation took place, where man was created.

Whereas the children who looked black were frequently faced with questions about their ethnic origins, the white-looking children in England were just assumed to be British. However, several of them liked to refer to their non-British background to make themselves more interesting, to stand out in the crowd of ordinary Britishness. A 17-year-old girl living in a southern English village explained:

> It is nice to have family all over the place. To have not just a normal English family with an auntie two miles down the road, and another

auntie, and another auntie, and that is what you've got. I couldn't bear that.

Her cousin of the same age similarly found that her ethnic background made her more unusual:

It is more interesting, you have more to talk about when you meet somebody. You don't just come from Portsmouth.

She was of both German and Jamaican background, but preferred the Jamaican origins, she explained, 'because of Hitler'. For these young people, their multiple places of origin therefore offered additional sources of belonging and identification that they could draw on when they were creating their own identity among friends.

Whereas most of the children had a pragmatic, sometimes even playful approach to their ethnic identity, their relationship with their actual place of origin in the Caribbean varied a great deal according to their particular experience of the place. Laura, as already noted, remembered Dominica in terms of the heat, the swimming and the friends she had made there. One 7-year-old boy described Jamaica in terms of the dogs he had met there; a 14-year-old girl related having encountered reverse discrimination in Jamaica in being called names because of her light skin; and a girl in her late teens depicted Dominica in terms of the relatives she had met there, describing the overwhelming feeling of being related to everyone and being 'totally welcome' that she had experienced.

Few embraced their Caribbean place of origin entirely, largely because they were not born in the Caribbean themselves and had only limited exposure to the region. Thus the only children who identified themselves as Caribbean had stayed there for longer periods: one was born in Jamaica, though she had moved as a small child to the United States; the other had lived a full year with grandparents in Dominica while her mother in Great Britain completed a university degree. These girls had no plans to move to the Caribbean, however, one having mixed experiences about living with grandparents, who had been rather strict about how she could dress and behave, the other having been exposed to racial hostility.

With their limited exposure to their Caribbean place of origin, most children were evidently concerned about sources of belonging that would ground them where they lived. For the younger children, the local community seemed to be the most important place of belonging. Some of the older, more racially conscious children, who were 'non-white', opted for an identity as black, often in combination with the nationality of their country of residence, because this was associated with modern life in the society where they lived. One 18-year-old boy in Canada identified with the pride and resistance of being black and related this to the particular history of independent spirit in Dominica. A 19-year-old boy, whose father was black American, had similarly adopted a black identity, noting that 'there is not much difference between my black American and my Jamaican family, except that, instead of being shipped here as slaves, they were shipped there as slaves'. Yet others refused to be pigeon-holed as having any sort of identity, such as Nicole in Toronto, who resented the whole idea of having a particular ethnic identity, or her younger cousin living in a suburb of New York, who exclaimed: 'I don't know what I am. What am I? I am what I am. I don't care what they think.'

Places of belonging

In this chapter, I have explored the places of belonging that emerged in life-story interviews with the children and grandchildren of immigrants. Such places included the local community and local neighbourhood where they had lived with their parents and siblings; the school where they had spent much of their time, obtaining an education and making friends; and the clubs where they had played sports against sports teams from other local areas. Places also included various places of origin that could be evoked to find common ground with, or make themselves more interesting in relation to, school friends and playmates in the local community. Finally, places of belonging also included the country where the children were born, had lived virtually all of their lives and expected to remain in their future lives as adults. These places of identification, moreover, were not mutually exclusive, but were employed in particular situations, as the children sought to define a social place for themselves in relation to their particular context of life; they were therefore woven together into multifaceted forms of identification.

In migration research, there has been an increasing interest in the continued importance of migrants' transnational or diasporic ties to the homeland in the place of origin, whereas others have noted that many migrants do not become integrated into the mainstream middle-class culture of the receiving society, but experience segmented integration into a marginalised subculture (Waters 1999; Zhou 2001). This increasing awareness of the significance of the immigrants' place of origin – especially if this place is located in the developing world – and the emergence of alternative avenues of integration into the receiving society is important, in so far as it is grounded in careful research on particular immigrants and their way of life. There is, however, a danger that research that sets out to study the transnational, diasporic or subcultural life of immigrants may miss an important aspect of the processes of integration in which migrants and their families are involved. My life-story interviews with children, where they talked about themselves as they wished, and not as immigrants or the children of immigrants, suggested that children construct places of belonging informed by their locally lived lives as well as the wider society of which they are a part, and that they did not particularly stress having a strong sense of belonging rooted in the place of origin of their immigrant parents or grandparents. Rather, they identified with various different places of significance in their everyday lives. This may be related to the fact that these children were from families of middle-class background, who came from social strata in the old colonies that were heavily influenced by British culture. Most of them settled comfortably in white, middle-class areas of the receiving societies. As they settled, the social focus on place of origin therefore increasingly came to define them in relation to an elsewhere – an empty category that served primarily to accord them the position of being a minority in society unable to develop credible local places of identification that ground them within society. This is particularly the case for those who are 'visible minorities' and therefore marked as different. However, my research included a number of children whose parents had not experienced social and economic mobility, and who had grown up in households located in immigrant neighbourhoods with their fair share of social and economic problems. Nevertheless, their recounting of their life stories and views concerning ethnicity were not markedly different from those of the other children interviewed. As in the case of their more privileged cousins, their life stories reflected the importance of local, national and transnational places of belonging, woven together in the context of children's life experiences.

This conclusion accords well with a study of multicultural education in Canada conducted by Ackroy and Pilkington (1999). They argue that 'children do not have one essential identity but switch identities in different contexts and, subject to diverse cultural influences, often produce new identities' (ibid.: 445). According to Heath and McLaughlin (1993a), being able to play out such shifting, contextualised identities is an essential aspect of growing up:

> Many young people told us repeatedly, 'Ethnicity ain't what it's really all about.' To them, ethnic labels could mean something only later on; achieving a sense of belonging and of knowing that they could *do* something and be someone in the eyes of others had to come first. Ethnicity came to carry import only as it functioned within a host of embedded identities that could get a young person somewhere in the immediate community.
>
> (Heath and McLaughlin 1993a: 6)

This analysis of the dynamics of children's construction of place in immigrant societies offers insights into wider processes of inclusion and exclusion in society. It suggests that children draw on a variety of local, national and global sources of belonging to create a social place of relevance in their context of life, but that as they grow up, they may find that their construction of places of identification becomes constricted by the multicultural or ethnic structure of the wider society. This structure and the policies associated with it teach them which place is expected to be their primary site of belonging and identification in society. They are then likely to discover that their main source of public identification is expected to be located in a geographic elsewhere. This situation raises important issues concerning children's place in multicultural societies. In multicultural societies, it has been argued, everybody has the right to their own cultural identity. Yet, if children operate with multiple, shifting identities, as this and other studies suggest, it is not enough to grant people the right to a cultural identity. One should rather, as Ackroy and Pilkington suggest, 'envisage children as having a right to construct their own cultural identities' (1999: 453). By acknowledging children's right to develop their own cultural identities, thus giving them a place of belonging in society, it may also be possible to envisage a future in which the more fluid and complex sociocultural fields of relationships that characterise many communities today do not have to contend with the ethnic regimes that tend to constrict present-day multicultural societies.

Notes

1 In anthropology, migration research has had a broader regional focus and includes studies of regional migration in the developing world. There has also been greater interest in examining migration processes from the perspective of migrants and their social relations in their place of origin, as well as in the receiving society. For a review of the literature, see Brettell 2000.
2 This research was part of a research programme entitled 'Livelihood, Identity and Organisation in Situations of Instability' and funded by the Danish Council for Development Research. For analyses of other aspects of this research, see Olwig 2002a, 2002b, 2002c.

References

Ackroy, J. and A. Pilkington (1999) 'Childhood and the construction of ethnic identities in a global age', *Childhood* 6(4): 443–54.
Anderson, M. (1999) 'Children in-between: Constructing identities in the bicultural family', *Journal of the Royal anthropological Intitute* (NS) 5(1): 13–26.
Appadurai, A. (1996) *Modernity at Large: Cultural Dimensions of Globalization*. Minneapolis: University of Minnesota Press.
Basch, L., N. G. Schiller and Cristina Szanton Blanc (1994) *Nations Unbound: Transnational Projects, Postcolonial Predicaments and Deterritorialized Nation-States*. Basel: Gordon and Breach.
Baumann, G. (1999) *The Multicultural Riddle: Rethinking National, Ethnic, and Religious Identities*. London: Routledge.
Brettell, C. (2000) 'Theorising migration in anthropology: The social construction of networks, identities, communities, and globalscapes', in C. B. Brettel and J. F. Hollifield (eds) *Migration Theory*. New York: Routledge, pp. 97–135.

Clifford, J. (1994) 'Diasporas', *Cultural Anthropology* 9(3): 302–38.

Cohen, R. (1997) *Global Diasporas: An Introduction*. London: UCL Press.

Gulløv, E. (1999) *Betydningsdannelse blandt børn*. Copenhagen: Gyldendal, Socialpædagogiske Bibliotek.

Heath, S. B. and M. W. McLaughlin (1993a) 'Introduction: Identity and inner-city youth', in S. B. Heath and M. W. McLaughlin (eds) *Identity and Inner-City Youth: Beyond Ethnicity and Gender*, New York: Teachers College Press, Columbia University, pp. 1–12.

——— (1993b) 'Ethnicity and gender in theory and practice: The youth perspective', in S. B. Heath and M. W. McLaughlin (eds) *Identity and Inner-City Youth: Beyond Ethnicity and Gender*. New York: Teachers College Press, Columbia University, pp. 13–35.

Mackey, E. (1997) 'The cultural politics of populism: Celebrating Canadian national identity', in C. Shore and S. Wright (eds) *Anthropology of Policy: Critical Perspectives on Governance and Power*. London: Routledge, pp. 136–64.

Mahler, S. (1998) 'Theoretical and empirical contributions: Toward a research agenda for transnationalism', in M. P. Smith and L. E. Guarnizo (eds) *Transnationalism from Below*. New Brunswick: Transaction Publishers, pp. 64–100.

Olwig, K. F. (2001) 'New York as a locality in a global family network', in N. Foner (ed.) *Islands in the City: West Indian Migration to New York*. Berkeley: University of California Press, pp. 142–60.

——— (2002a) 'The ethnographic field revisited: Towards a study of common and not so common fields of belonging', in V. Amit (ed.) *Realising Community: Concepts, Social Relationships and Sentiments*. London: Routledge, pp. 124–45.

——— (2002b) 'A respectable livelihood: Mobility and identity in a Caribbean family', in N. N. Sørensen and K. F. Olwig (eds) *Mobile Livelihoods: Life and Work in a Globalized World*. London: Routledge, pp. 85–105.

——— (2002c) 'A wedding in the family: Home making in a global kin network', *Global Networks*, 2(3): 205–18.

Olwig, K. F. and N. N. Sørensen (2002) 'Mobile livelihoods: Making a living in the world', in N. N. Sørensen and K. F. Olwig (eds) *Work and Migration: Life and Livelihoods in a Globalising World*, London: Routledge, pp. 1–19.

Portes, A., L. Guarnizo and P. Landholt (1999) 'The study of transnationalism: Pitfalls and promise of an emergent research field', *Ethnic and Racial Studies* 22(2): 217–37.

Schiller, N. G., L. Basch and C. Szanton Blanc (eds) (1992) *Toward a Transnational Perspective on Migration*. New York: New York Academy of Sciences.

Schwartz, J. (1998) 'Visions of diaspora in contemporary social science', in U. Haxen, H. Trautner-Kromann and K. L. Goldschmidt Salamon (eds) *Jewish Studies in a New Europe*. Copenhagen: C. A. Reitzel International Publisher, pp. 757–69.

Sutton, C. R. (1987) 'The Caribbeanization of New York City and the emergence of a transnational socio-cultural system', in C. R. Sutton and E. Chaney (eds) *Caribbean Life in New York City: Sociocultural Dimensions*. New York: Center for Migration Studies, pp. 15–30.

Synnott, A. and D. Howes (1996) 'Canada's visible minorities: Identity and representation', in V. Amit-Talai and C. Knowles (eds) *Re-Situating Identities:*

The Politics of Race, Ethnicity, and Culture. Peterborough, Ontario: Broadview Press, pp. 137–60.

Thorne, B., M. F. Orellana, W. S. E. Lam and A. Chee (forthcoming) 'Raising children, and growing up, across national borders: Comparative perspectives on age, gender, and migration', in P. Hondagneu-Sotelo (ed.) *Gender and U.S. Immigration: Contemporary Trends*. Berkeley: University of California Press.

Tölölyan, K. (1996) 'Rethinking diaspora(s): Stateless power in the transnational moment', *Diaspora* 5(1): 3–36.

Vertovec, S. (1999) 'Conceiving and researching transnationalism', *Ethnic and Racial Studies* 22(2): 447–62.

Waters, M. C. (1999) *Black Identities: West Indian Immigrant Dreams and American Realities*. New York: Russell Sage Foundation.

Zhou, M. (2001) 'Growing up American: The challenge confronting immigrant children and children of immigrants', *Annual Review of Sociology* 23: 63–95.

Epilogue
Children's places

Vered Amit

To whom, with whom and where do children *belong*? What are or should they be *doing*, where, when, with whom? What should they *not* be doing? Where and with whom should they *not* be? These and the other questions which issue from a focus on the 'place of children in society', the concern of the chapters of this book, are not, in themselves, new. As Karen Fog Olwig and Eva Gulløv note in their introduction, attention to such questions has featured in numerous anthropological monographs from the earliest days of the discipline's formation. And in one form or another, the social location of children has also been the preoccupation of many other academic disciplines and a host of public institutions, professional and popular discourses.

The prevalence of this interest is not surprising since to attempt to account for children is to inherently invoke fundamental issues of social reproduction. Given that over time they do not remain children, questions about the place of children in society inevitably imply queries about the ways in which social institutions, practices, relationships and cultural meanings are reproduced (or not) from one generation to the next. Within anthropology, however, issues of social reproduction have been rendered increasingly problematic over the last few decades by general shifts towards more processual views of culture and the unpacking of a conflation of culture, community, geography and time which often characterised earlier anthropological writing.

Contemporary anthropologists are much less likely to regard shared cultural knowledge, practices or communality as a necessary or self-evident concomitant of territorial proximity. Shared identities may be claimed by people who reside at great distances from each other while localised relationships may be characterised by disputes over meaning, experience and belonging. This reading of the relationship between locale, culture and identity as contingent renders the trajectory of social and cultural development over time far less predictable, and it is this analytical shift which explicitly frames the inquiries broached in this volume. So, if the questions the editors pose are longstanding, the same cannot be said of the answers they and their fellow contributors attempt to provide. Yet the study of children's places is not only framed within this broader theoretical repositioning, it can also crucially inform it. In this essay, I want to focus on two areas which are especially brought to the fore by this focus on children but which have import far beyond it: social transformation and individual agency.

'Futurity' and tutelage

In his analysis of the iconography of Norwegian nationalism, Thomas Hylland Eriksen (1997) argued that the development of the nation and the bourgeois individual have been treated as mutually referential. Metaphorically, the nation was a human being. One could extend Eriksen's argument further to the even more general homology that is often drawn between the stages of human development and the historical development of societies. Indeed one could argue that the very concept of generational order relies on this conflation of personal biography and social history. Within this reading of history as life course, whither goes the child in his/her movement towards adulthood, so too goes the history of the wider community. In principle, however, such an interpretation endows all the members of that general collectivity with an intrinsic moral stake in the development of one constituent social category and its individual members. For if the future of a collectivity depends on what kind of adults today's children will in due course become, then surely all its members have a vested interest in how these children develop? The logical implication of such an argument is to transform the personal biographies of members of one social category of persons into legitimate subjects of public scrutiny.

This morally proprietary positioning also draws its inspiration and legitimacy from a pervasive identification of childhood as the archetype for tutelage systems.[1] Indeed such is the strength of this association that the adult subjects of other forms of tutelage tend by analogy to be represented as childlike. It is with this association in mind that Noel Dyck has compared the tutelage orientation of the Canadian system of Indian administration with the adult supervision of organised children's sports in the suburbs of Vancouver (Dyck 2003) Tutelage systems are typified by a definition of clients as specially vulnerable and therefore legitimately and appropriately requiring the protections entailed in the exercise of restraint or care by a guardian (Dyck 1991: 24). Thus in this volume, we see children defined as a 'weak' population segment in Denmark (Anderson, Chapter 7 in this volume), traditionally requiring the special care of patrikin and only gradual incorporation into the adult Luo world of western Kenya (Nyambedha and Aagaard-Hansen, Chapter 8 in this volume), especially vulnerable to the Evil Eye among Tigrayan returnees in Ada Bai (Hammond, Chapter 4 in this volume), needing the safe havens of NGO children's projects in Addis Ababa (Nieuwenhuys, Chapter 5 in this volume) and so on. In short, tutelage systems are inherently paternalistic systems of moral regulation.

Thus, when Olwig and Gulløv note that '[p]laces for children . . . are defined by adult moral values about a cherished past' (see also chapters in this volume by Gulløv (Ch. 1), Hammond (Ch. 4), Nyambedha and Aagaard-Hansen (Ch. 8) as well as Olwig (Ch. 11)) 'and a desirable future' (see chapters by Meinert (Ch. 9) and Anderson (Ch. 7)), 'clothed in commonsense notions about children's best interests' (Introduction: page 3), they are identifying the interaction of particular versions of history and tutelage as these are applied to the moral regulation of children. The emotional and regulatory wallop packed by this brew of dependency, 'futurity' (Jenks 1996) and paternalism is perhaps most crudely apparent in repeated moral panics about children (Cohen 1972) which intrinsically combine all these elements. Panics about crime, music, styles, consumerism, pornography or abuse have been rung as alarm bells about the future of society and the need to extend constraints over children's bodies, movements and activities (see Nieuwenhuys on Addis Ababa NGOs in this volume) to protect them and, through them, the wider collectivity. At its extreme, this argument can even be used to justify physically hurting children as insurance against the risks of an unsafe world (see Hammond in this volume on the practice of cauterising and cutting Tigrayan returnee children to protect them from the Evil Eye).

Moral panics are inherently reactionary movements but another common representation of children which also draws from the association of life course with social development places the emphasis instead on innovation and experimentation. The endowment of childhood with special properties of movement and change (James 1998; James et al. 1998) in turn encourages a presumption that its incumbents are more open to and better able to master the new and the unfamiliar: new technology, forms of movement, creativity, connections and so on. For example, the 'dot.com bubble' of the late 1990s was pervasively identified with the young. In media imagery and reporting, government and corporate policies, hiring policies and popular discourses, the 'New Economy' was represented as the special province of youth, at least until the bubble burst. The future is or was the new, and both belong to the young.

Scholarly interest in children, while often critical of these kinds of representations, has nonetheless tended to be driven by them. The combination of tutelage or in James' terms, 'images of dependency' (James 1998: 140) and 'futurity' have been criticised as the limiting elements of longstanding Western theories of socialisation which have been incorporated into certain scientific discourses about the 'child' such as those appearing in developmental psychology (James 1998; James et al. 1998; James and Prout 1990). As these and other critics have noted (Stephens

1995; Amit-Talai and Wulff, 1995), this approach often emphasised the future of adults in the making, at the expense of considering the present of children in its own right. The emphasis on how children were socialised into adulthood often seemed to have more to say about the adults who were charged with this process of socialisation than the young they were supposedly shaping. Hence the critics of this approach tended to call (in terms similar to those espoused in the Norwegian government programme of 'Try Yourself' described by Kjørholt in this volume) for more attention to children's culture *sui generis*.

I will have more to say about the unintended limitations of this approach later but that aside for now, in spite of such critiques, orientations towards both futurity and tutelage continue to underlie a good deal of research on children. Even anthropologists are prone to identifying the young as most attuned to the changes being wrought by processes of globalisation, movement and new technologies (Hannerz 1996: 29). And across a number of disciplines, the most enduringly prolific genres of child studies focus on the subject matter of one moral panic or another: gangs, media violence, child abuse and so on. Nor does one have to search hard amongst other more nuanced studies on a variety of topics involving children in order to detect a ubiquitous subtext of protective advocacy. Among anthropologists, for example, whether in relationship to poverty (Susser 1993), violence (Scheper-Hughes 1992), or politics (Stephens, 1995), there appears to be a subtle presumption that children are structurally weak and hence particularly vulnerable to exploitation, to ill-advised government policies, even to the misguided missionary zeal of well-meaning Western activists (Gailey 1999). Accordingly, it is the scholar's, and perhaps especially the anthropologist's, duty to speak on their behalf. One might even go farther and suggest that the vulnerability and invisibility anthropologists once accorded generally to their 'exotic' ethnographic subjects is now being transferred to certain classes of informants. If anthropological paternalism is no longer considered to be acceptable on behalf of adult 'informants', who could deny its legitimacy on behalf of children, the quintessentially proper object of nurturing and protection? As inappropriate as it was to patronise non-Western adults as if they were children, surely and especially it can't be wrong to treat children in this way, wherever they may be. After all, they are children! In short, even the considerable efforts among anthropologists to atone for and jettison the presumptions and distortions of an older North/South tutelage has not prevented the adoption of similar stances vis-à-vis children.

There is nothing intrinsically wrong with advocating on behalf of certain children in particular circumstances. But there are some serious epistemological problems if the global categories of children are imbued a priori, even implicitly, with this orientation. First of all, it prematurely closes off the investigation of variations in children's social and juridical statuses whether in comparison to other sets of children or to membership of other social categories. As many of the chapters in this volume and others elsewhere (Gailey 1999) have pointed out, in many situations, children are not necessarily any weaker or more disadvantaged and sometimes less so than their adult counterparts. Second, whatever the circumstances under scrutiny, over-privileging protective advocacy risks the reduction of children to issues, rather than encouraging the careful investigation of the varied and difficult human complexities which attend engaging with the world, whatever your age and status. As the chapters in this volume illustrate so well, one of the most effective correctives to this form of reductionism is detailed, systematic ethnography. And, perhaps because of the dominance of a tutelage orientation, that kind of rounded ethnographic portrait of children is still more often marked by its absence than its prevalence. Hence this volume serves to address a crucial gap in this field. But it also happily avoids another more subtle form of reductionism.

For there is another form of reductionism that can attend even the explicit efforts to transcend both tutelage and futurity which characterised critical repositionings in the study of children and youth. In seeking to reassert the cultural integrity and agency so often categorically denied children in longstanding Western discourses such as socialisation theory or moral panics, such critiques sought to shift the emphasis instead on to peculiarly youthful cultural creations. Because the moral onus placed in these dominant discourses had tended to fall on the successes or failures of adult surveillance, efforts to move on from these shifted the focus on to peer contacts between children and the zones in which children or youths were most likely to encounter each other. Yet as a result, this focus on children's culture sometimes seemed to be trying to divorce it (also reminiscent of the official aims of the 'Try Yourself' project described by Kjørholt, Chapter 10 in this volume) from the multi-aged social context in which all young people live. This has been most glaringly evident in the literature that focuses self-consciously on 'youth culture' and which has been heavily influenced by the pioneering 1970s and 1980s work of the University of Birmingham's Centre for Contemporary Cultural Studies (the 'Birmingham School' or CCCS).

Rejecting the conservatism and stereotyping which characterised repeated moral panics about teenagers, the Birmingham School focused on and valorised highly stylised subcultures of white male rebellious youths such as punks, skinheads and so on. Although propelled by an interest in the historical implications of post-Second World War transformations of production, labour and consumption in Britain, the members of the Birmingham School were if anything quite fatalistic about the capacity of youths to effect broader structural transformations (Hall and Jefferson 1976). Particularly influential studies such as Paul Willis' *Learning to Labour* (1981 [1977]) represented the rebelliousness of working-class youths as ironically delivering them into the class position of their fathers. While, with a few exceptions such as Willis' study, the CCCS publications were not characterised by especially strong ethnographic accounts, the same cannot be said for their successors. Subsequent research on youth culture, while positioning itself within the tradition of the Birmingham School, has been characterised by detailed, often monograph-length, ethnographies (e.g. Pilkington 1994; Thornton 1995; Alexander 1996). More recent studies have also moved well beyond the limited focus of the CCCS on British white male working-class youth. They have moved on to examine the experiences of young women (Mirza 1992), youths from a wider range of ethnic backgrounds (Alexander 1996; Yon 2000) and so on. But this more recent work has for the most part, explicitly retained the CCCS definition of 'youth culture' as constructed in the course of peer interactions between youths, in opposition to other cultural forms, and taking shape most fully in the domain of leisure beyond the institutional controls exerted in more formal realms. Thus while producing a detailed and nuanced ethnography of young black men in London, Clare Alexander still defined youth culture in terms of agency exercised in the public leisure sphere (Alexander 1996: 19). In short, youth culture has been reduced to enactments only within specific places and domains for youths, and the ensuing portraits, however ethnographically detailed, have been narrowly circumscribed. As a result, an approach and field of study that started off as a theoretically influential effort to work through the ramifications of social transformations has ended up having less and less to say about broader processses of social reproduction and change. Not surprisingly, it has also become increasingly marginalised across a number of academic disciplines.

There is, as Olga Nieuwenhuys (Chapter 5) notes in this volume, an analogous danger that a focus on children's places will become a focus on places restricted to children. This danger is explicitly addressed in this volume not through a concerted focus on extending the range of sites being investigated – although a variety of sites are included – but through a critical engagement with the interaction between place and generation. This focus helps avoid several of the limitations that have characterised the approaches I outlined above. First, it centres on generational order as a vehicle for critically investigating the kinds of social identities and moral evaluations which are mobilised in the cultural construction of historical progression. Second, it uses the concept of inter-generational relations to ensure that the locations and positions of children are never studied through the lens of or by a priori focus on only one category of social actors. Children are not simply the objects of adult interventions but neither do they operate in a world without adults. And finally it uses the interaction between generation and place to interrogate social changes and in so doing offers more nuanced analyses not only of the uneven and contradictory nature of social reproduction but also of agency.

Social reproduction and agency

In a Luo community in Bondo District, western Kenya, the spread of HIV/
AIDS has orphaned many children, in the process dramatically changing
the institutions for socialising children (Nyambedha and Aagaard-Hansen,
Chapter 8). Orphaned children have employed a variety of strategies to
deal with these changed circumstances, in the process both challenging
aspects of traditional Luo models of childhood as well as drawing upon
them. Children in Ada Bai, a Tigrayan returnee settlement in Ethiopia,
transcended spatial boundaries their parents could or would not, creating
new bonds for themselves with their environment, and yet neither were
these processes of emplacement unaffected by adult constructions of previous
highland homelands and lineage orders or the dangers of this new lowland
settlement (Hammond, Chapter 4). Indeed, the bodies of Ada Bai children
bore the scars of their parents' efforts at protecting them from the
distinctive illnesses of this place. It was up to Aboriginal children in
Southeast Cape York, Australia to decide whether or not they would
attend school, which school they would attend as well as with which kin
they would reside (Lorimer, Chapter 3). As Kuku-Yalanji children made
choices and moved between places in which they held land rights and
where different sets of their kin lived, they were both following the place-
making constituted by the movements of a previous generation as well as
activating and actualising kin networks which cut across place. Yet the
agency exercised by these children in choosing to remain at home rather
than return to the loneliness and alienation of 'out of the way' mainstream
schools also ensured that they missed out on the kind of education which
might allow them to improve upon their inferior socio-economic situation
in Australia. In Belfast, children were restricted to local areas defined in
terms of the divisions between Protestants and Catholics (Gilliam, Chapter
2). While within everyday life within these areas, children could assert the
importance of other identities such as gender and age, the impact of
religious segregation was sufficiently comprehensive to limit the reconfiguration of conflict identities intended by sporadic anti-sectarian efforts to
bring Protestant and Catholic children together. In marked contrast, the
children attending an Open Gym in Copenhagen or residing in an ethnically integrated neighbourhood in Oslo encountered children of diverse
backgrounds on a regular basis. This proximity however, did not however
necessarily impart autonomy in or convergence of the place-making in
which these children participated. Thus, the children attending a temporary
Open Gym at a publicly funded sports facility in Copenhagen seemed to
have no particular difficulty in organising and enjoying their play at this
venue, whether or not they were members of more formal associations
(Anderson, Chapter 7). Yet lack of club membership and its symbolic
denotation, at least in the eyes of sports organisers, of the bewildered

inability of immigrant parents to satisfy certain forms of civic exchange resulted in the exclusion of their children from this venue and their relocation to more modest facilities shared by other marginalised categories. While research on childhood in Norway has emphasised the importance of self-governed involvement in mixed play groups and their role in defining and integrating shared places, shifts in the activities organised for children, family organisation and the ethnic and social diversity of urban neighbourhoods are challenging this understanding (Lidén, Chapter 6). The cases of four children all residing in a working-class inner-city Oslo neighbourhood reveal considerable variation in their use of their local residential area, the degree of autonomy granted them for exploration outside, movement in and out of the area, responsibilities within the domestic household, uses of the local playground and so on.

> Parallel networks thus introduce a paradox: despite several children living next door, the experience of many children, such as Maria, may be one of nearly 'empty' places.
>
> (Lidén, Chapter 6: 129)

In Denmark, there has been an enormous expansion over the last 25 years in the number of children enrolled in the day-care system. While the explicit goal of day-care practice emphasises teaching children to be self-managing and to make decisions for themselves, their placement in day-care is determined by adults. Thus the complaints of children about the discomfort of the spartan forest kindergartens their parents worked hard to get them into are not likely to be heeded (Gulløv, Chapter 1). In Kwapa, a rural area in Uganda, children have been caught in a battleground between the policies of the central Education Ministry and the pathways of social and residential mobility espoused by their parents and teachers (Meinert, Chapter 9). Central government planners seek to make school a means of improving agricultural practices, while for parents and teachers it is the city and hence the skills that are most marketable in an urban environment which offer the best chance of changing social position. Caught between these opposing goals as well as the difficulty of raising secondary school fees, education can be experienced as an existential and moral trap by Kwapu children.

The chapters in this book build up an impressive compendium of varied circumstances, histories and places that remind us of several key issues in the relationship between individual agency, social personhood and change. First they illustrate that the latitude of individual autonomy is not simply a progressive function of age categories. Notwithstanding the apparent prevalence of 'images of dependency' in Western models of childhood, government and domestic regimes in Norway and Denmark (Chapters 10 and 1) have self-consciously, albeit somewhat paradoxically, attempted to contrive situations which expanded on the autonomy and independence even of very young children's explorations and self-development. And in some circumstances – returnee Tigrayan children's spatial mobility (Chapter 4), children in Addis Ababa offsetting one adult tutelage system against another to evade the harsh obligations of parental authority (Chapter 5) – children appear to have a wider ambit in which to manoeuvre than their adult counterparts. Nor of course is this a matter of either/or. Children can exercise considerable agency in one set of circumstances and over certain choices while still facing confining strictures in other domains. A hoary anthropological canon still aptly warns us against assuming a straight-forward relationship between norms and social action and hence against assuming a correspondence between the individual exercise of agency by children and the normative delineation of childhood. If these are obvious points, their implications are not.

If the choices made and practices enacted by particular children do not simply correspond with generational categories and these categories in turn may not be stable over space and/or time, how do we account for processes of social reproduction or change? In this volume some of the children least constrained in terms of the choices they made about their daily routines were also least able to effect changes in the broader socio-economic structures which disadvantaged them. And some of the children most explicitly denied agency both by cultural precepts of generational hierarchies as well as opportunistic relationships of exploitation were nonetheless, out of necessity, carving out new structures of kinship and generational order. If, *à la* Anthony Giddens, we accept that structure and agency interact, this volume reminds us that we can make no facile assumptions about the direction of this relationship or its implication for historical transformations.

In considering the workings of both agency and structure, we might remember the distinction between situational and historical change posed half a century ago by Clyde Mitchell in the Copperbelt towns of then Northeastern Rhodesia (Mitchell 1966). People may change their practices and categorical understandings to meet the exigencies of different situations without necessarily changing or even seeking to change the broader structures within which these situations are located, and macro structures can change considerably without necessarily producing easily discernible changes in practices on the ground. Will shifts in the identities claimed by children of Caribbean origins living in Canada and Britain affect changes in patterns of migration, transnational connections and government policies of multiculturalism or vice versa (Olwig, Chapter 11 in this volume)? Over the course of changes in North American ideologies of the connection between children and migration, from one that constructs children as the vanguard of integration to another that vests them with the guardianship of ancient identities and relationships to distant homelands, it is not clear that the 'place-making' of immigrant children has correspondingly changed much.

In considering the agency exercised by members of a social category often used as the archetype for systems of tutelage, we might also do well to remember another observation, in this case, by Michel de Certeau on the 'tactics of the weak' (1984). Most of us, children, adults, old and young, exert very little direct control or influence over the institutions that govern our lives. This does not, however, render or even allow us to be passive. To prosper or even simply to survive within these institutional constraints requires a constant elaboration of tactical agency. Thus I am not persuaded that children in Belfast are bereft of agency. They may not be able to change the religious dichotomy that canalises so much of life in this society, but within the compelling strictures of that broader regime they are still busy working out how to live in and how to be a child in Belfast. To be Catholic or Protestant in Belfast determines much, but it does not determine everything. Thus the 'tactics of the weak' matter because they are the web and woof of the experiences through which our lives and our cultural understandings take shape, of being social and alive. And in some circumstances the tactics of the weak may become complicit in paradigmatic changes and structural transformations. The $64,000 questions for us are when? How? This volume may not provide the answers to these questions but to pose them in such ethnographically complex and telling ways is a considerable achievement in itself.

Note

1 I would like to thank Noel Dyck for reminding me of this point.

References

Alexander, C. (1996) *The Art of Being Black: The Creation of Black British Youth Identities*. Oxford: Clarendon Press.
Amit-Talai, V. and H. Wulff (eds) (1995) *Youth Cultures: A Cross-Cultural Perspective*. London and New York: Routledge.
Certeau, M. de (1984) *The Practice of Everyday Life*. Translated by Steven F. Rendall. Berkeley, California: University of California Press.
Cohen, S. (1972) *Folk Devils and Moral Panics: The Creation of the Mods and Rockers*. London: MacGibbon and Kee.
Dyck, N. (1991) *What is the Indian Problem: Tutelage and Resistance in Canadian Indian Administration*. St John's, Nfld: ISER.
—— (2003) 'Tutelage and the engineering of selves: A comparison of children's sports and Indian administration in Canada'. Paper presented at the Meetings of the Canadian Anthropology Society, Halifax, Nova Scotia, 2003.
Eriksen, T. H. (1997) 'The nation as a human being – a metaphor in a mid-life crisis?', in K. Fog Olwig and K. Hastrup (eds), *Siting Culture: The Shifting Anthropological Object*. London and New York: Routledge, pp. 103–22.
Gailey, C. Ward (1999) 'Rethinking child labor in an age of capitalist restructuring', *Critique of Anthropology* 19(2): 115–19.

Hall, S. and T. Jefferson (eds) (1976) *Resistance through Rituals: Youth Subcultures in Post-war Britain*. London: Hutchinson.

Hannerz, U. (1996) *Transnational Connections: Culture, People, Places*. London and New York: Routledge.

James, A. (1998) 'Imaging children "at home", "in the family" and "at school": Movement between the spatial and temporal markers of childhood identity in Britain', in N. Rapport and A. Dawson (eds) *Migrants of Identity: Perceptions of Home in a World of Movement*. Oxford: Berg, pp. 139–60.

James, A., C. Jenks and A. Prout (1998) *Theorising Childhood*. Oxford: Polity Press.

James, A. and A. Prout (eds) (1990) *Constructing and Reconstructing Childhood*. Basingstoke: Falmer Press.

Jenks, C. (1996) 'The postmodern child', in J. Brannen and M. O'Brien (eds) *Children and Families: Research and Policy*. London: Falmer Press.

Mirza, H. S. (1992) *Young, Female and Black*. London and New York: Routledge.

Mitchell, C. J. (1966) 'Theoretical orientations in African urban studies', in M. Banton (ed.) *The Social Anthropology of Complex Societies*. London: Tavistock.

Pilkington, H. (1994) *Russia's Youth and Its Culture: A Nation's Constructors and Constructed*. London and New York: Routledge.

Scheper-Hughes, N. (1992) *Death without Weeping: The Violence of Everyday Life in Brazil*. Berkeley: University of California Press.

Stephens, S. (ed.) (1995) *Children and the Politics of Culture*. Princeton, NJ: Princeton University Press.

Susser, I. (1993) 'Creating family forms: The exclusion of men and teenage boys from families in the New York City shelter system, 1987–91' *Critique of Anthropology* 13(3): 267–83.

Thornton, S. (1995) *Club Cultures: Music, Media and Subcultural Capital*. London: Polity Press.

Willis, P. (1981 [1977]) *Learning to Labor: How Working Class Kids Get Working Class Jobs*. New York: Columbia University Press.

Yon, D. A. (2000) *Elusive Culture: Schooling, Race and Identity in Global Times*. Albany: State University of New York Press.

Index

Aagaard-Hansen, Jens 15, 242
Aboriginal life: children 11, 73, 242;
  marginalisation 70–1, 73; school
  67, 71, 75n15, 192;
  traditional/urban 61; *see also* Kuku-
  Yalanji people
Ackroy, J. 232, 233
Ada Bai: Baptism 87–8; emplacement
  79, 80, 92; home 91–2; identity
  91; marriage 86; religion 94n9;
  returnees 84
Addis Ababa 100–1, 102, 108–13
adults: children 12–13, 99–100, 156,
  203–4; conflict 42–3; control 2, 12,
  143; emplacement 93–4; protection
  239; *see also* child care workers;
  club pedagogues; parents; teachers;
  volunteer helpers
advocacy 239–40
age differences: emplacement 93–4;
  home 90–1; identity 227; Kuku-
  Yalanji children 66; mobility 64;
  safe/dangerous places 85
agency: autonomy 116; Belfast 50,
  56, 245; communities of practice
  50; emplacement 79–80;
  independence 86–7; individuals
  244; inter-generational relationships
  204, 241; orphans 164, 167–8,
  171; place 8; poverty 175;
  restrictions 56; social reproduction
  17, 236, 242–5; structure 172
agriculture: land ownership 181;
  lessons in 187–8; life chances
  191–2

AIDS 15, 163, 242
alcohol problems 162, 181
Alexander, Clare 241
Amin, Idi 185, 193–4n3
Amit, Vered 17
Anderson, B. 198, 215n7
Anderson, M. 229
Anderson, Sally 14, 142–3
Anglican Church 168–9
anthropology: children's place 6, 99;
  fieldwork 4, 5, 180–1; liminality
  113; paternalism 239; place 4, 99,
  107; social reproduction 236
anti-materialism 27–8
anti-sectarianism 43, 51–2, 54–5
Appadurai, A. 15, 219
Ariès, Philippe 100
associationless children 140–2;
  identifying 148–9, 150, 153–5;
  local children 138–9, 155;
  locating 154–6; loose
  children 158; marginalisation
  139
Atieno-Odhiambo, E. S. 167
Augé, M. 101–2, 110, 115, 192
Australia 11, 73; *see also* Aboriginal
  life
authority 244; anti-authoritarianism
  33–4
autonomy: agency 116; self-
  development 244; social studies
  203; supervision 24, 36, 126

Baptism 87–8
Barth, F. 32, 48, 123

Belfast: categorising people 51–2; children's agency 50, 56, 245; cross-community projects 52–4, 55; political understanding 43; restricted areas 242; sectarianism 40–1, 245; segregation 44; youth 41

belonging: control 236; home 200–1; identity 233; immigrant children 217–18, 231; place 15–17, 120, 121, 133; social status 164

Bender, B. 78

Berdoulay, V. 200

Birmingham School 240–1

birthplace 90–1

Bodenhorn, B. 94n4

body/space 88

Bourdieu, Pierre 46, 53, 55; doxa/heterodoxy 40, 46, 53; habitus 72; place 120–1; universe of the un-discussed 55–6

boys: employment 115; fishing 114, 128, 170; Luo people 165–6; mobility 85, 181–2; see also gender

Britain 219–20, 229–30

bullying 146

burial 87, 88

burning/cutting 88, 89–90

Burton, F. 51–2

bus kindergartens 26

Canada: immigrant children 221–2; migration research 218; multiculturalism 219–20, 222–3, 232; sports 237

capital, social 116

carers 170–2

Caribbean 191–2, 220, 221, 225–6, 230

Carsten, J. 157

Carter, J. 72

Casey, E. S. 62–3, 70, 82, 94n2

Catholic Church 168

Catholics 40–1, 42, 43–4, 47–8

Certeau, Michel de 245

charitable acts 213

child care 23

child care workers 14, 29–31, 37n10

childhood 9; folk model 7; modernity 28; NGO 109–10, 114; Norway 243; place 2; segregation 99–100; social exclusion 3–4; social inclusion 3–4; social status 31

childhood icons 100

Children's Farm 119–20

Christianity 184

citizenship: community 36; exclusion 34; participation 25–6, 197–8, 214–15n1; public space 201; Sweden 35–6

civil relatedness 155–7

civil war, Uganda 185

closure, social 157–8

club pedagogues 148; collaboration 149–50; Open Gym project 145, 146–7, 151–3, 156

Cockburn, T. 34

Cohen, A. 200

Cohen, D. W. 167

Cohen, S. 238

collectivity 171–2

community: children's 203; citizenship 36; identity 121; imagined 198, 203, 206–8; of practice 50; see also local communities

conflict: adults 42–3; children's attitudes 41; discourse 46–7; identity 47–50, 55; involvement 56; other 51–2; sectarianism 41–4

conflict avoidance 54–5

control: adults 2, 12, 143; belonging 236; children's place 9–10, 40; parents 44–5; power 209

Copenhagen 159n1

Copperbelt towns 244

co-wives 165, 174

cross-community projects, Belfast 52–4, 55

culture 4; children's own 202, 239; difference 28; identity 220, 233; local 194n8; marked 219; neighbourhood 120–1; of opposition 71; place 5, 7, 70–4; public forms 220; transmission 217

custodianship 66

Dahrendorf, R. 185, 194n7
dala (homestead) 164
Danish Gymnastics and Sport
    Associations 138, 139, 155
Danish Youth Council 139
daughter-in-law status 190
decoding 44
defilement law 193n2
democracy 214
Denmark: compulsory education 37n4;
    ideal children 24, 142–3; immigrant
    children 14, 25–6, 37n3, 159n4;
    parents/child workers 14, 29–30;
    public day-care system 23, 24–7,
    243; socialisation 150; *see also*
    kindergartens
dependency, images of 238–9, 243–4
Derg 83
difference: cultural 28; democracy 214;
    egalitarianism 201–4; home 116;
    imagined communities 206–8; Open
    Gym project 242–3; social 160n13,
    210; visible 223–4, 226, 232
discipline 87, 116
discourse 46–7, 54–5, 199, 202–3
discrimination, reverse 230
domestic sphere: Luo people 167–8;
    public sphere 158
domestic work 104, 171; *see also*
    household chores
Dominica 230, 231
dowry money 108, 115
doxa 40, 46, 53
Dyck, Noel 237

education: Denmark 37n4;
    employment 107–8, 112; life
    chances 185; marriage 190;
    modernisation 179–80; moral trap
    186–7, 243; parents 60, 86, 184;
    ruralised 179, 187–8, 189; urban
    centres 184–5; vocational 188; *see
    also* school; Universal Primary
    Education
egalitarianism 201–4, 213–14
Ehn, B. 31, 33
elderly people 90–1, 140, 164
electronic media 133–4

emplacement 78; Ada Bai 79, 80, 92;
    adults/children 93–4; age differences
    93–4; agency 79–80; gender 93;
    home 80, 90–1; identity 78; lineage
    93; refugee camps 80–3; space
    83–6; *tebib* 82
employers 170–2
employment: boys/girls 115, 128, 168;
    education 107–8, 112; Luo 165;
    mothers 121; orphans 169–72;
    rural–urban migration 170
Eriksen, Thomas Hylland 237
Eritrea 77
Ethiopia 11–12, 13, 77, 94n11; *see
    also* Ada Bai; Addis Ababa
Ethiopian People's Revolutionary
    Democratic Front 83
ethnicity: gender 14; identity 48,
    224–6, 228–9, 232; visible
    differences 223–4, 226, 232
ethnography 5
Evans-Pritchard, E. E. 174
everyday lives: experience 39, 123–9;
    neighbourhood 120; peer relations
    127; religion 125
Evil Eye 81, 89–90, 94n7, 237, 238
exclusion 34; social 3–4, 232–3
exogamy 172–3, 181–2
experience 39, 123–9, 135
extended case analysis 71–2

family: children 35; extended 58–9,
    125, 126; home 122–3; leaving
    114; places 129–30; protection
    171; split 123–4, 128–9, 130; street
    children 110–13
Ferguson, J. 5, 7, 15
fieldwork 4, 5, 180–1
Firth, Raymond 17n1
fish-landing place 102, 104, 106, 107
fishing industry 128
food from the land 61–2, 65
football games 56n10
forest kindergartens 26, 27–8, 243
Foucault, Michel 12, 116, 199
freedom of choice 11, 144, 145–6
friendship 203
futurity 237, 238, 239

gated sites 110
Geertz, Clifford 4
gender: emplacement 93; encoding of
    space 84–5; ethnicity 14; identity
    63; immigrant children 159n5; Luo
    children 165–6; mobility 85;
    neighbourhood 130–2; place
    189–91; rural–urban migration
    191; segregation 102, 103–5;
    socialisation 106–7; space 94n4;
    workplace 104; youth culture 241
gerontocracy 9–10, 45
Giddens, Anthony 172, 244
gift exchange 104
Gilliam, Laura 11, 42
girls: dowry money 108, 115;
    employment 115; Luo people
    165–6; mobility 85, 181–3;
    siwindhe 165–6, 175; sports ground
    131–2; see also gender
globalisation 15–16
gold mines 170
Gorm, P. 151
grandparents 166, 174
group identity 206–7
Gullestad, Marianne 2, 143, 200, 207
Gulløv, Eva 10–11, 236, 238
Gupta, A. 5, 7, 15

habitus 72
Hammond, Laura 11–12, 92
Hannertz, U. 185
Heath, S. B. 225, 232
hepatitis 88
heterodoxy 40, 53, 55
Hindus 101
Hirsch, E. 78
HIV/AIDS: see AIDS
Holland, D. 167, 172, 179
home: Ada Bai 91–2; age differences
    90–1; belonging 200–1;
    emplacement 80, 90–1; family
    122–3; institutions 32–3;
    obligations 126–7; place 73, 92–3,
    129–30
household chores 126, 166; see also
    domestic work
Hughes, Elizabeth 41

Hultqvist, Kenneth 29, 35–6

Ibsen, B. 140
idealised view of children 2–3, 142–3
identity: Ada Bai 91; age 227;
    belonging 233; black 225, 226,
    230–1; community 121; conflict
    47–50, 55; cultural 220, 233;
    diasporic 219; emplacement 78;
    ethnic 48, 224–6, 228–9, 232;
    expressive 207; gender 63;
    geographical 217; group 206–7;
    immigrant children 17, 221; inborn
    50; land ownership 63; local
    communities 121, 228; multiple
    220, 223, 227–8; national 215n7,
    227–8; negative 111; place 80,
    233; public spaces 211; racial 134,
    223, 224; sectarianism 43–4,
    48–50; shared 236; telling system
    52; transnational 219; visible
    characteristics 232; visible
    differences 226
immigrant children 16–17; belonging
    217–18, 231; Britain 229–30;
    Canada 221–2; Caribbean 230;
    Denmark 14, 25–6, 37n3, 159n4;
    gender 159n5; identity 17, 221;
    integration 14, 23, 26, 218–19; life
    stories 221–6, 231–3; loose children
    141–2, 157; Norway 122; Open
    Gym project 146, 158; Pakistani
    125–6, 134; parents 14, 157, 243;
    places of origin 226–7
incest 92–3
inclusion, social 3–4, 212, 214, 232–3
independence 86–7, 162, 175, 244
India, South: see Poomkara
indigenisation of modernity 108, 116
individualism, egalitarian 201
indoctrination 52–3
institutions 6–7; appropriated 3;
    home 32–3; labour market 23–4;
    parents 29–31; time spent in 30;
    see also kindergartens; public day-
    care system
integration: immigrant children 14, 23,
    26, 218–19; inter-generational

relationships 214; sports 138–9,
140–1
inter-generational relationships 2, 6;
agency 204, 241; children's place
1, 204–6, 241; cultural transmission
217; electronic media 133;
integration 214; place 12–15;
power 45; socialisation 6, 122
intermarriage 44
Ireland, Northern 11, 39–40, 41–2;
see also Belfast

Jamaica 230
James, A. 9–10, 39, 40, 56, 100,
156–7, 201, 203
Jenks, C. 39, 238
Jørgensen, M. 150, 154

kakwaro (lineage) 164, 168, 171
Katalamma sea goddess 104
Keith, M. 209
Kenya: AIDS 15, 163, 242; kinship
systems 15; orphans 162; parental
death 162; patrikin 237–8
kindergartens 10–11, 24; child carers
37n10; home concept 32–3;
ideologies 26–8, 29, 243; mother's
paid work 121; night kindergartens
26
kinship systems 6, 15, 63–4; *see also*
lineage; matrikin; patrilineage
Kjær, B. 32
Kjørholt, Anne Trine 16, 198, 201,
202, 203, 213
knowledge: distinct 119–20; how to
61; power 10; situated 129–30;
skills 188–9; traditional 166,
174–5
Koran school 126, 134–5
Kugu-Nganychara people 64, 74n12
Kuku-Yalanji children: age differences
66; kinship 64; land rights 242;
school 67–8, 72–3, 192; school
attendance 58, 59–60, 64–8, 242
Kuku-Yalanji people: land ownership
58–9, 63, 74n13, 242; mythology
68–9; opposition, culture of 71;
place-making 58

labour market 23–4
labour migration 183
land ownership: agriculture 181;
identity 63; kinship systems 63–4;
Kuku-Yalanji 58–9, 63, 74n13, 242
landscape, social/cultural 198–9
Lave, J. 50
Levinson, B. A. 23, 179, 192
Lidén, Hilde 14, 122, 243
life chances: agriculture 191–2;
education 185; school 179, 180
life stories 70, 221–6, 231–3
life style changes 171–2
liminality 100, 102, 105, 112, 113,
116; *see also* marginalisation
lineage 93, 95n15; *see also kakwaro;*
patrilineage
livelihood strategies 163, 169–72, 174
local communities: globalisation
15–16; identity 121, 228; narratives
200–1; relationships 200–1;
social/cultural landscape 198–9; Try
Yourself project 202–4
Lorimer, Francine 11, 192
Luo people 242; children 165–6;
domestic sphere 167–8; patrilineage
164–5; socialisation 163, 174
Lutheran Church 69
Lutheran missionary schools 65–6, 69

McDermott, R. 158
McDowell, L. 203
Mackey, E. 223, 224–5
McLaughlin, M. W. 225, 232
Malinowski, Bronislaw 17n1
Manchester School 71–2
marginalisation: Aboriginal life 73;
Aborignal life 70–1; associationless
children 139; forest kindergarten
28; NGO projects 113; social 2, 7,
100; *see also* liminality
marriage: Ada Bai 86; education 190;
exogamy 172–3, 181–2;
intermarriage 44; mobility 114–15;
monogamous 190; polygyny 165,
174; restraints 115; social status
108; women 86
masculinity 130–1

matrikin 172–3
Mbuya, P. 168
media narratives 134
Meinert, Lotte 16
men: masculinity 130–1;
    safe/dangerous places 84–5; see also
    gender
Merlan, F. 63
Merleau-Ponty, Maurice 121
Mexico 194n8
middle-class 115–16, 117, 220, 221
Middle East jobs 108, 115
Migdal, J. 79
migration: employment 170; gender
    191; immigrant children 141–2,
    158; life style changes 171–2;
    poverty 179; Uganda 191, 193
missionary schools 65–6, 69, 74–5n14
Mitchell, Clyde 244
mobility: Aboriginal children 73; age
    differences 64; boys/girls 85,
    181–2; gender 85; marriage
    114–15; orphans 169–70, 172;
    Poomkara 105; relationships 64;
    returnees 244; social 184
modernisation 179–80, 182
modernity: childhood 28;
    indigenisation 108, 116
mortality rates, refugee camps 80–1
multiculturalism: Canada 219–20,
    222–3, 232; richness of 225
Museveni, Yoweri 185
Muslims 100, 127
mythology 68–9

narratives: local communities 200–1;
    media 134; Try Yourself project
    200; visibility 209–12
nature 28, 35, 203
neighbourhood: culture 120–1;
    different experiences 135; everyday
    lives 120; familiarity with 127–8;
    gendered 130–2; patriotism 131
Nevis 191–2
Nieuwenhuys, Olga 13, 109, 192, 241
non-governmental organisation: Addis
    Ababa 108–13; childhood 109–10,
    114; marginalisation 113; projects

113, 237–8; protection 109–10;
    space for staff 110; street children
    102, 108–13; street children's
    families 110–13
non-places: Augé 101–2, 115; school
    106, 107, 108, 192; zones of
    passage 113, 114
Norway: childhood 243;
    egalitarianism 201; immigrant
    children 122; Muslims 127; Oslo
    14, 119–20, 122; outdoors play
    places 121, 134
Norwegian Council for Cultural Affairs
    197, 202, 208
Nyambedha, Erick Otieno 15, 168,
    174, 242

obligations 6, 126–7
observation, mobile 103
Ocholla-Ayayo, A. B. C. 168, 171
Olwig, Karen Fog 16, 143, 191–2,
    199, 236, 238
Ominde, S. H. 166, 171
opposition, culture of 71
orphans: agency 164, 167–8, 171;
    AIDS 163; as carers 163–4; carers
    of 170–2; domestic work 171;
    employment 170–2; Kenya 162;
    matrikin 172–3; mobility 169–70,
    172; paid work 169–70;
    patrilineage 162–3; public
    workplaces 170; school 171; social
    relations 173–4
Oslo 14, 119–20, 122
Ottesen, L. 140
outdoors play places 45, 121, 134,
    203

Pakistani immigrants 125–6, 134
parents: alcohol problems 162;
    authority 244; child workers 14,
    29–30; children 30–1, 32–3; control
    44–5; death of 162; education 60,
    86, 184; education, own 124–5;
    immigrant children 14, 157, 243;
    institutions 29–31; non-
    reciprocating 156–7; pedagogy
    37n6; project organisers 53; respect

for 111–12; teachers 53, 188; unemployment 25

participation/citizenship 25–6, 197–8, 214–15n1

passage, rites of 6, 17n1, 100

passage, zones of 111, 113, 114

passivity, social 140–1

paternal ancestors 93

paternalism 238, 239

patrikin 237–8

patrilineage 74n12, 162–3, 164–5

pedagogy 32–3, 37n6

peer relations 120–1, 127, 129, 133–4, 212

personhood 101

physical environment 61

Pile, S. 209

Pilkington, A. 232, 233

place 1; belonging 15–17, 120, 121, 133; Bourdieu 120–1; childhood 2; culture 5, 7, 70–4; experience 39; family 129–30; home 73, 92–3, 129–30; identity 80, 233; inscribed on body 88; inter-generational relationships 12–15; links between 69–70; meaning 6–9, 44, 78, 93, 199; of origin 226–7; peer relations 120, 121; phenomenology 82; poverty 170; school 68–70, 72, 192–3; social construction 198, 210; social difference 160n13; social status 191–3; space 78, 94n2, 121–2, 199; subversive use 2, 142; visibility 198

place types: anthropological 4, 99, 101–2, 102–6, 107, 115; distant/near 132–5; empty 129; gendered 189–91; local 132; neutral 52–4; safe/dangerous 84–5; social/physical 163–4

placelessness 112

place-making 58

play places: liminal 105; mixed gender 131; outdoor 45, 121, 134, 203; streets 45

polygyny 165

Poomkara 100–1; children's place 105–6; mobility 105; non-places

106; poverty 101; school 106, 107, 108

poverty: agency 175; place 170; rural–urban migration 179; rural areas 183, 186–7; school 101; urban 179

power: control 209; inter-generational relationships 45; knowledge 10

pregnancy 167, 193n2

Project Vesterbro 139–40

protection: adult perceptions 239; Evil Eye 238; family network 171; NGO 109–10; safety 40; sectarianism 46

Protestants 40–1, 42, 43–4, 47–8

Prout, A. 39, 56, 167

public day-care system, Denmark 23, 24–7, 243; see also kindergartens

public funding 209–10, 212–13

public space 201–4, 211

public sphere 158

Qvortrup, J. 214

Rapport, N. 157

refugee camps 80–3

refugees 11–12, 77

relationships 60–3; co-wives 165, 174; local communities 200–1; mobility 64; Open Gym project 148–50; tracking 62

religion: Ada Bai 94n9; Baptism 87–8; everyday life 125; social status 184

remittances 108

repatriation 77, 80

resettlement of refugees 11–12

resource-weak populations 140, 142

restrictions 39, 44–5, 55, 56, 242

returnees 77, 78–9, 84–6, 244

Rhodesia, Northern 244

rights/obligations 6

Rodman, M. 198–9, 200

Rose, G. 198, 203

Rose, Nicolas 10, 36

rural areas: modernisation 182; poverty 183, 186–7

ruralisation of education 179, 187–8, 189

Sack, R. D. 115
safety 2, 40, 85, 109–10, 171
saga (collective work groups) 162
Sahlins, M. 108
Scandinavia 143
school: Aboriginal people 67, 71,
    75n15, 192; access to 73–4, 129;
    Anglican Church 168–9; boarding
    182; Catholic Church 168; fishing
    crew 114; Kuku-Yalanji 67–8,
    72–3, 192; life chances 179, 180;
    local culture 194n8; non-places
    106, 107, 108, 192; orphans 171;
    personal histories 70; place 68–70,
    72, 192–3; Poomkara 106, 107,
    108; poverty 101; refugee camps
    82–3; socialisation 113; Try
    Yourself project 205–6; UNHCR
    85–6; *see also* education
school attendance, children's choice
    58, 59–60, 64–8, 86–7, 242
school drop-outs 162, 173, 183, 185
Schwab, R. G. 72
secondary schooling 186–7
sectarianism 11, 39–40; avoidance 52;
    Belfast 40–1, 245; conflict 41–4;
    identity 43–4, 48–50; other 45–7;
    protection 46; violence 46–7
segregation 100, 154–5; Belfast 44;
    children/adults 12–13, 99–100;
    cultural differences 28; gender 102,
    103–5; violence 45–7; welfare states
    115
self 7, 12
self-determination 201
self-development 244
self-management 33–4
self-realisation 207–8
Serpell, R. 186
Sharp, L. R. 74n12
Shore, C. 141
simba (boys' dormitory) 166
siwindhe (girls' dormitory) 165–6, 175
skills/knowledge 188–9
social construction 1–2, 100, 198, 210
social networks 84, 85, 129
social relations 30, 116–17, 173–4,
    175

social reproduction 17, 236, 242–5
social status: belonging 164; childhood
    31; marriage 108; place 191–3;
    religion 184
socialisation 2, 6; children's place
    113–14; demand-sharing 74n11;
    Denmark 150; gender 106–7; inter-
    generational relationships 6, 122;
    Luo people 163, 174; public day-
    care 23; school 113; spatial
    fragmentation 116
sociality 14, 142
Somali refugees 77
space: body 88; discursive construction
    199; emplacement 83–6; encoding
    of 84–5; forbidden 110; gendered
    94n4; meaning 93; place 78, 94n2,
    121–2, 199; private 79; public 79,
    201–4, 211; socialisation 116;
    supra-local 110
spirit possession 82, 90, 95n12
sports: Canada 237; Copenhagen
    159n1; gender 131–2; government
    policies 150–3; integration 138–9,
    140–1; subversive use of projects
    142; voluntary organisations
    139–40
Stambach, A. 191
Stephens, S. 203
stereotypes 47, 53
street children 2, 3; NGO 102,
    108–13; personhood 101
Structural Adjustment Programme 185
structure/agency 172
Sudan 77, 84–6
Sutton, M. 23
Sutton, P. 74n12
Sweden 29, 35–6

Tanzania 191
teachers 53, 188
tebib 81–2, 89; *see also* Evil Eye
television 62–3, 133
Thompson, D. 62
Tigrayan children 79
Tigrayan People's Liberation Front 80,
    83
Toren, C. 50

Trigger, D. 71
Try Yourself project 197–8; adult–
    children relationships 203–4; adult-
    free 208–9; children's culture 202,
    239; discourses 202–3; examples
    204–9, 211–13; local communities
    202–4; narratives 200; public
    funding 209–10; school 205–6
Tuan, Yi-Fu 1, 2, 191, 200, 210
Turkish immigrants 134
Turner, Victor 17n1
tutelage systems 237–8, 244

Uganda: civil war 185; defilement law
    193n2; rural–urban migration 191,
    193; Universal Primary Education
    16, 179–80, 193; wealth 184
UN Convention on the Rights of the
    Child 33, 37n9
unemployment 25
United Nations High Commissioner for
    Refugees 80, 82–3, 85–6
United States of America 218, 219–20
Universal Primary Education 185, 186;
    skills/knowledge 188–9; Uganda
    16, 179–80, 193
urban areas 2, 3, 115–16, 117, 179
urbanisation 182

Valentine, G. 200
Vesterbro after-school clubs 147,
    154
Vesterbro Sport Union 139–40, 151

Vigh, H. 41
violence 40–1, 45–7
visibility: differences 51–2, 223–4,
    226, 232; narrative 209–12; place
    198; public spaces 211
vocational education 188
voluntary organisations 100, 139–40
volunteer helpers 148; collaboration
    149–50; Open Gym project 144,
    145, 151–3, 156
von Sturmer, D. E. 64, 74n12
vulnerability 40, 52–3, 81

welfare societies 24, 115
Wenger, E. 50
Whisson, M. 174
Whyte, J. 44
Whyte, S. R. 184
Willis, Paul 240–1
Winter, M. de 214–15n1
women: daughters-in-law 190;
    employment 121; marriage 86;
    safe/dangerous places 84–5; social
    networks 85; workplace 104; see
    also gender
working-class youth 240–1
workplace 104, 170
Wright, S. 141

Young, Allen 94n7
youth 41, 240–1

Zambia 186